Key Writings on British Cinema

Edited by Andrew Higson

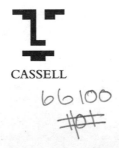

CASSELL

Rethinking British Cinema
Series Editor: Pam Cook

This series is dedicated to innovative approaches to
British cinema. It expands the parameters of debate,
shedding new light on areas such as gender and
sexuality, audiences, ethnicity, stars, visual style, genre,
music and sound. Moving beyond narrow definitions of
national cinema, the series celebrates the richness and
diversity of British film culture.

Pam Cook lectures in film at the University of East
Anglia and is editor of *The Cinema Book*.

Cassell
Wellington House
125 Strand
London WC2R 0BB

215 Park Avenue South
New York, NY 10003

© the editor and contributors 1996

First published 1996

British Library Cataloguing-in-Publication Data
A catalogue record for this book is available from the British Library.

Library of Congress Cataloging-in-Publication Data
Dissolving views : key writings on British cinema / edited by Andrew
   Higson
      p. cm.
   Includes bibliographical references and index.
   ISBN 0–304–33528–2.   ISBN 0–304–33529–0
   1. Motion pictures—Great Britain—History.   I. Higson, Andrew.
PN 1993.5.G7D56 1996
791.43'0941—dc20   95–44729
                                                                         CIP

ISBN 0 304 33528 2 (hardback)
      0 304 33529 0 (paperback)

Cover photograph from *Bhaji on the Beach* courtesy of
Christine Parry

Typeset by Ben Cracknell
Printed and bound in Great Britain by Biddles Ltd,
Guildford and King's Lynn

330449

Contents

Acknowledgements

I originally conceived this book as an attempt to bring together in one volume a number of important discussions of British cinema history that had already been published elsewhere. While it does still perform this function, the book is in its final shape a far more original collection than I had at first envisaged. For this I must thank the several contributors who agreed, at very short notice, to revise in often quite substantial ways work that already existed in some form or other. I am also very grateful to the several contributors who agreed, again at very short notice, to write completely new pieces for this volume.

None of this would have come to fruition without the help and advice of a number of people who have worked on the book in one form or another. Pam Cook has been a very supportive series editor and made many useful suggestions which I hope she feels have found their rightful place in the final product. Jane Greenwood at Cassell has sorted everything out at her end in an admirably efficient and helpful manner. Special thanks to Sue Winston, who worked with me on the book as editorial assistant over several months; her work has been both substantial and invaluable – the book would certainly not have gone to press without her help. Thanks too to Kevin Donnelly for his help in scanning one of the articles, and to Bob Neaverson for preparing the index.

I am grateful to the Research Committee of the School of English and American Studies at the University of East Anglia, who provided me with a grant to prepare the manuscript, and to the University's Study Leave Committee who approved the sabbatical during which I did some of the initial planning for the book.

Finally, my thanks to my family – my partner Val, and our two daughters, Billie and Luisa – who allowed me to hide away in my study in our new house for long periods when I should have been with them.

Andrew Higson

'Hitchcock's British Films Revisited', by Charles Barr, is a revised version of a conference paper delivered in Rome in 1960; the original paper appeared in translation in Edoardo Bruno (ed.), *Per Alfred Hitchcock* (Montepulciano, Italy: Editori del Grifi, 1981), and was reprinted as 'Hypnagogic structures: Hitchcock's British period', in *The Maguffin*, no. 6, February 1992.

'The Production Designer and the *Gesamtkunstwerk*: German Film Technicians in the British Film Industry of the 1930s', by Tim Bergfelder, is a translated and revised version of 'Rooms with a view: Deutsche Techniker und der Aufstieg des Filmdesigners', first published in Jorg Schöning (ed.), *London Calling. Deutsche im britischen Film* (Munich: Edition Text und Kritik, 1993). Our thanks to the publishers and to Cinegraph for allowing us to use this version.

Parts of the argument in 'Engendering the Nation: British Documentary Film, 1930–1939', by Kathryn Dodd and Philip Dodd first appeared in 'Representing the nation: the British documentary film, 1930–1945' by Robert Colls and Philip Dodd, in *Screen*, vol. 26, no. 1, January–February 1985. Our thanks to *Screen* and to the original authors for permission to reprint parts of that article here.

'The Quality Film Adventure: British Critics and the Cinema, 1942–1948', by John Ellis, is a substantially revised version of 'Art, Culture, and Quality', which was published in *Screen*, vol. 19, no. 3, Autumn 1978. Our thanks to *Screen* for permission to reuse material from the original version.

'From *Holiday Camp* to High Camp: Women in British Feature Films, 1945–1951', by Sue Harper, is a substantially revised version of 'The representation of women in British feature films, 1945–1950', which appeared in *Historical Journal of Film, Radio and Television*, vol. 12, no. 3, 1992. Our thanks to Carfax Publishing Company (PO Box 25, Abingdon, Oxfordshire, OX14 3UE) for permission to reuse material from the original version.

'*Victim*: Text as Context', by Andy Medhurst, is a revised version of the article which first appeared in *Screen*, vol. 25, nos. 4–5, July–October 1984. Our thanks to *Screen* for permission to reprint the article here.

'Space, Place, Spectacle: Landscape and Townscape in the "Kitchen Sink" Film', by Andrew Higson, is a revised version of an article which first appeared in *Screen*, vol. 25, nos. 4–5, July–October 1984. Our thanks to *Screen* for permission to reprint the article here.

'Landscapes and Stories in 1960s British Realism', by Terry Lovell, was first published in *Screen*, vol. 31, no. 4, Winter 1990, and appears here by permission of Oxford University Press and the author.

'A Post-national European Cinema: a Consideration of Derek Jarman's *The Tempest* and *Edward II*', by Colin MacCabe, first appeared in Petrie, D. (ed.) *Screening Europe: Image and Identity in Contemporary European Cinema* (London: BFI Publishing, 1992); an earlier and shorter version appeared in *Sight and Sound*, vol. 1 (NS), no. 6, October 1991, under the title 'Throne of Blood'. Our thanks to the British Film Institute and to the author for permission to reprint the chapter here.

Notes on Contributors

CHARLES BARR is a Senior Lecturer in Film Studies in the School of English and American Studies at the University of East Anglia. His numerous publications on British cinema include *Ealing Studios* (Cameron and Tayleur/David and Charles, 1977) and, as editor, *All Our Yesterdays: 90 Years of British Cinema* (BFI Publishing, 1986).

TIM BERGFELDER is a Lecturer in Film and German at the University of Southampton. He has previously taught film at the Merz Akademie in Stuttgart and at the University of East Anglia in Norwich. He has contributed to several German publications, including Schöning, J. (ed.) *London Calling. Deutsche im britischen Film der dreissiger Jahre* (Edition Text und Kritik, 1993). He is currently researching issues of European, British and German cinema.

PAM COOK is a Lecturer in Film Studies in the School of English and American Studies at the University of East Anglia. She has published widely on feminism and cinema and is editor of *The Cinema Book* (BFI Publishing, 1985) and co-editor of *Women and Film: A Sight and Sound Reader* (Scarlet Press, 1993). Her study of national identity and costume in British cinema, *Fashioning the Nation*, is to be published by the British Film Institute in 1996.

KATHRYN DODD is Senior Lecturer in Sociology at Thames Valley University, having previously held posts at the Thomas Coram Research Institute and Leicester University. Her most recent publications include *A Sylvia Pankhurst Reader* (Manchester University Press, 1993), which she edited, and (with Ann Oakley and Julia Brannen) *Young People, Health and Family Life* (Open University Press, 1994). She is currently working on a book-length study of women's writings between the wars.

PHILIP DODD is Editor of *Sight and Sound*. He was an academic for fourteen years, and has published five books, including *Englishness: Politics and Culture, 1880–1920* (Croom Helm, 1986), co-edited with

Robert Colls. He has written several scripts for television, including for the BBC series *Relative Values*. He is co-curating an exhibition at the Hayward Gallery in 1996 on the relation between art and film.

JOHN ELLIS is Associate Head of Media Production at Bournemouth University, and is an active independent producer. His many television programmes include the *Visions* series (1982–5), *Distilling 'Whisky Galore'* (1988) and *The Man Who Ruined the British Film Industry* (1995) for Channel 4, and *Dream Town* (1994) and *French Cooking in Ten Minutes* (1995) for BBC2. His book *Visible Fictions* (Routledge, 1982) was published in a revised edition in 1992. In 1991 he was appointed Professor II at the Institute of Media Studies, Bergen University, Norway.

SUE HARPER is Senior Lecturer in Film and Cultural History in the School of Social and Historical Studies, University of Portsmouth. She has published widely on British cinema of the 1930s and 1940s, including *Picturing the Past: The Rise and Fall of the British Costume Film* (BFI Publishing, 1994).

ANDREW HIGSON is Course Director for Film Studies and the Deputy Dean of the School of English and American Studies, University of East Anglia. He is the author of *Waving the Flag: Constructing a National Cinema in Britain* (Oxford University Press, 1995), and has contributed papers on British cinema history to several books and journals. He is currently preparing a book on heritage discourses and British cinema.

JUSTINE KING teaches English and Cultural Studies at City College, Norwich, and is researching a PhD on British women film-makers at the University of East Anglia.

TERRY LOVELL is the Director of the Centre for the Study of Women and Gender and a Reader at the University of Warwick. Her recent publications include *Feminist Cultural Studies* (ed., 2 vols., E. Elgar, 1995), *British Feminist Thought: A Reader* (ed., Blackwell, 1990), *Consuming Fiction* (Verso, 1987) and *Pictures of Reality* (BFI Publishing, 1980).

COLIN MACCABE is Head of Research and Education at the British Film Institute and Professor of English at the University of Pittsburgh. His books include *James Joyce and the Revolution of the Word* (Macmillan,

1979) and *Godard: Images, Sounds, Politics* (BFI Publishing, 1980). He was Head of British Film Institute Production from 1985 to 1989 and has previously taught at Strathclyde and Cambridge Universities.

SARITA MALIK is based at the British Film Institute, where she is researching a PhD on Black representation on British television from 1936 to the present, jointly supervised by the BFI and the Open University. She has published various articles on British Asian cinema in *Black Film Bulletin*.

ANDY MEDHURST is a Lecturer in Media Studies at the University of Sussex. He has published widely on film, television, popular culture and sexuality, and contributes regularly to *Sight and Sound*, *The Observer* and *Gay Times*.

MICHAEL O'PRAY is Reader in Art and Design, University of East London. He has edited *Andy Warhol: Film Factory* (BFI Publishing, 1989) and, with Jayne Pilling, *Into the Pleasure Dome: The Films of Kenneth Anger* (BFI Publishing, 1989). He has contributed recently to *Dark Alchemy: The Films of Jan Svankmajer* (P. Hames, ed., Flicks Books, 1995). At present he is editing an anthology of writings on British avant-garde film and completing a book on Derek Jarman. He has published widely, especially on avant-garde film, and is a contributing editor of *Sight and Sound*.

1

Introduction

Andrew Higson

Dissolving views: this was one of the terms used to describe the work of the magic lanternists. The magic lantern, of course, was one of the precursors of cinema; in particular, it is generally recognized that it had a major impact on the formation of British cinema. Throughout its hundred year history – the first public exhibition of films in Britain took place in 1896 – British cinema has drawn on and reworked pre-existing cultural practices and technologies of entertainment and education. In the early years, besides the magic lantern, British films learnt much from photography and other forms of visual representation, from popular melodrama, pantomime, music hall and legitimate theatre, and from the novel, the short story, and other more transient forms of story-telling. With the conversion to sound, we need to add radio and musical revue to the list, and, later still, television and music video. There was also of course the influence of social reportage, public relations activities and public service ideals on the documentary idea, and modernist artistic theories and practices on the avant-garde film.

Given the diversity of cultural forms on which British cinema has drawn, the richness and vitality of that cinema is hardly surprising. For it is one of the insights of this book that, contrary to a whole tradition of critical writing on film, there is much of value in British cinema. Of course, the industry has forever been plagued by financial and structural crises, not least because of the strength of its competitors. Since the 1910s the most significant competitor has been Hollywood, a force not just in its own domestic market, but in the British market as well. The British film industry, British film-makers, critics and audiences have responded to the prominence of Hollywood in various ways. There have at various times been concerted efforts to construct or embrace a specifically national British cinema, distinct from American cinema; but there have also been many, both inside and outside the industry, who have preferred to work with Hollywood and its traditions rather than against it.

The contributors to this book are, at least on this occasion, mostly concerned with the efforts to construct an indigenous cinema. One of the most refreshing aspects of what follows, however, is the recognition that the indigenous is actually forever in flux. There is no core identity to British cinema – it is far too diverse, far too rich to be reduced to a fixed essence. And it is far from pure too; on the contrary, the national cinema is a hybrid formation, drawing on both local tradition and the cosmopolitan influence of European cinema, both contemporary popular culture and elite heritage culture, both Hollywood and the documentary idea.

British cinema is at once music hall humour and the quality literary adaptation, Hitchcock and Grierson, Gainsborough melodrama and working-class realism, Powell and Pressburger and Derek Jarman, the imperialist epics of the 1930s and the post-imperialist Black British cinema of the 1980s – and so on. Previous commentators on and historians of British cinema have rarely embraced all of these traditions; they are more likely to promote one or other aspect as the truly national cinema and to marginalize those other traditions which least fit the model.

This book cannot be exhaustive either and is of necessity bound to be selective. What I have tried to do is to bring together some of the best writing from the last twenty years or so, by some of the most interesting scholars of and commentators on British cinema history and the contemporary scene. I have tried to gather in one volume both writing which has already received due acknowledgement from other workers in the field and material which deserves to be better known but has so far reached only a limited audience in Britain because it was originally published in a foreign language. Few of these pieces have been reproduced exactly as they were when first published; most have been revised, some of them quite substantially; others have new sections specially written for this volume.

To this already impressive array of work I have added several pieces which appear here for the first time, and which in various ways break new ground, extend existing debates in unexpected ways or present unfamiliar areas of British cinema to a wider audience. With this new material, I have tried to fill important gaps and address neglected issues – although inevitably some remain.

The contributions I have selected concentrate on the period after the coming of sound (the 'silent' period surely deserves its own volume) – although I have not applied this principle too rigorously, because it seemed important to be able to deal with the work of the one internationally recognized *auteur* of the inter-war years, Alfred Hitchcock. Thus Charles Barr's opening chapter deals with some of Hitchcock's pre-sound films as well as some of the better known thrillers and melodramas of the 1930s. Thereafter, the book proceeds more or less chronologically until it reaches the early 1990s.

The contributions I have selected also deal with film culture more than with the film industry. Thus the book is about British film and the culture on which it draws and in which it emerges and is taken up. And it is about film culture, that network of often contradictory ideas and activities, institutions and practices, some of them carefully defined or delineated, others more or less taken for granted, which form our understanding of cinema, whether in the guise of funding strategies and production policies, the aesthetic assumptions of film-makers, the critical discourses of those commentators who have written British films into history, or the popular taste and cultural competence of audiences.

Thus my own two contributions as well as the chapters by Kathryn and Philip Dodd, Pam Cook, John Ellis and Michael O'Pray – the list could go on – are as much concerned with prevailing debates about cinema as they are with the films themselves. Their object of investigation is in part the discourses of film criticism which have established and promoted certain ways of understanding British cinema. In some of the other chapters – those by Sue Harper, Andy Medhurst, Terry Lovell and Sarita Malik, for instance – the cultural context of the films in question is thrown into sharp focus.

Looked at from another perspective, the fourteen chapters which follow fall into four chronological clusters, thereby offering a range of often quite different insights about the same key historical moments. First of all, the chapters by Charles Barr, Tim Bergfelder and Kathryn and Philip Dodd each deal centrally with the British cinema of the 1930s, but it is a very different cinema which emerges in each case. Barr explores in a fascinating and detailed way the relation between fantasy and the real in a number of silent and sound films from Hitchcock's British period, arguing that the textual richness of these films is such that they deserve to be as highly regarded as Hitchcock's later American films. Bergfelder examines the influence of the many German film-makers, and others who had worked in the German film industry, who came to work in Britain in the 1930s. This allows him to reflect on the politics of this particular diaspora, and on the question of national cinema in a European context. But most importantly, it allows him to look at what he shows to have been the highly significant impact of German art directors on British films of the period and on film production methods more generally. Kathryn and Philip Dodd tackle the question of national cinema from a rather different perspective. They ponder the culture of documentary, and issues of masculinity and Englishness in relation to British film practice, and especially docu-mentary practice, in the 1930s. Of particular interest here is the link they draw between the writings of John Grierson about cinema and the state in the 1930s and longer-standing social-democratic traditions from the earlier part of the twentieth century and back into the nineteenth century.

The second cluster of chapters deals centrally with British cinema of the 1940s. Pam Cook investigates the highly popular cycle of costume dramas produced by Gainsborough Studios between 1943 and 1950, and in particular the sexual politics and the pleasures of costume in films and in the culture at large. Once again, she uses this case study as a way in to debates about national identity and national cinema. Quite rightly, she argues that too many studies of British cinema as a national cinema deal with the predominantly realist 'consensus' films. Her own look at a rather different set of period romances with few pretensions to cultural respectability replaces the experience of hegemony with the experience of hybridity. Identity is shown to be fluid, the national as unstable and impure. John Ellis, in a carefully revised version of an earlier, much longer and very influential article, lays out for us in great detail the discourse of those film critics of the 1940s who sought to promote a particular version of British cinema, a quality national cinema that could appeal to all audiences. As he notes, this discourse, this way of making sense of cinema and its responsibilities, was to have a profound effect on subsequent thinking about British film in Britain itself. The central concern of Sue Harper's chapter is the representation of women in a range of popular and prestige films in the latter half of the 1940s. Harper situates her study in the context of wider social and political developments and relates her findings to the gender of the film-makers concerned, though she finds little evidence of a feminist sensibility in the films of the period, even those with a woman director or producer. Harper argues that the producer holds the key to the relation between text and audience and has the greatest creative control over the production process. Her study is accordingly organized by producers and their films, so situating the films firmly in their industrial context.

The third historical moment on which this book focuses is the period of the late 1950s and early 1960s, a period which has been of such interest to film critics and to historians of British cinema over the years. Andy Medhurst ostensibly concentrates on one film, *Victim*, released in 1961. But he situates this film so carefully in the social, cultural and historical circumstances of the moment of its production that the chapter becomes much more than a study of a single film. *Victim* was the first British film to organize its narrative around male homo-sexuality and Medhurst explores the film in relation to contemporary conceptualizations of homosexuality, and to the ways in which sexuality in general is dealt with in British film culture.

Medhurst argues for a properly historical approach to film, an approach which is also adopted – albeit in different ways – in the two chapters on the New Wave 'realist' films of the late 1950s and early 1960s, one by me and the other by Terry Lovell. My own chapter considers the films in relation to the prevailing critical discourses, arguing that the concept of poetic realism enabled reviewers to adopt an ambivalent position which could celebrate the films both for their realistic depiction of contemporary working-class experience and for their aesthetically pleasing deployment of spectacular imagery. The chapter traces various links between the feature films of the period and the documentary movement of the 1930s and 1940s, and considers the function of and relation between narrative space and real historical place in the unfolding dramas of the films. Lovell looks at the same films, building on aspects of my argument, but also developing a different perspective, not least in her concern with the representation of women in the New Wave films, and in other texts of the period. Like

Medhurst, Lovell situates the films firmly in their contemporary context, looking in great detail at the formation of a new working-class culture in the 1950s and at new ways of understanding that culture in texts as diverse as Richard Hoggart's *Uses of Literacy*, first published in 1957, the television soap opera *Coronation Street*, first broadcast in 1960, and the New Wave films themselves, especially *A Taste of Honey* (1961), the only one of these films to focus on a female protagonist.

The fourth and largest cluster of chapters covers a much longer period, from the 1970s to the present. Each of the five contributors here takes a different strand of contemporary cinema. Michael O'Pray looks at avant-garde and art cinema, and charts the development from the 1970s, when the boundaries between different types of cinema seemed to be very heavily policed, to the late 1980s, when those boundaries appeared to have dissolved. Colin MacCabe reflects on Derek Jarman's adaptations of Shakespeare's *The Tempest* and Marlowe's *Edward II*, and at the ways in which they raise vital questions about national culture and national cinema. Sarita Malik surveys the development of Black British cinema from the 1960s to the present, concentrating particularly on the work of the various Black film workshops of the 1980s, developments in British-Asian film-making, and recent populist narratives by directors such as Isaac Julien and Gurinder Chadha. Justine King identifies a cycle of films of the 1980s, from *She'll Be Wearing Pink Pyjamas* (1985) to *Shirley Valentine* (1989), which she regards as woman's films, a perspective which surprisingly has not been applied previously to these films, but which King shows makes eminent sense. And in my final contribution to the book, I return to the question of the so-called heritage film, re-examining some of the claims I made about those quality British costume dramas of the 1980s and 1990s in an earlier publication. Apart from MacCabe's chapter, these essays were all written specially for this collection; together, they offer a fresh and often highly original perspective on the remarkable richness and diversity of contemporary British cinema.

There are several interesting overlaps in these chapters. Jarman's work is seen by O'Pray as an instance of a cinema which eclectically combines the traditions of both the avant-garde and the art-house film, and by MacCabe as an example of what he sees as a properly post-national European cinema. Both MacCabe and I explore how Britain's cultural heritage is taken up in contemporary films, and how different film-makers use the past. The work of young Black film-makers is considered in an avant-garde context by O'Pray, and in relation to questions of ethnicity and identity by Malik. Similarly, feminist film practice is taken up by O'Pray as another instance of avant-garde practice, and by King in relation to the idea of the woman's film. King refers to *Orlando* (1992) and *Bhaji on the Beach* (1993) as examples of recent attempts by women film-makers to build on the strengths of the woman's film; I consider *Orlando* in relation to the idea of the heritage film; Malik looks at *Bhaji on the Beach* as a British-Asian film.

Dissolving views: many of the received wisdoms about British film, and about national identity and the formation of the national film culture and the national cinema, dissolve under the steady gaze of the contributors to this book. Far from dismissing British cinema out of hand or taking it for granted, several chapters here look at the ways in which earlier commentators and historians constructed particular 'core' versions of national cinema, marginalizing other strands of the film culture in so doing. Thus the chapters by Dodd, Ellis, and me (on the New Wave films) show how a particular essentialist version of British cinema was constructed around the idea of the quality realist film, an idea which was founded on liberal-humanist and social-democratic ideals.

If these chapters examine how a particular centre was established in the national film culture, writers such as Cook, on popular costume drama, and Malik, on ethnicity, move away from this centre to look at other versions of national identity as mobilized in quite different traditions of cinema. O'Pray, Medhurst, Harper, Lovell and King also foreground traditions of representation, defined here in terms of avant-garde practice, sexuality and gender, too often marginalized in existing accounts of British cinema.

Most of the chapters in one way or another explore film in relation to the wider cultural formation. The divisions and tensions within that cultural formation are more than evident. Kathryn and Philip Dodd on 1930s documentary, and Lovell and I on the New Wave films of the late 1950s and early 1960s, all focus on the way in which a certain strand of cinema centrally involves one class, or one fragment of a class, looking at another. Other chapters deal with the gendering of culture, its homophobia, and the different ways in which the past can be used in the present. Malik notes that 'the emergence of a wide range of Black

British films in the 1980s and 1990s has broadened the somewhat narrow repertoire of British national cinema by interrogating otherwise taken-for-granted notions of British culture and British film'. And King suggests that the cycle of woman's films from the 1980s which she focuses on offer women a highly fruitful means of escaping from the constraints and tensions of the national culture. From such a range of views, British cinema and British film culture can only be understood as hybrid and impure, as something that needs to be unfolded and revealed as continually spilling out beyond its own boundaries into the complexities of a European or even global culture. I hope that the essays in this book collectively demonstrate that the centre of national cinema is forever shifting, forever dissolving.

2

Hitchcock's British Films Revisited

Charles Barr

Preface (1995)

The text that follows was given as a paper at a conference on Hitchcock held in Rome in May 1980, and published the following year, in Italian translation, in the book of the conference proceedings (Bruno, 1981). The justification for publishing the original version now is that it did address a significant issue at a significant time.

The 1980s were a decade of rapid expansion in film study courses and in film publications, two closely linked fields. Among the main growth areas were British cinema (in Britain at least) and Hitchcock (just about everywhere). Since Hitchcock made his first twenty-four films for British companies, and did not leave for Hollywood until he was aged forty, in 1939, it might seem that the two go naturally together, and that you could hardly study one without the other, but it's not so simple. British cinema study has tended to take 1939 as its serious starting point, and modern Hitchcock scholarship is accustomed to privileging the Hollywood films.

Hitchcock's death at the start of the decade, in fact a week before the Rome conference (he died in Hollywood on 29 April 1980), had the effect of intensifying public, critical and academic interest in him and his work. It cleared the way for a high-profile warts-and-all biography by the American writer Donald Spoto (1983) and, later in the same year, for the exhibition of the famous 'missing Hitchcocks': five films which had long been unseen for contractual reasons, and for which his estate now negotiated a release. Their revival was a big media event, and sparked off a lot of reviews and weightier critical studies.[1] All five of the films were Hollywood ones: *Rope* (1948), *Rear Window* (1954), *The Man Who Knew Too Much* (1955), *The Trouble with Harry* (1956), and *Vertigo* (1958). Although one or two critics commented on *The Man Who Knew Too Much* that they preferred the 1934 British film of which it was a remake, the event as a whole – like the Spoto biography – powerfully reinforced the standing of the 'mature' American work; rightly so, given the extraordinary richness of, in particular, *Rear Window* and *Vertigo*.

However, the British films too were beginning to attract a more serious kind of attention, of which the following paper was an early example. It can have had little or no direct influence, but it was a straw in the wind.

The Rome conference was a lavish international event, funded by the regional government. Speakers were invited in generous numbers from France, America and Britain, as well as Italy. Although several of the twenty-nine papers included reference to a British film or two, mine was the only one to concentrate on them. Apart from some minor technical adjustments, I have left the text in the form in which it was written up for publication at the time.

Hypnagogic structures: Hitchcock's British period (1980)

I intend to focus on Hitchcock's British work (the period before 1940), partly because it seems an appropriate contribution for a British critic to make in this context, but more importantly because of the need to question an imbalance that is familiar in the critical literature on Hitchcock and evident in the structure of the conference itself: that is, a concentration on the American films at the expense of the British. Why does this imbalance seem so inevitable, so natural? Firstly, the British films have become distant in time – it would have been hard to bring together a cross-section of collaborators from the British period to match the group who have spoken here about the experience of working on Hitchcock's American films.[2] Secondly, the British films have been less widely distributed and have remained less widely available; indeed, we have been told that only five out of Hitchcock's twenty-four British films had a normal commercial distribution in Italy.[3] But, thirdly, there is a powerful critical orthodoxy created by writers who have had no problem of access to the films, notably Robin Wood, himself English, whose immensely influential book of 1965 treated them as mere works of apprenticeship (Wood, 1965).

Ironically, Hitchcock himself contributed to the neglect of these pre-1940 films by the terms in which he described them even when he was expressing a preference for them over his Hollywood work. As we know, he was always ready to tell interviewers what they seemed to want to hear, to privilege the British or alternatively the American work according to the preferences and prejudices and nationality of his questioners. Here is what he told a British-born interviewer, W.J. Weatherby, in a late interview published shortly after his death:

> I think my English films are more realistic. I not only knew the way of life better, but I could risk subtler observation. My American films are more romantic, more like my dreams. The personal touch, what means most to me, has to be slipped in surreptitiously. (*Sunday Times*, 4 May 1980)

The words set out a contrast between realism on the one hand and dream or fantasy on the other, and the context clearly suggests that the former is more highly valued. They also define the 'personal touch' in terms of the 'slipping in' of eccentric details. Now it was in very similar terms that Anglo-Saxon critics of the 1940s and 1950s consistently elevated the British films above the American ones. It was a line most powerfully expressed by Lindsay Anderson, writing in England in the late 1940s (Anderson, 1949, reprinted in LaValley, 1972). The view is not yet completely dead, but it has become an anachronism which it is hard to take seriously – I refer not to the liking expressed for Hitchcock's British work but to the terms in which this liking is expressed. We have many models for reading the personal signature and thematic of a film-maker, within a film and an *oeuvre*, which transcend the notion of individual touches or of explicit subject matter. Likewise, the critical attitude that uses the words dreamlike, fantastic, escapist, romantic, unrealistic, fabricated, as terms of dispraise, putting them *ipso facto* lower than 'realistic' stories and films with a 'documentary' base, has also been overturned.

So it has seemed simple to accept the terms of the conventional contrast and to turn them upside down: to neglect the British work precisely as being what its champions (Anderson and co.) presented it as being: more realistic, more eccentric, and thus, by a slight extension, more superficial and less rich than the American films were now found to be. That is the attitude which still generally obtains and which Hitchcock himself in his understandable nostalgia went on from time to time abetting.

I don't wish to reverse the process again and denigrate the American period, which I believe does contain Hitchcock's richest work, but I do wish to argue, briefly and as lucidly as I can, for a different approach to the British films on the grounds that in general they have the same kind of complexity and the same kind of dreamlike narrative structures as his American work does.

Let me start by recalling a sequence from Hitchcock's final silent film, and one of the finest of all his films, *The Manxman* (1929). Like many of the early films this is a triangle story: a woman hesitates between two men. It is set on an island, the Isle of Man. Kate, the heroine, promises to marry Peter. He goes abroad, she promises to wait for him. While he is away, Kate and Philip – who is Peter's friend from childhood – fall in love. Peter is reported killed. Kate and Philip continue meeting secretly and discuss whether to bring their love into the open. Suddenly, Hitchcock reveals to the audience that Peter is alive after all: we see him despatch a joyful telegram to Philip to say he is coming home. In the next scene, Kate leaves her house and runs to the shore to keep a rendezvous with Philip. He starts to speak to her (remember that the film is silent). Cut to the image of a ship at sea, sinister-looking, puffing out black smoke.

What is the impact and meaning of this image, the reading of it made by the spectator, at this point? It seems to me there are four possibilities:

– It is Kate's, or the couple's, mental image, located in no specific space; Philip is telling her the news that Peter is on his way back.

– It is their visual image: the next shot may show them looking at it.

– It is a narrative transition to a distant scene: Hitchcock is showing us Peter, *en route*.

– The ship is nearer, offshore, but the characters haven't seen it.

That is, the status of the image may be subjective/far (mental image), subjective/near, objective/remote, or objective/near.

What happens is that as the scene proceeds we are shown that the boat *has* come within the couple's field of vision: he sees it, and she sees it, and they react to it, in turn. But this placing of the boat within the scene does not, I suggest, resolve the previous ambiguity. It is ñot a case of a *confusion* which has now been *cleared up*. The boat remains both actual and symbolic, both present to their imaginations and present in reality: we get these impressions in quick succession, and they merge, to give, very powerfully, the sense that *their fears are coming true, they are starting to live through their nightmares*. And this is a process which the film rigorously follows through. That hesitation between subjective and objective, actual and symbolic, evoked by the image of the boat, could have been illustrated in many other images and sequences in *The Manxman*, and it is the principle on which the whole film, one might ultimately say the whole of Hitchcock's work, is structured. On the one hand we see characters living their lives in an external world objectively presented, on the other the flow of images is subjectively motivated, catching us up in the dreams, fantasies, nightmares of these characters. In this context, it is worth citing the passage in the Truffaut interview book where Hitchcock recalls taking 'the chance to experiment' in his fourth film, *Downhill*, in 1927. 'In those days dreams were always dissolves and they were always blurred. Though it was difficult, I tried to embody the dream in the reality, in solid, unblurred images' (Truffaut, 1968, pp. 43–4).

I want to say more about how this principle operates by referring to some of the sound films of the 1930s. As in the silent films, Hitchcock does not simply present an exotic dream-world on screen in which a spectator can lose himself, or herself. Nor, often, does he insert dream or nightmare sequences in which we see a representation, clearly marked as such, of the character's dream. Nor, I think, does Hitchcock ever use the device of showing us an ostensibly 'real' sequence which is revealed in retrospect as subjective – 'it was all a dream'; perhaps the closest he comes to this is in the tongue-in-cheek ending of *North by Northwest* (1959), with the near-magical transition from extreme peril on the cliffs of Mount Rushmore to the top bunk of the railway cabin where Eve and Roger went to sleep midway through the film – *as if* it was all their dream. The delicacy, the non-explicitness, of this 'hint' is crucial. Dream or reality (within a narrative that is in any case fiction)? We need a concept that is at once more fluid and more precise, and for this I would propose, at least half-seriously, the idea of *hypnagogia*. The term is related to hypnosis but it is not identical with it. It has been used to describe the state *between* sleeping and waking in which an intense, fevered succession of images passes through the mind: the sequence is more rational, more subject to control, than the images of a dream, but less rational and inhibited than our waking perceptions. Hypnagogia is a sort of trance, and hypnagogic images are images seen in a heightened trance-like state. I suggest that this kind of state links spectator and protagonist in many Hitchcock films.

If one had to define, in a single phrase, the dominant subject of Hitchcock's British films, the best attempt at a definition might be this: a woman in a trance. Sometimes there is a man in a trance, sometimes the conflict within a character is presented without a strong subjective dimension, but frequently at the centre, as in *The Manxman*, there is a woman in a trance. Think of *Murder!* (1930), Hitchcock's early sound film, where the woman accused of the crime enters the plea that if she did it, it must have been when she was not conscious of herself, that it was, to quote her words, 'daytime sleepwalking'. Think of Alice, the daytime sleepwalker of *Blackmail* (1929), a film absolutely full of the kind of hesitation between subjective and objective that I pointed to in *The Manxman*, and as complex, as multi-layered, a film as any Hitchcock ever made. Think of Madeleine Carroll in the latter half of *Secret Agent* (1936), and of Sylvia Sydney in the latter half of *Sabotage* (1936). And consider the process by which, in the three purest adventure films of the 1930s, the act of sleeping is systematically inscribed in the narrative.

Every textbook on editing records, from *The Thirty Nine Steps* (1935), the famous cut from the scream of the landlady discovering the dead body to the whistle of the train carrying Hannay to Scotland, but remember too that Hitchcock dissolves from the railway line to Hannay's sleeping face.[4] It is part of a rigorous pattern whereby, until the final resolution, whenever Hannay is absent from the action we are shown either before, or retrospectively, that he is asleep or otherwise unconscious.

If one segments the narrative of *The Lady Vanishes* (1938) in terms of time and location, it falls into four very uneven sections: day one, the hotel; day two, the train; day three, the ship (a single image); day four, London. The real structuring principle of the film is seen if one divides it in terms of the periods of unconsciousness experienced by the heroine, Iris, and the blocks of action that take place during, and between, these periods. In succession, Iris sleeps, swoons, sleeps, swoons, hallucinates, swoons, sleeps, sleeps, and finally *pretends* to sleep. The whole film proceeds like a fantastic dream from which she intermittently awakes, and into which she then plunges again, just as it is a fantastic adventure for the spectator, who is simultaneously conscious and unconscious of his/her own location in the cinema. And this hypnagogic discourse, based on the central character's fluctuations between sleep and waking, is very precisely motivated both in this film and *The Thirty Nine Steps*. Both Richard Hannay and Iris become the focus of strong conflicts connected with sex and marriage. A chaotic world of unfulfilled sexual energy is created in the opening scenes in the music hall, and in the hotel. Hannay himself is unattached; Iris is reluctantly engaged. Hannay is shaken up, meets a provocative woman, sleeps, wakes to nightmare, sleeps again, wakes (on the train), and so on. Iris is shaken up, sleeps, wakes to find by her bed (to fantasize?) a handsome man who creates new conflicts, is stunned by a blow on the head, wakes (on the train), and so on. At each stage it is *as if* she (like Hannay) is dreaming or hallucinating, but at no point is this made explicit; the double status of the discourse, subjective/objective, is scrupulously maintained. The effect created is of a heroine playing out, living through, her fantasies, nightmares, conflicts. Or, to express it in reverse: what is being played out in objective narrative terms is a projection of meaningful *interior* fantasies, nightmares, conflicts, and it works in that way, for the characters and through them for the audience.

Finally, *Young and Innocent* (1938) – one of Hitchcock's purest and most self-conscious narratives, the last of his 'Golden Sextet' of the 1930s (the others being the two films just discussed, plus *The Man Who Knew Too Much* (1934), *Sabotage* and *The Secret Agent*), and the only one of the six that has no political dimension. Like all of them it is centred on the formation, or consolidation, of a couple.[5]

Analysis divides the film into nineteen scenes, marked by change in location (the scene on the beach, the visit to the aunt and so on). What this analysis does is to reveal an extraordinary and perhaps calculated symmetry in what might be termed the hypnagogic structure.

We start with the young man, Robert: caught up in violence, accused of murder. In scene 3, in the police station, he swoons, faints; and Erica enters the room and the film, as if summoned up by his unconscious. In scene 8, on the run, he sleeps: Erica finds him and rescues him, thereby for the first time committing herself to helping him. In scene 12 – the eighth from the end – *she* sleeps, and he saves her from danger. And in scene 17 – the third from the end – she swoons, faints, on her bed, and he enters her room by the window to save her as in the fulfilment of *her* dream. Which sets it up for the happy ending: their unmasking of the real murderer, and their union. Remember that Robert has been established at the start as a writer of film scripts. It's as though he created a screen fantasy for himself, summoned up a woman to love, and then projected a reciprocal (symmetrical) fantasy on to her; and this also makes a satisfying fantasy or fairy-tale for his film's audience.

This anticipates very closely the intricate structure of reciprocal fantasies in *Suspicion* (1941), made by Hitchcock in Hollywood three years later – not to mention later films. The surface disparities between these two films (for example, in acting style, and location versus studio shooting) are less important than the structural connections. There is no clear dividing line between Hitchcock's British and American work. I suggest that a close, and unpatronizing, study of the British films can lead us to a more accurate grasp of his work as a whole, and to a thorough and long overdue revaluation of the British films themselves.

Afterword (1995)

Fifteen years on, this revaluation has certainly got under way, though it can hardly be described yet as 'thorough'; nor can I claim to have contributed much to it, apart from the introductory essay in the 1986 collection *All Our Yesterdays: 90 Years of British Cinema*, which discussed the case of Hitchcock in similar terms but for a wider audience, and in a wider historical and critical context.

> 'These [British] films ... are rich in precisely those elements which make Hitchcock so important to a new and very productive school of structuralist and psychoanalytic criticism.' (Barr, 1986, p. 20)

That claim was already implicit in the non-technical language of the 1980 paper: behind the segmentation of *Young and Innocent* lies the influence of Raymond Bellour, and the account of the 'woman in a trance' theme relates to issues raised both by him and by Laura Mulvey (Bellour, 1979; Mulvey, 1975).

Mulvey's celebrated essay 'Visual Pleasure and Narrative Cinema' used Hitchcock as a prime illustration of her central arguments: that classical film narrative is commonly 'cut to the measure of male desire', and that it operates through a trinity of *looks* (three in one and one in three). The male protagonist, looking at a female object of desire or fascination within the fiction, acts as surrogate both for the male director, and for the male spectator. Example: the obsessively looking James Stewart characters in *Rear Window* and *Vertigo*. In *All Our Yesterdays* I made the point that this kind of structure was already highly developed in the early British films:

> The 1928 [silent] film *Champagne* is exemplary: it opens with a strongly marked *look*, aligning spectator with (male) character, and expressing a fantasy or desire which is then worked through in a narrative tightly controlled in terms of structure and point of view. Exactly the same formula could be used to summarise *Young and Innocent* (1938); Hitchcock's British work consists of a series of busy variations worked on this basic structural model, always involving (apart from some interruption in the early years of sound) play with point of view and fantasy. (Barr, 1986, p. 20)

Moreover, the male bias of this model is at least to some extent undercut by the films' formal self-consciousness, and by the way they frequently centre on, and align the spectator with, the figure of a 'woman in a trance'.

It is above all the combination, and interconnection, of formal issues and gender issues that has recently begun to get more scholars seriously interested in British Hitchcock. In 1986, as in 1980, I'd expressed regret at the intransigence of Robin Wood, who ever since his original book of 1965 had kept returning to Hitchcock and revising and fine-tuning his judgements, but without any new engagement with the British films. Wood is a figure of such eloquence and authority that his stance demonstrably mattered. And then at the end of the decade, in *Hitchcock's Films Revisited*, came what Tom Ryall describes as a 'conversion' (Ryall, 1993, pp. 35–6). Looking back on his original 1965 text, Wood apologized for this embarrassingly ignorant and supercilious dismissal of the first half of Hitchcock's career ... a sweeping rejection of a body of work that includes numerous admirable and fully realised films and that at once establishes the thematic and structural bases of the work to come and suggests other paths that were not followed. (Wood, 1989, pp. 230–1)

The new book contains a very substantial chapter on *Blackmail*, and another on *The Thirty Nine Steps* and *Young and Innocent*. I disclaim any influence here; my own tentative writings were simply in tune with the same range of ideas that Wood had already shown himself to be interested in, and all that he had to do was, by his own account, to see past his strong personal antipathy towards 'the British middle-class milieu in which most of [the pre-1940 films] are set' (Wood, 1989, p. 231).

Equally important is Tania Modleski's 1988 book, subtitled *Hitchcock and Feminist Theory*. Of her seven main case-studies, one is on *Blackmail* and another on *Murder!*, and one regrets that she then jumps a decade between that and Hitchcock's first Hollywood film, *Rebecca* (1940). One of her concerns is to question, and to refine, the (initial) Mulvey model of uncompromising male-centredness. She does this by, for instance, showing how the Grace Kelly character in *Rear Window* offers an alternative to James Stewart as a locus of identification; this is analogous, I think, to the movement I sketch in *Young and Innocent* between Robert, the early focus of the narrative and bearer of the look, and Erica, who comes to share these functions.

The 1980s also brought, among a stream of other books, *Hitchcock: the Murderous Gaze* by William Rothman, and *Alfred Hitchcock and the British Cinema* by Tom Ryall, respectively American and British. The former selects for rigorous shot-by-shot analysis five films, of which three are British (*The Lodger* (1926), *Murder!*, *The Thirty Nine Steps*) (Rothman, 1982). The latter, without much in the way of textual analysis, explores Hitchcock's relation to the British film industry and film culture of the period (Ryall, 1986).

On the one hand, these varied publications fulfil the wish of my Rome paper's last sentence by exploring British Hitchcock in ways that are indeed 'unpatronizing', serious, and full of insights. On the other hand, they all remain partial and selective. We still lack any holistic account that would both analyse and adequately contextualize the full range of Hitchcock's work up to 1940 (memo to self: get on with it). But meanwhile we can afford to stop being defensive and feeling the need to speak up for the British work as such – that battle has evidently been won. It would surely now be impossible for a conference taking as its subject simply 'Hitchcock' to marginalize his British films in the manner of Rome 1980.

Notes

1. On the revival of the five 'missing Hitchcocks', and critical responses, see Kapsis, 1992, pp. 119–21.
2. Along with biographer Donald Spoto, the contingent from America consisted of actors Farley Granger and 'Tippi' Hedren, screenwriter Ernest Lehman, and the British-born Peggy Robertson, who worked as script editor and personal assistant to Hitchcock for most of his career from 1949.
3. Information about the difficulty of access in Italy to Hitchcock's British films was given by a previous speaker. It is not documented in the conference book.
4. 'Every textbook' is an exaggeration. To my surprise, the scene is not referred to in the standard work on editing written by a close associate of Lindsay Anderson (Reisz, 1953). However, it does crop up in many other books on film technique (e.g. Stephenson and Debrix, 1965, p. 67; Salt, 1983, p. 284).
5. Just to avoid any confusion about the identity of these films: *Young and Innocent* was released in America as *The Girl Was Young*; its working title had been that of the novel on which it was based, *A Shilling for Candles* (by Josephine Tey). *Sabotage* was released in America as *A Woman Alone*; it couldn't use the title of the original novel, *The Secret Agent* (by Joseph Conrad), since that title had been used for Hitchcock's previous film, which was based on the *Ashenden* stories by Somerset Maugham.

$$\boxed{3}$$

The Production Designer and the *Gesamtkunstwerk*: German Film Technicians in the British Film Industry of the 1930s

Tim Bergfelder

Refugees, residents and the mobility of labour

The last ten years have witnessed a renewed interest in the concept of a 'European film', with interventions ranging from the rhetoric surrounding French resistance to the American film industry in the 1993 GATT negotiations about international trade tariffs, to the establishment of cross-cultural media organizations such as EURO-AIM and EURIMAGES and the Euro-Oscar 'Felix'. All these interventions are more or less explicit reactions to a perceived dominance of Hollywood. Almost inevitably, the problem of how to define 'European cinema' in the first place has equally resurfaced as a strongly contested subject in the field of film studies and has led to a variety of different approaches (most notably Petrie, 1992b; Dyer and Vincendeau, 1992). These debates are of course far from new, and have their precedents, most prominently perhaps in the 'Film Europe' movement of the 1920s and 1930s. In analysing this movement, one is confronted with various complications, most notably how to reconcile the issue of national identity with the wider context of a European identity. In other words, how is one to do justice to a movement that intersects the film cultures of three nations (Britain, France and Germany), and how can we develop a discourse which is both inclusive and comparative? The second complication in talking about the 'Film Europe' movement of the 1920s and 1930s is that it coincides historically with the narratives of German Fascism, the Jewish diaspora and exile. The exodus of innumerable talented artists (including film-makers) from Germany after 1933 has proved to be a potent symbolic image. Consequently the developments of 'Film-Europe' have been seen mainly as the product of the political situation after 1933 rather than as developments in their own right.

Tracing the trajectories of those German film technicians who worked in Britain during the 1930s, however, it becomes apparent that the discourse of political exile from Nazi Germany cannot adequately explain the various migrations in this period. Seen from a purely industrial perspective, 1933 was in no way the beginning of a wide-ranging emigration, but was rather the politically motivated intensification of a process that had started in the early 1920s (see, e.g., Elsaesser, 1993).[1]

Several economic factors determined this development, notably the attempts by various national film industries, and especially those in Germany, Britain and France, to consolidate their position against Hollywood's hegemony through strategies of product differentiation and inter-European co-operation (Higson, 1993a). Equally important, however, were Hollywood's interventions in Europe, for example the attempts to neutralize potentially threatening markets by signing up their foremost talents (note, for example, the career paths of Lubitsch, Sjöström, Murnau and Hitchcock). One result of such strategies in Hollywood and Europe was that the film industries of the 1920s and 1930s witnessed an increasingly mobile work force and the emergence of a new type of film professional, the mobile freelancer. This situation was well established years before artists and technicians were forced out of Germany for political reasons. More importantly, this professional mobility continued as a practice alongside the Nazi-enforced diaspora of the 1930s. It is therefore extremely problematic simply to label all German technicians active in the British film industry of the 1930s as political refugees. It is important to remember that after the Nazification of UFA in 1933, which resulted in a large-scale purge of politically and ethnically undesirable employees, the German film industry was less isolated within Europe than one would imagine. Anglo-German co-operation and co-production continued up to 1938, and Franco-German film relations do not seem to have suffered substantially under the changed political circumstances. Even after 1933 the major incentive and motivation for a film technician to move seems to have been economic, not political. Yet while there is no common experience of political exile, one can nevertheless identify several distinctive groups among the technicians in terms of employment and residence status.

The first group are the 'professional travellers'. They moved extensively within Europe, mainly in the film-industrial triangle of Berlin, Paris and London, but also to Italy and Holland. On the whole they were freelancers without binding contracts to studios. Most of them ended up in Hollywood by the end of the 1930s, their travelling made impossible by the impending war. For the art director Ernö Metzner, once a collaborator of Pabst's and director of agit-prop shorts, Britain was merely a stopover on his way to the United States. This itinerary from Berlin to Hollywood via Paris and London characterizes many careers including those of the cinematographers Franz Planer, Eugen Schüfftan and Curt Courant. The Russian-born art director André Andreiev provides an interesting variation. Having gained his reputation in German films of the 1920s, he worked throughout the 1930s in Britain as well as in France, moving back and forth before settling in France in 1937. During the years of the Occupation, Andreiev remained busy designing the sets for films made by Continental, a French subsidiary of UFA. In 1946 he was back in Britain, designing Alexander Korda's *Anna Karenina* (1947).

As the case of Andreiev suggests, the travel boom among film technicians during this period was not always rooted in existential fears and political exile. Even more obvious is the case of the cinematographer Hans Schneeberger, who worked on three films for Alexander Korda in the mid-1930s (*Conquest of the Air*, 1936, *Forget-me-Not*, 1936, *Farewell Again*, 1937) before returning to Germany as one of the Nazi cinema's most prestigious cameramen. Another visitor in the same league was his colleague Franz Weihmayr, who went to Britain in 1936 to shoot *Calling the Tune* (1936) for director Reginald Denham. A year later he was back in Germany, and became instrumental in creating a distinctive photographic style for UFA's biggest star at the time, Zarah Leander. There were even some more settled émigrés who occasionally travelled back. Günther Krampf, by the mid-1930s firmly established as a cinematographer in the British film industry, returned one last time to the UFA studios in 1935 to photograph Gustav Ucicky's Joan of Arc epic, *Das Mädchen Johanna*.

It was certainly in the interest of Nazi propaganda, at least up to the mid-1930s, to capitalize on such international exchange of personnel, upholding the illusion of continued mobility and an unproblematic, cosmopolitan co-operation of national cultures, and camouflaging the German film industry's outrageous ethnic cleansing measures. (One should remember that the 1936 Olympic Games in Berlin was an equally propagandist gesture.) Germans abroad, whether they were there on 'business trips' or forced into exile, could still be exploited for propaganda purposes. In 1936, for example, the party-controlled journal *Film Kurier* ran an article headlined 'German film artist is honoured in England', reporting on the awarding of an honorary degree from Oxford University to the film architect Alfred Junge (26 February 1936). By 1936, however, Junge could no longer be described as a German film artist, having worked consistently in Britain since the late 1920s.

Junge, in fact, belonged to the second group of immigrants who might be labelled 'residents' – that is, technicians who envisaged a long if not permanent stay in Britain. Most of them had been in the country since the late 1920s and had gained their experience in silent films and later multilingual co-productions. What is more important, however, and indeed quite unusual for film technicians working in Britain at the time, is that some of them had solid long-term contracts with well established companies such as Gaumont-British and Gainsborough. The more common production practice at the time was to sign technical crews for individual films only – thereby actively encouraging internationally mobile film technicians. For those aiming at a stable home base and a secure career, however, this practice entailed many risks. In particular, the only German technicians who were given long-term contracts and who were fully integrated into the British film industry were cinematographers and art directors – that is, members of those branches of the film industry on which the international reputation of German cinema in the 1920s was based.

If one wants to trace the German influence on British cinema in this period, one therefore needs to focus precisely on these technicians rather than on the more perfunctory and erratic careers of directors such as Berthold Viertel, Karl Grune or Friedrich Feher. Art directors such as Junge, Oscar Werndorff or Vincent Korda and cinematographers such as Günther Krampf, Otto Kanturek or Mutz Greenbaum (later Max Greene) had left Germany or the German film industry years before Hitler's rise to power. They came to help with the development of the British film industry, lured by opportunities which UFA – after a series of financial crises in the late 1920s – could no longer guarantee them.

Continental know-how for British films

The brains behind the boom in the British film industry in the late 1920s, particularly Michael Balcon, were acutely aware of the fact that in order to consolidate the national film culture it was necessary to create distinctive products for an international market. What was needed, therefore, was both a recognizable and distinctive national film style and a rationalization of production, an increased efficiency. In the late 1920s there were only two dominant industrial and stylistic paradigms that offered themselves as potential blueprints for the British industry, namely Hollywood and the German UFA. What producers like Balcon effectively had in mind was a synthesis of both models, combining the fast-paced, fluid narration of American cinema with the *mise-en-scène* and visual craftsmanship of UFA. In practice this meant reconciling a considerable paradox. In German films of the 1920s the *mise-en-scène* quite often takes priority over the requirements of the plot, whereas in Hollywood the image is constricted by the imperatives of the narrative flow. Judging by the majority of British films in this period, the Hollywood mode of narration emerged triumphant, with German technicians providing the *mise-en-scène* more as a decorative than as a narrational contribution.

Looking at the employment patterns of British studios from the late 1920s through the 1930s the producers' dual orientation towards Hollywood and Germany and their respective strengths is quite evident. Scriptwriting, editing and direction were clearly informed by American standards, and a considerable number of workers in these branches were directly imported from the United States. The art and cinematography departments, on the other hand, modelled themselves more on

24

German studios and were on the whole staffed with British as well as Continental technicians who had gained experience in the production teams of UFA or DECLA in Berlin. This employment strategy helps to explain why such a high proportion of German film immigrants are to be found in these departments and why there were hardly any German editors in British films.

The British studios expected from their German imports professionalism, technical know-how and economic efficiency, using them to help bring outmoded studio facilities up to UFA standards. Indeed, several changes and innovations in British studios of the late 1920s and early 1930s were introduced by German immigrants. Alfred Junge, for example, revolutionized scaffolding and crane technology, which led to an increased mobility for both sets and cameras. Günther Krampf designed special soft-focus lenses that were especially made for him in Budapest and were later used by other colleagues as well (to stunning effect by Curt Courant in John Brahm's *Broken Blossoms*, 1936). Another cinematographer, Otto Kanturek, doubled as an entrepreneur for the short-lived Chemicolour technology (showcased in the Karl Grune film *Pagliacci*, 1936). With more success he also acted as a sales representative for the Czech Cinephon camera, an apparatus with low noise levels – an important advantage in the early days of sound technology. Kanturek sold eight cameras to Gaumont-British alone, and the Cinephon became for a while the industrial standard. More generally, the Continental technicians had learned in Germany special effects techniques of false perspective and the use of miniatures, models and mirrors. (The 'Schüfftan effect' became one of the best-known of these devices.) As *Sight and Sound* acknowledged towards the end of the decade: 'Tricks of the camera which look so easy today and which we take for granted were worked out with great skill and imagination by Werndorff and his associates' (*Sight and Sound*, Winter 1938/39, p. 181). Compared with this technical input, the immigrants' artistic merits were less important to the studios. In fact, too idiosyncratic a personal style was actively discouraged. This is particularly true for the field of art direction, as the case of László Moholy-Nagy proves. The prestigious Bauhaus artist was fired as art director from the H. G. Wells adaptation *Things to Come* (1936) because the film's producer, Alexander Korda, evaluated his designs as too expensive and incompatible with the requirements of the narrative action. Moholy-

Nagy was replaced by another immigrant, the producer's brother, Vincent Korda, who – incidentally – had begun his career as an assistant to Alfred Junge (on the Franco-German co-production *Marius/Zum goldenen Anker*, 1931).

The more successful art directors (like Junge, Werndorff or Korda) were those who blended most efficiently into the studio mode of production and who adapted most perfectly to the studio's style. From a purely pictorial or aesthetic perspective one might value the sets designed by Metzner or Andreiev as more original and artistically daring. Yet within the context of production, their style was often considered too expensive or too time-consuming.

On the whole, art directors restrained their artistic ambitions, subsuming them under the requirements of a particular mode of narration, as these comments by Oscar Werndorff indicate:

> I always think of art directors that the less you hear about them the better they are. Good art direction must give you the atmosphere of the picture without being too noticeable. The best 'sets', in my experience, are those which you forget as soon as the film is over and the lights go up again in the theatre. The first essential in the film is the action of the characters. The art director's job is to provide them with a background – and a background it should remain at all costs. (Winchester, 1933, p. 445)

Given these constraints, partly enforced by the studios, partly internalized by the artists themselves, the art directors nevertheless had a power and influence in the production process which cannot be overestimated. The case of Gaumont-British and Gainsborough serves as a good example here. These affiliated companies owned two studios in the early 1930s. The complex at Lime Grove/Shepherd's Bush opened in summer 1932 (the location had housed a film studio since 1914). In its heyday, three to five films were shot simultaneously on five sound stages, a situation that understandably required flexibility and mobility on the part of the art director in charge. This position was filled by Alfred Junge up to 1936, when Lime Grove was temporarily closed because of the general financial collapse of the British film industry. Oscar Werndorff, 'Uncle Otto' to his British colleagues, had a similar managerial position at the Gainsborough studio at Islington. This lot, founded in 1919 by the American Lasky Corporation and reopened by Gainsborough in the spring of 1931, was equipped to shoot one film at a time, using two sound stages. (On occasions the Islington crew would move to Shepherd's Bush.) Gainsborough employed twenty-five carpenters and thirty-five technicians a day here. Both the Gaumont-British and the Gainsborough studios were situated in densely populated areas and had practically no outdoor facilities. This made the art department even more important and to an extent dictated the type of film the studios could produce.

It is fair to say that with Junge in Lime Grove, Werndorff in Islington and Vincent Korda at Elstree (and later at Denham), art direction in British films of the 1930s was dominated by the 'Continentals'. It was during this time that the role of the art director in the British film industry underwent a fundamental and, as it turned out, lasting change. It is generally acknowledged that British films up to the mid-1920s showed no sign of a coherent or systematic approach towards art direction, let alone the idea of a 'designed' film. Edward Carrick, one of the early historians of British film design and an art director in his own right, remembers this time:

> In the early days of film-making in England, the job of 'supplying' the scenery or sets was left to carpenters and painters who worked under the 'instructions' of the director. A room was a room and there could be no argument about it ... The only thing that mattered was that continuity should be fairly smooth. Occasionally an artist was called in to help with one or two of the lavish sets, but he was a kind of luxury that no one wanted because he was always suggesting too many changes. He bothered about detail, atmosphere and similar things that exasperated the producer. (Carrick, 1948, p. 12)

It was a new generation of producers, above all Balcon and later Korda, who insisted on these aspects of detail and atmosphere and who understood the importance of 'film design'. The cutting edge of art direction at the time was of course German, with the work of film architects such as Erich Kettelhut, Robert Herlth and Walter Röhrig, impressively showcased in the films of Lang, Murnau and Lubitsch. It was not only the artistic genius that impressed producers abroad, however, but the technical skills and organization of studios like

Babelsberg that made a *Nibelungen* or a Lubitsch epic possible in the first place. In the early 1930s none of the studios in Britain could compare with UFA's fourteen separate sound-floors and forty-two administrative and technical buildings in the Berlin suburb of Babelsberg (Elstree, with nine production stages in three blocks, came closest). That Germany provided the best-equipped studio facilities in Europe at the time did not go unnoticed abroad. Indeed, UFA made considerable profits during the 1920s by renting its facilities to foreign companies. Since the mid-1920s British producers had encouraged film-makers and technicians to study the German film industry's approach to art direction, and sent them for occasional films to Berlin or Munich. Among them was Alfred Hitchcock, whose first two directorial efforts were shot in southern Germany. Untrained beginners, usually university graduates, were sent by Balcon on special exchange courses to Berlin, under the auspices of a co-operation agreement between UFA, Gaumont-British and Gainsborough.

Britain fared well with this exchange. By the late 1920s, Alfred Junge had come to Britain alongside the director E. A. Dupont, and Oscar Werndorff came over after being involved in Anglo-German co-productions shot in Berlin (Higson, 1992). It is clear that German film design was not just admired from a distance by British producers, but was seen as the model future British productions should emulate. The German-Hungarian art director Ernö Metzner published several articles between 1929 and 1933 in the highbrow film magazine *Close Up,* on his collaborations with Pabst, on the craft of the film architect, and on the organization of production in German studios. And when film artists were commissioned by the *World Film Encyclopedia* in 1933 to write briefly about their work, the ones that were published were – tellingly – mostly Germans: Werndorff on art direction, Curt Courant on photography and Ernst Lubitsch on direction (Winchester, 1933).

There is no doubt that the widespread prestige German film design enjoyed abroad boosted the status of the art director in British films in general. Between the 1920s and the 1930s the power and influence of the art director within the production process changed dramatically. A supervising art director like Alfred Junge at Lime Grove, for example, could rely on a department such as his British colleagues a few years earlier could only have dreamt of. Under his command were historical and artistic consultants, teams of sketch artists and draughtsmen, as well as plasterers, carpenters and painters. Junge and his successors in the 1930s and 1940s had total control over almost all aspects of the conception and execution of the sets, except targeted budgets and deadlines. Furthermore Junge was given a contractual right to decide upon and co-ordinate any aspect of *mise-en-scène* (lighting, camera position) that affected the overall visual impact of the setting. In practice this could mean that the art director became a director in his own right. And it is clear that the art directors of the 1930s enjoyed a special status within the studio. They were hierarchically removed from the other technicians and knew it, as many survivors of this period recall. The open rivalry between Junge and the director Berthold Viertel during the shooting of *Little Friend* (Gaumont-British, 1934) has been well documented by Christopher Isherwood in his brilliant *roman-à-clef* about the British film industry, *Prater Violet*. And Michael Powell in an interview with Kevin Gough-Yates, remembered Junge half-sarcastically, half-admiringly as the man who ran Shepherd's Bush 'like a machine' (Gough-Yates, 1971).

The direct impact of the German or German-trained art directors manifested itself as a change in the organization of labour. People like Junge approached film design from a conceptual angle – what they aimed for was the overall designed film. As a result the number of tasks supervised by the art director increased during the decade. Since the mid-1930s new hierarchies and professions emerged within the field. The previously independent set decorators and art directors were now led by the 'production designer', whom Carrick defines as the person who supplied 'the "ideas" about the visual composition of the film, costume, customs, lighting, background, etc., while the art directors, dress-designers, cameramen, and even the director, carried them out' (Carrick, 1948, p. 17). Alfred Junge was one of the first production designers in British cinema to supervise all the visual aspects of a production without carrying out all the individual tasks himself. Most of the sketches attributed to him, for example, were in all likelihood drawn by someone else in his large team delegated for this purpose. Among these associates a whole generation of future British art directors and production designers received their training. Michael Relph, one of the most important British film architects of the 1940s and 1950s, began his career as Junge's assistant, an influence he always acknowledged and which is evident in some of his later works (see, for example, the Priestley adaptation *They Came to a City,* 1944).

In the same way that Junge relied on his storyboard and sketch artist team, André Andreiev worked in close collaboration with the painter and draughtsman Ferdinand Bellan. Carrick notes the influence of the Viennese-born Bellan on his British colleagues:

> Bellan's first sketches, full of exquisite figures, were admired by all, his use of 'conte' crayon was very skilful and he knew all the tricks of light and shade. ... The new style he set in drawing in some ways did more harm than good because his method of drawing was copied by many less skilled artists. (Carrick, 1948, p. 14)

Indeed, if one looks at some of Bellan's and his contemporaries' drawings and designs, notes their precision in relation to lighting and spatial composition and finally compares these sketches with their realization on film, one can only be surprised how much of the designer's imagination found its way into the end product. This certainly owes a lot to the close working relationship between the production designer and the cinematographer, something that had been common practice at UFA. In particular, the pairing of Junge or Werndorff with Kanturek or Krampf proved extremely fruitful collaborations.

The dominant art directors of 1940s British cinema (John Bryan, Roger Furse, Edward Carrick, Michael Relph, Hein Heckroth, W. C. Andrews, Paul Sherriff and Peter Proud) inherited the status as well as the influence of the immigrants of the 1920s and 1930s. Ironically most of the Continental art directors who brought about these professional changes had disappeared from the British film scene by then. Oscar Werndorff died prematurely in 1938, his career tracing a full circle. One of his first films in Britain had been the Edgar Wallace adaptation *The Wrecker* (1928), co-produced by Balcon's Gainsborough. His last film was one of Balcon's first at Ealing, and again an Edgar Wallace adaptation, *The Gaunt Stranger* (1938). By the end of the 1930s Metzner and Andreiev had left Britain. Vincent Korda, like his brothers, spent the war years in Hollywood and his subsequent career (lasting to the early 1970s) was increasingly international. A definitive survivor of the 1930s, however, was Alfred Junge. After leaving Shepherd's Bush he worked for two years at MGM-British before teaming up with Powell and Pressburger's company, The Archers, in the early 1940s. After *Black Narcissus* (1947), for which he won an Academy Award, he became the head of MGM-British's art department, designing many prestige productions, including *Ivanhoe* (1952), *Mogambo* (1953) and *A Farewell to Arms* (1957). He remained a fixture in British films until his death in 1964, at the age of 78.

Public opinion and the Union

It is of course neither coincidence nor 'destiny' that the overall visibility of German film personnel in the British film industry waned by the end of the decade. For political refugees, Britain's geographical proximity to Germany was worrying enough for them to consider moving on. Furthermore public opinion in Britain, even within the film industry, was less than encouraging. With Britain declaring war on Germany in 1939, many immigrants were interned or subjected to severe restrictions, among them Alfred Junge, Hein Heckroth and Emeric Pressburger. Feelings of animosity had in fact been growing for some time. Since the mid-1930s press reports on the Continental presence in the British film industry had used the metaphor of an invasion, thereby blurring any distinction between refugees, international markets and national concerns.

Continental film artists, producers and directors were seen as an alien and subversive influence, and deep mistrust accompanied the activities of producers like Alexander Korda and Max Schach. The famous 'Polish Corridor' at Gaumont-British, referring to Balcon's international production partners Josef Somlo and Hermann Fellner (neither of them actually Polish, but Hungarian and German respectively), was noted with deep suspicion. Fellner, a true cosmopolitan, had been active in films since 1912, as a writer and producer for German-Danish co-productions, later as a representative of Fox-Europe. It is clear that Balcon himself regarded him less as an intrusion than as a definitive asset in his designs for a European film centre based in London ('British films benefited much from our association with Fellner.' [Balcon, 1969, p. 54]).

The financial crash of the British film industry in 1936/37, in reality at least as much the fault of the lending banks as of producers such as Korda or Schach, seemed to confirm all suspicions. Even intellectuals of the political left supported theories about sinister foreign conspiracies. Graham Greene's now notorious review of the otherwise forgotten Karl Grune film, *The Marriage of Corbal* (1936), is indicative of the public mood of the time:

> The Quota Act has played into foreign hands, and as far as I know, there is nothing to prevent an English film unit being completely staffed by technicians of foreign blood. We have saved the English film industry from American competition only to surrender it to a far more alien control. ... Watching the dark alien executive tipping his cigar ash behind the glass partition in Wardour Street, the Hungarian producer adapting Mr Wells' ideas tactfully at Denham, the German director letting himself down into his canvas chair at Elstree ... I cannot help wondering whether from this great moneyed industry anything of value for the human spirit can ever emerge. (Taylor, 1972, pp. 79–80)

Recent analyses of Greene's review have tried to downplay these comments, interpreting them merely as a personal attack on Alexander Korda (see Parkinson, 1993). Yet there are similar statements by others, infused in varying degrees with the xenophobia and anti-Semitism that can be found, worryingly often, in many subsequent assessments of British film history (see for example C. A. Oakley's history of British cinema, *Where We Came In* (1964), and its chapter on 'The German Invasion').

What weighed even more than the public opinion, however, was the increasing pressure the immigrants were under within the studios. The driving force behind this pressure was the newly founded union of film technicians. The Association of Cine-Technicians (ACT) had been formed in June 1933, as a response to the abysmal working conditions of British film technicians at the time. Unpaid overtime, shifts lasting well into the night, low wages and practically no financial or legal securities were the norm. This situation determined the ACT's interventions and policies for the rest of the 1930s. Issues of increasing wages and contractual security were high on the union's agenda. It is easy to see how the question of foreign personnel became a central rallying point for the ACT. In a time of general financial crisis within the industry the union's solution was to close ranks and opt for a policy of 'splendid isolation'. Ironically, the soundly left-wing ACT was one of the first voices within the industry to condemn Hitler's Germany, and the tension between political idealism and economic imperatives must have been nearly impossible to balance. That some desperate refugees, coming into the country after 1933, offered their services to the industry below the minimum wage did not help to endear them to their British colleagues. The various actions the ACT undertook to stop the employment of foreign personnel have been well documented elsewhere (for example, Low, 1985; Gough-Yates, 1989, 1992). The British film industry changed within less than ten years from being a European, cosmopolitan film centre to a nationally defined trade guild, at least partly owing to the ACT's interventions. This effectively marked the end of the professional mobility that had been the dynamic force behind the European cinema of the 1920s and early 1930s. It has rarely been acknowledged how much the emergence of a national British film culture in the late 1930s owes, not only to the documentary style of Grierson and his colleagues, but also to the political pressure and lobbying of the ACT.

Established immigrants such as Junge certainly felt this pressure ocasionally, but were mostly secure in their positions, some of them becoming thoroughly adapted. Ferdinand Bellan, for example, became an active ACT member: 'He was more English than the English', remembered a fellow unionist in an obituary decades later (*Film and TV Technician*, 1976). Subsequent immigrants, however, particularly the truly political refugees after 1933, faced a much more closed industry. For them as for the 'travelling technicians' of the 1920s, the only career option left was Hollywood. The 'international years' of the British film industry were put on halt for the time being – although Rank's foreign aspirations revived this international dynamic to an extent after the war, the productions of Powell and Pressburger's company The Archers being the most prominent examples.

A 'Teutonic' aesthetic?

Looking at this period of British cinema in retrospect, the question remains whether the Continental technicians had any lasting discernible influence. In other words, is it possible to identify a distinctive style or aesthetic in British films of the 1930s which could be labelled specifically 'German'?

The idea of a 'Teutonic' influence has long been suggested, from review articles published in the 1930s, for example in Greene's and C. A. Lejeune's criticism during this period (Lejeune, 1991; Parkinson, 1993), to recent film historical analyses (Harper, 1995). Importantly, most of these approaches use the term 'Expressionism' as a kind of shorthand for German cinema as a whole.

German film scholars, particularly those associated with the Hamburg-based research group Cinegraph, have insisted for some time that the Weimar cinema was much more diverse than the label 'Expressionism' implies. Indeed they have contended that the majority of German films in the 1920s conformed rather to the conventions of indigenous popular genres (social melodrama, circus films, exotic epics, detective thrillers, and so on). It has been argued that of all the films produced in Germany between 1918 and 1933, less than a handful (including, of course, the ubiquitous *The Cabinet of Dr Caligari*, 1919) can be associated stylistically and in content with Expressionist principles. Furthermore, Expressionism was far from dominant in cinema or in German culture at large, and was always in competition with other influences and movements such as Constructivism, New Sobriety, and documentary naturalism, to name a few. To these influences one must add the style of early Danish cinema, which was widely copied by German film-makers well into the 1920s (see, for example, the films of Murnau). Furthermore, many Danish film-makers had worked in the German film industry since the pre-Weimar period, for example Urban Gad, Carl Theodor Dreyer and Benjamin Christensen. Their cinema, however, was widely regarded as 'Impressionist' (Behn, 1994). Weimar cinema of the late 1920s, on the other hand, was clearly influenced by the Russian political avant-garde. By the end of the decade austere social dramas and agit-prop documentaries had become common, and Russian film-makers such as Fedor Ozep, Alexander Rasumny and Victor Trivas worked in Germany (Schöning, 1995).

'German Expressionist Cinema' can thus be seen as a restrospective theoretical invention creating its own problematic canon. Some writers have argued that the term might have originated as a marketing strategy for exporting German films in the aftermath of World War One in general and *Caligari* in particular (see, for example, Jacobsen, 1989). Yet it is this perceived stylistic coherence and imagined unity of Weimar cinema that still informs a lot of current writing (most recently, in Thompson and Bordwell, 1994). This has also resulted in some misconceptions about the German influence in British films. A good example is Sue Harper's otherwise excellent analysis of art direction and costume design at Gainsborough in the 1940s, referring to the influence of the Continental immigrants of the 1930s:

> Gainsborough provided a space for those art directors who were opposed to the decor realism of other art directors like Morahan, Relph, and Sutherland ... to practise in a non-realist way. ... The influence of continental art directors such as Andre Andreiev, Ferdie Bellan, Vincent Korda and Alfred Junge can be seen far more clearly at Gainsborough than elsewhere. ... The art directors from Germany are widely recognised as anti-realist. ... Their expressionism was filtered through to Gainsborough art directors and tempered their concern with craftsmanship.' (Harper, 1983, pp. 40–1; see also Harper, 1994)

Apart from the notorious difficulty in defining what constitutes 'realism', particularly in the field of art direction, one should not forget that the UFA film architects of the 1920s regarded decor realism as a high priority (let alone the even more radical attempts at documentary realism of films such as *Menschen am Sonntag*, 1929). It is very doubtful that the German art directors 'filtered expressionism' through to their successors. Alfred Junge's disciples at Gaumont-British, for example, included not only later Gainsborough artists, but also Michael Relph, characterized by Harper as a decor realist.

It is very difficult to find a trace of an explicitly Expressionist aesthetic in the British films of the Continental technicians. It is in fact almost impossible to identify any stylistic coherence whatsoever, even within the *oeuvre* of a single artist. Ernö Metzner's work provides a perfect example: his sets for the science fiction film *The Tunnel* (1935) relate to the principles of the Bauhaus movement; *Chu Chin Chow* (1934), an exotic melodrama, is dominated by mannerist fake-Oriental sets; whereas the diagonals and steep angles of the dreamlike *The Robber Symphony* (1936) possibly come closest to being Expressionist. It is evident from these examples that stylistic choice was usually determined by generic requirements. This is particularly true for the work of Junge and Werndorff. The latter's sets for the Hitchcock thrillers *The Thirty-Nine Steps* (1935), *The Secret Agent* (1936) and *Sabotage* (1936) provide primarily functional spaces for action, while Junge's contributions to *The Man Who Knew Too Much* (1934), which incorporated a lot of outdoor scenery, and *Young and Innocent* (1937) strongly emphasize the verisimilitude of the sets.

All of this should come as no surprise. As I have argued, British cinema of the 1930s was mostly dominated by the Hollywood model of narration and *mise-en-scène* was not a means of producing meaning independently from the narrative, as it had been in German cinema of the 1920s. Most Continental art directors adhered in their British period to a 'classical' organization of space (Bordwell, Staiger and Thompson, 1985), and most of the rare aberrations from these principles can be explained as 'highlighting' markers for isolated dramatic effect. But this does not amount to a German aesthetic. German technicians had to adapt to a new working environment in Britain, to new styles and new narratives. In fact, in the end it was those technicians who managed to camouflage their national background, those who, like Bellan, blended in, who turned out to be the most successful.

I would argue, therefore, that what remains of these artists is not so much an individual legacy, but rather the way they reorganized the concept of *mise-en-scène* in the British film industry. This may also represent the only genuine and lasting influence in British films of German Expressionism, a movement that always stressed the importance of totalization and rationalization of design. Arthur Korn, an Expressionist theorist, wrote in 1923:

> Architecture is the royal leader. All the materials are put into its hands ... out of which develops a sense for material structure and the build-up of any substance. Architecture, ingenious as the machine, as the underground train, the air cabin. Anonymous. ...
> (Quoted in Behr, Fanning and Jarman, 1993, p. 80)

What counted more for the Expressionists than shades and angles was the belief that all expressions, art forms and media should combine in one unified artistic experience, a total work of art or *Gesamtkunstwerk*, designed and composed by the artist. I would argue that this Expressionist credo influenced the German film technicians more in terms of their approach to the organization of work, and less in terms of style. Their rationalization of technology and labour as well as the meticulous planning of filmic design can thus be seen as late manifestations of this credo. Expressionism as a distinctive style may not have had a great influence on British cinema, but the invention of the 'production designer' certainly did.

This article is a revised and updated version of a piece originally published in German in Jorg Schöning (ed.), *London Calling. Deutsche im britischen Film* (Munich: Edition Text und Kritik, 1993). Thanks to Charles Barr, Thomas Brandlmeier, Sidney Cole, Kevin Gough-Yates, Andrew Higson and Jorg Schöning for their support and help in my research.

Note

1. Primary research material for this chapter included the German and British trade press of the late 1920s and 1930s (mainly *Film Kurier* and *Kine Weekly*); the tapes of the Oral History Project of BECTU, held in the British Film Institute Library; and an interview with Sidney Cole, founding member of the ACT. My main secondary sources were Low, 1971, and 1985.

Engendering the Nation: British Documentary Film, 1930–1939

Kathryn Dodd and Philip Dodd

No one now shares Paul Rotha's judgement made in 1936 that the documentary film movement is 'this country's most important contribution to cinema as a whole' (Rotha, 1936, p. 96). The Gothic tradition within British cinema (from Powell and Pressburger through Gainsborough and Hammer) now seems more resonant for both young film-makers and critics. But unless we want to indulge in the 'enormous condescension of posterity', to use E. P. Thompson's phrase (1980, p. 14), and simply damn the British documentary film movement on ideological grounds, then we need to make intelligible its fascination with the remaking of the nation and its claim that the films enabled the nation to represent itself to itself.

Unfortunately, one dominant strand of film studies is ill-equipped to provide such intelligibility since it has deliberately cut itself off from the knowledges provided by the more traditional disciplines of History and Literature, in an attempt (understandable in certain ways) to establish its own disciplinary credentials and autonomy. This article, in contrast, is an attempt to place the study of documentary film in a wider context than is usual. It sets out from the premise best articulated by Raymond Williams in a posthumously published essay, that the meanings of contemporary forms of cultural production can only be fully appreciated by tracing their development in nineteenth century forms. Such precursors, he argues, 'are elements in the constitution of these precise contemporary forms, so that the tension between that history of social forms and these forms in a contemporary situation, with their partly new and partly old content, partly new and old techniques, can be explored with weight on both sides' (Williams, 1989, p. 159). Taking our cue from Williams, our argument is that we need to establish the provenance of the thinking about the national culture that informed dominant documentary practices in the late 1920s and 1930s, as well as some of the density of the 'current situation' in which the films were made, if we are to understand the specific contours of its imbrication with the national culture between the wars. In short, we need to work simultaneously on two fronts and provide both a diachronic and a synchronic analysis of those dominant documentary practices.

In analysing the documentary film movement, reference to a number of significant films of the period will be supplemented by a detailed examination of John Grierson's writings on the movement first published in the 1930s. What we would maintain is not simply that Grierson and his work were central to the movement, but that his writings had a definitive impact on the way documentaries were received as conscious interventions into current arguments about the 'State', 'Nation' and 'Film'. The most cursory glance through the 1946 collection of essays, *Grierson on Documentary*, reveals his concern with the construction of a national culture (Hardy, 1946, pp. 16, 140, 126). Dominating the volume are ideas of 'citizenship', 'national education', 'the corporate nature of community life', and their centrality to any serious thinking about film.

So what is the political provenance of Grierson's vocabulary? Like the man himself (he was born in 1898), it should be located in the period 1880–1920, the years of a massive reconstruction of capital, the rise of collectivisms, and the formation of a new kind of 'educative' interventionist state. Grierson's celebration of citizenship, his sense of 'the impossibility of pursuing the old liberal individualist and rational theory', and his belief that 'the great days of unmitigated individualism and governmental *laissez-faire* are over, and the day of common unified planning has arrived' (Hardy, 1946: 124, 193), echo the early twentieth century collectivists who, conscious of the bankruptcy of an ideology of economic *laissez-faire*, offered the state as the neutral site for resolving class conflict by elaborating a politics of citizenship and community.

Note the similarity between Grierson's vocabulary above and that of the Fabian collectivist Sidney Webb writing in the 1890s:

... if our aim is the transformation of England into a Social Democracy we must frankly accept the changes brought about by the Industrial Revolution ... [and] the subordination of the worker to the citizen, of the individual to the community. We must rid ourselves resolutely of all these schemes and projects of bygone socialisms which have now passed out of date. (Quoted in Yeo, 1986)[1]

Efficient social democracy was to be effected through individual self-realization which, to become a reality for all citizens, necessitated the state getting rid of social impediments such as ignorance and poor environmental conditions, while at the same time encouraging a sense of community and national belonging.

Webb's relegation of other kinds of socialisms to the realm of the unmodernized past is paralleled by Grierson's argument that the 'socialist dreams of workers' control in a classless society' represented an 'unpractical and inefficient [ideal]' (Hardy, 1946, p. 197). But if the continuity between the dominant documentary film tradition and the ideas of the turn-of-the-century collectivists was solely a matter of a shared political vocabulary, it would still be worthy of note, given our conviction that the specific processes of film must be seen in relation to a more general history. But the relation is much more substantial. Within a history of film the British documentary movement begins in, say, 1929 with *Drifters* directed by Grierson himself. With an awareness of a wider cultural history, the grammar and concerns of the movement can be traced back to the 'Into Unknown England' writing of the late nineteenth century, in which the older tradition of personal exploration blended, according to Peter Keating, 'into the newer techniques of sociological analysis' (Keating, 1976, p. 10). We are with Raymond Williams in his argument that there are 'really very few films, by proportion, for which there is not a nineteenth-century precedent in drama or entertainment', and also, we would add, in such social reporting (Williams, 1983, p. 17).

Like the documentary film – which Grierson tells us initially meant travelogue – such writing involves our travelling into a world unknown to us. The titles and subjects of some of the writings could serve for the much later projects of the documentary film-makers: consider Lady Bell's *At the Works* (1907), a study of iron foundry workers in

Middlesbrough, or Stephen Reynolds' *A Poor Man's House* (1909), or George R. Sims' *How the Poor Live* (1883). The continuity between these two groups of travellers is evident: George Sims writes of the need to travel 'into a dark continent that is within easy walking distance of the General Post Office' (quoted in Keating, 1976, p. 107), and Grierson of his desire to 'travel dangerously into the jungles of Middlesborough and the Clyde' (quoted in Hood, 1983, p. 107). Their intentions are also paralleled: if the writers discovered that the working class had a culture of their own, so the film-makers wished to discover 'tales of fine craftsmanship ... tucked away in the Black Country' (Hardy, 1946, p. 56) or to map the leisure of that class (for example, Humphrey Jennings' *Spare Time*, 1939). Like the documentarists (documentary is itself a nineteenth century word), such writers were convinced of the need to bring the middle classes and the poor into one nation, and of the necessity for the enlightened state to regulate social life. Grierson would even go so far as to claim that films such as *Housing Problems* (Edgar Anstey and Arthur Elton, 1935), which condemned the slum conditions of the poor and presented the alternative in the form of a model council estate, were meant to avert a working-class revolution, a 'bloodier solution' (Hardy, 1946, p. 181).

The inscribed audience of both groups has to be led into this unknown world. In *The Bitter Cry of Outcast London*, Andrew Mearns addresses his own class thus: 'Few who read mere pages have any conception. ... To get into [the rookeries] you have to penetrate courts' (quoted in Keating, 1976, p. 15). In *Housing Problems*, what are reductively called establishing shots, an aesthetic convention which like all such conventions inscribes variable social meaning, move the viewer into the slums from outside. The opening sequence of cuts is as follows (the voice-over is of a councillor introducing the area and its 'problems'): high distant shot of the slum area; pan on high from left to right of the building of new flats; medium long shot of back of slums; pan right to left of roofs; eye level shot from within the alley. The next five shots move us slowly and inexorably into a yard; three shots later we are inside one of the houses. We have arrived. It may be that the film-makers' actual audience was more heterogeneous than that of the earlier explorers, but there is no mistaking Grierson's pride in his (middle-class) audience's response to *Industrial Britain* (1933) or the continuity between that response and the one desired by the earlier writers: 'the workers' portraits of *Industrial Britain* were cheered in the West End of London. The strange fact was that the West End had never seen workmen's portraits before – certainly not on the screen' (Hardy, 1946, p. 139).

To gauge Grierson's achievement we have only to remember the other tradition of representing the urban poor by middle-class observers. This tradition, which has a much longer history, represents the urban poor as a cultureless class, lost in an abyss of filth, depravity, criminality and sin. Comparisons were made throughout the nineteenth century between the urban masses living in *terra incognita*, and the 'savages' of Africa (Schwarzbach, 1982, pp. 64–8). Ungodly, habitually drunk, sexually active from a young age, and physically debilitated – some observers were led to the belief that the degeneration was so extreme that the poorest classes had reverted to an animal state. In an early nineteenth century Parliamentary Report on the populations of the large towns, one witness, Southwood Smith, claimed that to understand how the poor live, you 'have only to visit the Zoological Gardens and to observe the state of society ... where every want is relieved, and every appetite and passion gratified' (*First Report of the Commissioners for Inquiring into the State of Large Towns and Populous Districts*, pp. 82–3, quoted in Schwarzbach, 1982, p. 74). The use of primitive analogues in relation to the working class did not disappear with the advent of the new century. In a 1933 BBC wireless programme on the slums of Tyneside, the presenter talked of 'stumbling along a pitch dark passage' at the end of which 'squat a dozen or so misshapen houses ... like a collection of mud huts in an African swamp. I didn't go because I wanted to ...' (*The Listener*, 18 January 1933, pp. 73–4, quoted in Scannell and Cardiff, 1991, pp. 142–3).[2]

Rather than fear and loathing, the film-makers' dominant stance towards the relationship between the audience and the working class, like that of many of the earlier writers in the 'Into Unknown England' tradition, can be summed up by one word, 'conscience'. The preciousness and value of *Housing Problems* according to Grierson was that it 'touches the conscience' of its audience (Hardy, 1946, p. 149). An invention of the late nineteenth century, 'social conscience', not to be confused with solidarity or affiliation, involves, according to Raymond Williams, 'a persistent sense of a quite clear line between an upper and a lower class. ... It is a matter of social conscience to go on explaining and proposing at official levels, and at the same time to help in organising and educating the victims' (Williams, 1980, p. 155). 'Explaining and proposing', 'organising and educating' – could there be a better description of a large part of Grierson's programme, and of his writing which is addressed to one class about the 'problem' of another? 'Film can really bring the outside world alive to the growing citizen,' he tells us. 'It really can serve an interpretative function ... it can, if it is mastered and organised provide this necessary umbilical to the community outside' (Hardy, 1946, p. 127). Note the spatial organization of the gaze, as the citizen, defined as an insider, is persuaded by the documentary film to take responsibility for looking 'outside'.

And how is the class which is looked at viewed? The simplest role they are cast in is that of 'victim'. *Housing Problems*, already referred to, offers a sequence of slum dwellers who, after being introduced to us through commentary, speak direct to camera, responding to an unseen interrogator (Mr Bruner: 'a lot of people don't understand what it's like living in one room'). We are never given in visual terms the point of view of any of the occupiers; the camera keeps a discreet distance, it simply looks and allows its audience to examine poor people in their own houses. What the film shows is that these people need our help and that we have nothing to fear if we provide them with better homes. The representation of the 'victims' is consolidated in the film's preference for the occupiers to address us from around the fire or by the mantelpiece, a preference paralleled in one of Orwell's pre-war comments about working-class interiors, 'when the fire glows in the open range ... when Father, in shirt sleeves, sits in the rocking chair ... and Mother sits on the other with her sewing' (Orwell, 1962, p. 104). There is a strain of English thinking on the 'poor' which stretches into the 1950s with Hoggart's *Uses of Literacy* (1957), which is happiest with the apparent gendered certainties *chez* the working class.

Working class as 'victim' is less prominent in documentary film than working class as working hero. In films such as *Industrial Britain* and *Coalface* (1935) the concentration on men at work is cause and effect of the determination to see 'the working man ... as a heroic figure' (Edgar Anstey, quoted in Hood, 1983, p. 107), and to celebrate 'the ardour and bravery of common labour' (Hardy, 1946, p. 86). The male body becomes the focus of this celebration, seen at its simplest in the countless close-ups of the male body at work. For example, in *Coalface*, a film in which the human being is so often displaced by the machinery to the margins of the frame, the only sustained close-ups are of semi-naked miners. Such celebration may also help to explain the (very common) preference for dusk/dawn shots in which the worker's individuality is effaced and he is seen – like the machinery he serves – as shape.

There are also moments within a number of films when the male body absorbs attention without regard to its work function. Consider that sequence in *Coalface* of two miners eating their snap. After a few shots which establish their presence against the visible coal seam, and via a shot of one of the men's sandwiches, a shot of a different order is produced. The coal seam has disappeared and foregrounded on the left of the frame in the blackness – lit and shot from above – is the radiant face and body of a miner; on the right hand side is a muscular arm around which is wrapped a large hand. In a film characterized by rapid cutting, this shot, absorbed in the male body, is held for some time. One might understand the significance of such a sequence by a quotation from Graham Sutherland, a commissioned Second World War artist, who painted miners. Uninterested in his own 'small and naturalistic' drawings of miners' heads, he felt that the deeper significance of the miners was that 'they were a kind of different species – ennobled underground, and with an added *stature* which, above ground, they lacked' (quoted in Ross, 1983, pp. 44-5).

Beatrix Campbell's attack in *Wigan Pier Revisited* on Orwell's 1937 celebration of the miners' 'most noble bodies; wide shoulders ... and small pronounced buttocks, with not an ounce of waste flesh anywhere' could also stand as a critique of the treatment of the bodies of manual workers in the dominant documentary tradition:

> ... miners are victims and heroes at the same time ... they command both protection and admiration. They are represented as beautiful statuesque shaded men. The miner's body is loved in the literature of men because of its work and because it works.'
> (Campbell, 1984, pp. 97–8)

What Campbell's attack on 'male narcissism' neglects is the class and homoerotic dimensions of such representations – these are representations of the men of one class by the men of another – and of their ideological significance. Concentration on the splendour of male working-class bodies (a simple complement to a matching obsession with their animality) fixes such men's competencies at the level of the physical and ratifies the distinction between mental and manual labour. Working-class women are simply read out of the picture or 'left' at home (see, for instance, *Housing Problems* or *North Sea*, 1938).

But there is another dimension to the documentarists' fascination with the construction of strong, virile working-class male bodies, one that can only be made intelligible if we recover some of the density of the 'contemporary situation' when the movement emerged – a moment when a dominant version of national identity as being vigorous and manly was in crisis. The 1920s was such a moment of crisis for the national culture for a variety of reasons, not least because those who were said to incarnate the best of the nation had perished in the Great War, leaving only the old and neurasthenic survivors behind. Through the period and particularly between 1928 and 1933 (when the documentary tradition begins), there was, according to the literary historian Robert Wohl, a flood of male autobiographical writing which attempted to come to terms with the devastating effects of the Great War on notions of middle-class manliness, established in the last quarter of the nineteenth century as the essence of Englishness (Wohl, 1980). That particular species of manliness nurtured in the reformed public schools and in the imperial domains has been described by one commentator as 'chivalric romanticism' (Mangan, 181, p. 135) and included the inculcation of values such as victory within the rules, courtesy in triumph and compassion for the defeated. The presumption is always that of the victorious overlord with responsibilities to the defeated; 'vigorous, manly, and English' was the popular collocation (Dodd, 1986, p. 6). It was this vision of chivalric Englishness which was declared either dead or anachronistic in the late 1920s. A whole generation of men educated in such a system was in the process of looking back to the apparent certainties of the pre-war years to make sense of a completely altered set of social relations; *Goodbye to All That*, Robert Graves' 1929 autobiography, has a representative title though he was to endorse the changes taking place. Others were much more ambivalent and the general cultural construction was of an overwhelming sense of masculine loss and discontinuity with the past. 'Supposedly,' says Wohl, 'the purest and noblest, the strongest and most cultivated had fallen; the weakest and the least courageous had survived. The process of reverse selection had meant "failure and calamity in every department of human life".' (Wohl, 1980, p. 113)

How that loss reverberated through the 1930s can be seen across a range of cultural practices – from literature, through music, into film. For example, its resonance can be felt in *The Four Feathers* (1939), a film set in the period when vigorous manly Englishness was forged, and ostensibly concerned to laud the qualities of the English officer class, as it moves its protagonists from what George Orwell called 'deep' England to the deserts of the Sudan. At the start of the film, Harry Faversham is seen as a dashing, handsome soldier in a tight-fitting uniform. But he rejects the military code of English manhood and resigns his commission when ordered to go to the Sudan to fight. Rejected by his family and branded as a coward by his colleagues, he is determined to prove himself. But what is interesting is that to do so he has to discard his English military uniform and dress himself as an Arab servant, in the usual robes and turban. It is impossible not to be reminded of that other Englishman turned Arab, T. E. Lawrence in David Lean's post-Suez film *Lawrence of Arabia* (1962), in which a different formation of English masculinity is scrutinized. But *The Four Feathers* is the more radical film; not only is the Englishman made a native servant, suitably passive and submissive (Lawrence gets to keep his officer status and his own servants), but he has to pass as dumb – the untouchable caste he joins are made pariahs by having their tongues cut out. The film conjugates all the elements of an imperial English masculinity in order to expose their inadequacy: for Faversham to become a hero, he has to strip himself of every one of these elements – his status, his whiteness, his lordliness over others, his clothes, and even his power of speech are given away. That the protagonist's extraordinary acts of heroism are private rather than public and that they can only be carried out in the guise of a feminized 'other' is suggestive of the extraordinary crisis which afflicted the dominant version of manly Englishness between the wars.

Although we do not want to be drawn into the error of believing the process was cause and effect, it appears clear that the documentarists' obsession with working-class masculinity should be seen as one of the ways that a new, alternative version of manly Englishness could be first imagined and then stabilized. The films themselves make clear that not only should virile, heterosexual, working-class masculinity be welcomed into the nation, but that such a masculinity might serve to incarnate it. This is said without any sense of condescension; there was clearly a desire to incorporate the class into the national culture and to give them a voice of their own for the first time in film, in much the same way that innovative BBC producers in the regions, especially in Manchester, had begun to incorporate local people into their 1930s documentary programmes (Scannell and Cardiff, 1991, pp. 341–5). But the process of incorporation necessarily involved a fixing of the class in the image of the film-makers. That the class was masculine, and working-class women were therefore marginalized, was not just an unfortunate omission. We will argue in the last section of this essay that the documentary film movement should be seen as an offensive against the feminization of Englishness in the 1930s, a process which was part of the crisis of dominant manly Englishness.

Kate Millett's analysis of anti-feminism in the fiction of such American writers as Norman Mailer as a reaction against the rise of second-wave feminism (Millett, 1972) provides a helpful analogue to the relation between first wave feminism and the documentary film movement. After all, in 1928, the year before the first Griersonian documentary was made about the hard lives of fishermen, not only did all women get the vote, but two landmark feminist publications also appeared: Virginia Woolf's *A Room of One's Own* and Ray Strachey's *The Cause*, the first authorized history of the feminist movement. Both publications argued for women's occupation of formerly masculine spaces – whether it was the Oxford colleges, the nation's political structures, or cultural forms which had been dominated by men. For Ray Strachey to write her history of the feminist movement in terms of a series of biographical portraits of 'great' women was to challenge the orthodoxy that said history was the biography of great men. Her argument was that metropolitan women (now liberated and in partnership with men of like minds) were to be the spearhead of the modernization of Britain (Strachey, 1928, p. 392; see also Dodd, 1990).

The documentarists appeared to be moving into the territory of a different class of men, just as middle-class male spaces were being forced open by women; nothing could be a greater contrast to Strachey's modernization of Britain than the documentary, *Drifters*. The film offered a representation of the nation as a predominantly male community, with images of physical, concentrated co-operation, which were to reappear in films such as *Night Mail* (1936) and *Coalface*. The fishermen in *Drifters* were essentialized, their essence located in their strength and endurance, a result of their experience struggling against the natural elements. The 'Into Unknown England' tradition had as usual been there first. Stephen Reynolds, in *A Poor Man's House* (1909) journeyed to Plymouth and observed the herring fishermen: 'the air here has been charged with excitement – the excitement of men who earn their livelihood by gambling with the sea' (quoted in Keating, 1976, p. 265). At this earlier moment, the concern was more about establishing the idea that the working class had a separate and vital culture of their own; by 1929 that same group was transformed into the very icon of the nation – drawing on ideas of true manliness and true Britishness, and thus contributing to a new modernizing cultural intervention. In this sense, *Drifters* should be seen as continuous with the discoveries being made by a group of contemporary metropolitan artists who made regular pilgrimages to Cornwall between the wars and found inspiration in the work of the fisherman and the untutored, 'primitive' painter Alfred Wallis. In Sven Berlin's biography, *Alfred Wallis: Primitive*, as much as in *Drifters*, the working-class male becomes the new icon of a manly nation, as far removed from imperial manliness as it is possible to imagine (Berlin, 1949).

That the seedbed for a new invigorated national identity should be discovered at the geographical peripheries of Britain, up 'north', or in the coastal fishing villages, was not incidental. The 'south' of England was in the process of being physically and culturally abandoned by male artists of all kinds as an increasingly feminized domain. The reasons for the abandonment of the 'south' as a possible location for manly Englishness are suggested by Alison Light in *Forever England*, in which she outlines what she sees as the 'conservative modernization' of Englishness through women's literary writing between the wars:

> What had formerly been held as the virtues of the private sphere of middle-class life take on a new public and national significance. I maintain that the 1920s and 1930s saw a move away from formerly heroic and officially masculine public rhetoric of national destiny ... to an Englishness at once less imperial and more inward-looking, more domestic and more private – and, in terms of pre-war standards, more 'feminine'. (Light, 1991, p. 8)[3]

Women's fictional narratives, according to Light, constructed an England which was populated by the new southern middle classes unsure of their social standing and looking to their suburban homes and their leisure sites to develop new identities. What was more likely to repel the documentary film-maker in his search for an essential masculine Englishness than being introduced by Agatha Christie to the inner thoughts of a hairdresser, 'uttering mechanically the usual clichés, "Let me see, how long has it been since your last perm, Madam?"' (Christie, 1935, p. 14, quoted in Light, 1991, p. 76)? Or having the contents of the bedroom of a respectable but shabby female shopkeeper described to him: 'a little stock of well-darned underwear in a drawer – cookery recipes in another – a paper-backed novel entitled *The Green Oasis* – ...a Dresden shepherd much broken, and a blue and yellow spotted dog – a black raincoat and a woolly jumper hanging on pegs – such were the worldly possessions of the late Alice Asher' (Christie, 1936, p. 33, quoted in Light, 1991, p. 82)? Such lives were not the stuff of heroism which the documentarists required for their project of remaking manly Englishness. And it is extraordinary how persistent the equation of southernness with femininity has remained, as can be seen in the words of novelist and screenwriter David Storey who in the early 1960s described two novels he had recently written:

> It was in order, so it seemed, to accommodate the two extremes of this northern physical world and its southern, spiritual counter-part that I started making notes which two years later, while I was still at the Slade, resulted in the writing of a novel which I called *This Sporting Life*. ... In this way, the northern terminus of that journey became associated with a masculine temperament, and when I came to write its southern counterpart – the intuitive, poetic and perhaps precious world to which I felt I had escaped – I immediately associated it with femininity, with a woman's sensibility and responses. The north–south dichotomy became a masculine–feminine one. The second novel, *Flight Into Camden*, was written in the first person by a woman. (Storey, 1963, pp. 159–60)

Our argument, then, is that the dominant British documentary tradition not only activated the late nineteenth-century project of binding antagonistic classes into one nation, by 'explaining' one to the other, but was also a source for the making of a new, masculine, post-imperial national identity in opposition to the feminization of that national identity between the wars. What the documentarists 'discover' is a heroic, masculine British working class. And as they do so, they renew their own manliness as they cut through to the 'jungles' of Middlesbrough, descend into the mines of Yorkshire or adventure out into the high seas with the fishermen. To understand this is not to encourage any simple condescension towards the project in which film-makers were involved. But it is to be reminded that those who do not understand history are condemned to repeat it.

Notes

1. On collectivism, see Greenleaf, 1983, and Collini, 1979.
2. For a discussion of the representation of the working class in post-war fiction, film and television in relation to the history of such representations, see Dodd and Dodd, 1992.
3. Raymond Chandler, an English *émigré*, criticized Agatha Christie's fiction on the basis that she wrote in 'the conversational accent of Surbiton and Bognor Regis' and believed that English female whodunits were like 'a cup of lukewarm consommé at a spinsterish tea-room' (Chandler, 1950, p. 7, quoted in Light, 1991, p. 75).

Neither Here nor There: National Identity in Gainsborough Costume Drama

Pam Cook

Since the turn of the century, the construction of national identity in and of British cinema has been debated with considerable intensity, not only by scholars and historians, but also by journalists, film-makers and official bodies. That the subject should arouse such passion is an indication of the power accorded to cinema, above all the arts, in representing (in both senses of the word) Britain's national culture. The heated arguments are also symptomatic of the importance of the concept of nation in the formation of individual and group identities, the sense we have of ourselves and others as both discrete and different yet belonging to a wider community. The stakes are high: what is at issue is the investment of each of us in the culture in which we live, even though we may not have been born into it, and the status of that culture in relation to others.

I do not have space here to trace the history of these debates; this essay is part of a wider project to investigate some of the ways in which national identity in relation to British cinema has been discussed in film studies (Cook, 1996). My argument in the following pages is intended to be an intervention in that discussion, and an attempt to shift its terms. Interesting though much of the work in this area is, it has been characterized by a narrow focus – not only in the restricted choice of films considered, but also in the way national identity has been conceived. Even the more sophisticated accounts, such as those in the British Film Institute monograph *National Fictions* (Hurd, 1984), for example, which posit national identity as a process in which conflicting discourses compete until one of them achieves hegemony, pay less attention to the marginalized discourses than to those that achieve consensus. This has not only impoverished the debates; it reproduces a view of British cinema as the parochial consensus cinema many believe it to be, neglecting the transgressive currents that keep any film culture alive.

My own focus on a handful of period costume romances produced by Gainsborough Studios between 1943 and 1950 may seem equally restricted. It is motivated by the fact that, despite the rediscovery of the Gainsborough melodramas by film historians in the early 1980s (Aspinall and Murphy, 1983), these costume dramas remain marginalized, ignored or subsumed into the consensus in discussion of national identity in British cinema (Hurd, 1984; Richards, 1988; Lant, 1991; Higson, 1995a). I hope to shed light on why this should be so by exploring the anti-consensual aspects of this brief cycle of films. I will suggest that their critical neglect has to do with their approach to costume and visual style and the ways in which they flouted demands for realism and authenticity in wartime and immediately post-war British cinema. It also has to do with their representation of history, their mobilization of a notion of identity in crisis that contravened contemporary official strictures, and the versions of femininity they constructed at this crucial period of social change.

The 1940s are characterized by an intensification of debates around national culture and the demand for a quality indigenous cinema that would represent the British character and ideals to both foreign and domestic audiences (Ellis, 1978, revised for this volume). They are also perceived as a golden age for British cinema after the economic difficulties of the late 1930s. British films held their own, at least at the home box office, against competition from Hollywood – a relatively unusual state of affairs (Lant, 1991, pp. 231–3). It is hardly surprising, then, that this period is constantly returned to by historians. As I have already indicated, discussion of national identity in wartime British cinema has tended to focus on what might be called the consensus films – that is, those on which an uneasy alliance of opinion between producers and critics (mainly from the quality press) and official bodies such as the Ministry of Information Films Division, the Foreign Office and the British Board of Film Censors conferred the status of quality British cinema. Audiences, however, often failed to agree with the consensus. The critically sanctioned films were not always successful at the domestic box office (Lant, 1991, pp. 231–3). In fact, a relatively small number of films achieved quality status. Some titles might be: *In Which We Serve* (1942), *Millions Like Us* (1943), *This Happy Breed* (1944), *The Way Ahead* (1944) and *Waterloo Road* (1945) (Lant 1991, pp. 41–56). Both *Millions Like Us* and *Waterloo Road* were produced by Gainsborough Studios.

The criteria for a quality national cinema were defined in terms of opposition to Hollywood spectacle in favour of an austere realism. Visual and acting styles were to be restrained, the emphasis was to be on ordinary people in contemporary settings. The documentary flavour of many of the consensus films emphasized their immediacy, their foundation in the 'here and now' (Higson, 1984a; 1995a). And, as Antonia Lant has pointed out, the deglamorized heroine, stripped of her American counterpart's trappings of stardom, was crucial to the realist project (Lant, 1991). As the home front became increasingly vital to national defence, women's role, their acquiescence to national goals of self-sacrifice and deference to the community (often conflated with family) were placed high on the cultural agenda. Lant has discussed in detail the official attempts to manage the mobilization of a specific kind of femininity – one that was desexualized, almost masculinized, though only up to a point. As women donned uniforms and dungarees and the boundaries of gender threatened to disappear entirely, the War Office commissioned a specially designed corset from Berlei that would 'preserve the feminine line and at the same time be practical under a uniform' (Lant, 1991, p. 110).

Lant's work is invaluable in opening up discussion of national identity to questions of gender and sexuality. Nevertheless, like many other commentators on the subject, she tends to concentrate on films which more or less subscribe to the quality consensus, treating as limit cases those such as Powell and Pressburger and the Gainsborough costume dramas which appear to flout the quality criteria. In fact, with notable exceptions, such as Ian Christie's work on Powell and Pressburger in *Arrows of Desire* (Christie, 1994), some wayward contributors to Charles Barr's *All Our Yesterdays* (Barr, 1986), and Sue Harper's *Picturing the Past* (Harper, 1994), British commentators on national identity appear to be remarkably attached to the realist canon.

A major problem for British film-makers and critics has been the desire to differentiate their national cinema from the Hollywood movies that have always dominated the domestic market. In many cases, the resistance to the internationalism of Hollywood has led to the impasse of an essential British identity. However, the documentary-realist option is not necessarily the most obvious or natural route to take in defining a quality British cinema. There are rich traditions of fantasy in British culture, manifest in our Gothic literature, for example; and decorative and anti-realist traditions in British architecture, painting and theatre (Pevsner, 1956). Many of these traditions have been reflected in British cinema – in the Alexander Korda extravaganzas of the 1930s, for instance, or in 1950s and 1960s Hammer horror. There seem to be two main reasons for the wartime consensus around realism as the optimum British aesthetic: the rejection, in wartime austerity conditions, of what were seen as the decorative excesses of Hollywood; and a general masculinization of culture during the war, because women were required to stand in for absent men in key tasks, with a consequent devaluing of 'feminine' frivolity in favour of 'masculine' restraint.

The masculinization effect was nowhere more obvious than in the areas of clothing and cosmetics, both subject to strict regulation, for obvious practical and economic reasons (Lant, 1991, pp. 68–72). But it is also striking, when looking at the designs for women's utility clothing, that they are based on a square, tailored look that flattens the female body, ironing out the signs of sexual difference. Utility clothing was not just utilitarian, it was a form of cross-dressing which allowed women to try on masculine drag – sanctioned, moreover, by official sumptuary regulations. Though resisted by some, this masculine androgynous look was perceived by many as democratic and egalitarian, offering women equal opportunities with men in the public sphere. That this equality was more apparent than real has been pointed out by many feminist writers (for example, Harper, 1988). However, there is no doubt that many women in wartime Britain felt empowered by masculinization, and after the war they were naturally reluctant to relinquish such freedoms (Phillips, 1963). Indeed, the scandal caused by French designer Christian Dior's extravagantly feminine 'New Look' in 1947 Britain has as much to say about sexual politics as about economics.

Since Elizabeth Haffenden's splendid costume designs for the Gainsborough costume cycle were promoted as heralding the New Look, it is worth investigating this scandal further. The New Look was launched at the peak of post-war austerity conditions in Britain, and although it eventually became fashionable, it had a difficult passage at first, inspiring heated debates in the press (Phillips, 1963). Many objected to its extravagance (the long, full skirt required an exorbitant amount of material) and others to its inconvenience (all those flounces were hardly suitable for working women). Some Labour Party feminists disliked its frivolity and its sexiness: the fitted jacket emphasized the breasts, waistline and hips that had all but disappeared during the war. (Also difficult to accept, perhaps, was its Europeanness – the New Look represented a bid by Paris to restore its status as leader in the world of high fashion, which had been seriously dented during the war.) Yet, as Elizabeth Wilson has pointed out, the New Look itself was curiously androgynous (Wilson, 1985). The models were tall and imposing, often with an erect military bearing or carrying a City-style umbrella. What seems to have been at stake in the arguments over the New Look was the shift from a masculine to a feminine androgyny. Perhaps, too, the New Look presaged the post-war dual role of women as both mothers and workers. It is interesting that in some manifestations, the style incorporated a strong element of masquerade. It was almost as if the women who had stood in for men during the war were now disguising this fact by displaying an assertive femininity. At any rate, the New Look did not simply represent a nostalgic return to an oppressive, domesticated femininity, as has sometimes been argued. It is better seen as a complex, hybrid cultural phenomenon signifying a process of social transition.

To return to the Gainsborough costume cycle, it is not difficult to find a precursor of the negative responses to the frivolity of the New Look in the scandalized reactions of the quality critics in particular, who derided the costume dramas' lack of seriousness. Simon Harcourt-Smith, writing in *Tribune* in response to *The Wicked Lady* (1945), could scarcely stomach it:

> Perhaps because I am, by inclination at least, an historian, *The Wicked Lady* arouses in me a nausea out of proportion to the subject. Perhaps I should not cavil at this complete mis-understanding of Restoration England, the tatty Merry English Roadhouse atmosphere, with the bowls of 'daffies' on the gate-legged tables, and the ladylike carousings of pretty Miss Margaret

Lockwood, with a James Mason so embarrassed and yet so competent as the highwayman, that he aroused at once both admiration and sympathy. The tedium, the grey ruin of modern life have obviously turned the costume picture into, perhaps, the most promising film gamble of today. ... By all means let us escape on the wings of the movies to less troubled epochs than the present. What more sumptuous, sexy and witty age could you find than the Restoration? But for the Lord's sake let's evoke it properly, let's use authentic material, the life of Pepys or of Charles II himself. ... In short, if the future of the British film industry hangs, as some say, on the success of *The Wicked Lady*, then let us dispense with that future. (quoted in Aspinall and Murphy, 1983, p. 74)

Apart from the significant conflation of authenticity with masculinity in this passage, it contains some interesting notions with respect to historical films: that they should be realistic, and not be seen to be 'restaging' history; that they should not take liberties with history; that they provide refuge from a troubled present in the past; and that the lives and works of great men are more appropriate subject matter than the misdemeanours of wicked ladies. It is interesting to note how many of Harcourt-Smith's remarks are echoed by more recent commentators – in Pierre Sorlin's ideas about the historical film as a vehicle which uses the past to process present concerns, for example (Sorlin, 1980). In Sorlin's analysis, 'history' (that is, the reconstructed past) is a mask for social, cultural and political concerns prevalent at a film's moment of production. The historian's task, then, is to demystify (unmask) the period reconstruction in order to reveal those concerns. So strong is the unmasking impulse in this approach that the visual processes of reconstruction – costume, decor and so forth – are rendered trans-parent. The 'present' (that is, the historian's analysis of it) is privileged, and authenticated, by virtue of being retrieved from behind the deceptive veneer of the past.

There are considerable advantages to Sorlin's argument. It recognizes the role of the present in reconstructing the past, for example, thereby challenging the authority of history as 'truth'. It also acknowledges the validity of the contributions made by popular fictions to a nation's understanding of its history. Yet there remains an ambivalence, also to

be found in Harcourt-Smith's comments, towards fictional recon-
structions of history, and a sense that the true historian transcends such
fictions to produce a more authentic (authoritative) analysis.

This ambivalence is also evident in an article by Andrew Higson on
the cycle of 1980s British heritage movies (Higson, 1993b). Higson is
suspicious of the heritage films' tendency to pastiche and self-conscious
visual splendour, which he sees as petrifying the past and detracting
from the ironic critique of Britain's imperialist history offered by the
narrative and dialogue. Although he does pay attention to the
contribution of visual codes to the process of historical reconstruction,
Higson defines spectacle negatively as the display of commodified
objects for consumption, and sees it as getting in the way of a more
authentic project which would enable the audience to take up a critical
position *vis à vis* the national past. In other words, the role of history,
even in its fictional forms, is to educate and instruct; it requires
analytical distance rather than a fetishistic fascination with the past; and
it must not be contaminated by commodification.

It is perhaps unfair to generalize about the assumptions underlying
Higson's argument, which is tied to a critique of a specific group of
films. His article represents a sophisticated and carefully elaborated
version of the 1980s left-inspired criticism of what was perceived as the
Thatcherite heritage movement (see also Corner and Harvey, 1991), and
his project is clearly different from that of Harcourt-Smith or Sorlin.
Nevertheless, he shares with both these writers a distrust of spectacle as
a potential distraction (or perhaps, following Gunning, 1990, 'attraction' would be a better word) from the more serious business of
historical analysis.

With such criteria at work, it is hardly surprising that the blatantly
spectacular, fanciful Gainsborough costume dramas should be so
troublesome. They are an uncomfortable reminder that history is
always masquerade, and they eschew the very idea of authentic, stable
identities. Of course, authenticity is a problem with all costume drama.
Costume and fashion are intertextual systems which play notoriously
on anachronism – something which is often less problematic for film-
makers and audiences than for critics. In spite of well-publicized
extensive research to get period detail right, audiences are aware of and
well able to accommodate the fact that liberties are taken by the film-
makers. Indeed, it seems to be a criterion of fantasy genres such as the

costume romance that boundaries of verisimilitude should be transgressed (Donald, 1992). Most of the studies by costume historians on historical films seem to bear this out: they are obsessed with pointing out inaccuracies and discrepancies (for example, Maeder, 1987). Yet it is clear from the Gainsborough costume films' playful visual jokes that the film-makers knew they were dealing in heterogeneity rather than accuracy. Since to the wartime quality critics lack of authenticity was identified with non-British identities (Lant, 1991), it is no wonder that they reviled the Gainsborough costume dramas. While much of British wartime cinema concentrated on contemporary British locations, several Gainsborough costume films were set in European locales, featured stories centred on European characters and dealt with cross-cultural romance. I shall return to this Europeanness later. First I should like to consider the relationship of the costume romance to the genre of the historical film.

The historical film is a hybrid genre which incorporates prestige literary adaptations, bio-pics, period musicals and comedies, Westerns, swashbuckling adventure and romantic melodramas – any of which can be and are mobilized in the interests of national identity. At the top end of this scale, what has been called the 'heritage' historical film allegedly serves to celebrate our glorious past (though if, as I have argued, authenticity is never achieved in costume drama, then the status of that celebration is brought into question). At the less reputable end, where the costume romances belong, the British past is mobilized more promiscuously. It can be a place of terrible injustice and inequality in contrast to the democratic present, as in *The Man in Grey*, the film that inaugurated the Gainsborough cycle in 1943. Indeed, most of the costume dramas depict the past as fraught with perversion, danger and risk; it is the locus of crisis and conflict as well as sensual pleasure. The contemporary wartime films were often set a few years in the past, so the invitation to relive the past seems to have been a vital, as yet little discussed, element in the audiences' pleasure, and in the endeavour to project a vision of the future of Britain (but see Lant, 1991, and Harper, 1994). In the case of the Gainsborough costume romances, the narrative resolutions of past conflicts were highly ambiguous. Frequently, the new-found equilibrium or the democratic egalitarianism that was to forge Britain's future were shadowed by past atrocities, but also by the loss of something important. If the costume romances, like the rest of

British cinema, looked forward to a modern Britain in which class and gender boundaries would be eroded, they also mourned the erasure of difference that this implied.

The films' questionable representation of the past extended to costume, set design and decor, which was not only playfully anachronistic but distinctly rococo. As Sue Harper has pointed out, the visual codes in the costume romances have their own language, which often works against the moralistic trajectory of the script in which the heroines received their comeuppance (Harper, 1983; 1994). It is interesting that Harper, using a similar argument to Higson's about the tension between spectacle and narrative, arrives at a diametrically opposed conclusion (Higson, 1993b). For Harper, spectacle plays a positive role in costume drama as the carrier of coded meanings which express the powerful status of femininity, overriding the narrative drive to disempower transgressive female protagonists. Audiences leaving a screening of *The Wicked Lady* (1945) were more likely to remember the stunning image of a fetishized Margaret Lockwood dressed in highwayman gear astride a stallion than to take on board the moral implications of her punishment by death.

Harper's validation of spectacle and fetishism ties in with recent feminist work on screen costume (for example, Gaines and Herzog, 1990). However, her position is relatively rare in discussion of British cinema. As I have already hinted, debates about identity in and of British cinema generally downplay the role of visual style, to which decor, the 'look' of a film, and costume are central. Visual and auditory codes are usually subordinated to questions of narrative. The costume cycle films are visually and auditorially very rich. The film-makers managed, under restricted economic conditions, to produce an extravagantly decorative 'look' which was in direct contrast to the understated realism of the consensus films (and, indeed, much closer to the critically despised Hollywood movies). Many of the designers (art director John Bryan and costume designer Elizabeth Haffenden, for example) were influenced by anti-realist currents in 1930s theatre design. Indeed, some of Haffenden's work for British theatre during this period had been criticized for its 'expressionism', a visual style associated by many British critics with German culture and problematic for that reason (see Bergfelder in this volume). There were also a number of European émigrés working in the British film industry at that time who had a particular impact on art direction – Vincent Korda, Alfred Junge, who was for a time head of art direction at Gainsborough/Gaumont-British, and Hein Heckroth spring immediately to mind (Harper, 1983; Bergfelder in this volume).

This influx of European personnel was in part the product of a strategy known as Film Europe, set in motion during the late 1920s and early 1930s when British film-makers attempted to challenge the hegemony of Hollywood by forming production alliances with European countries – particularly Germany, which was the most powerful market next to the US, and also possessed some of the most highly regarded technicians in the world. Gainsborough was deeply implicated in this Europeanization of British cinema. Michael Balcon, who founded the company with Graham Cutts in 1924, initiated many European co-productions until his departure in 1936 (Higson, 1993a). Indeed, Gainsborough was in this respect a very European company, importing many European personnel, so it is hardly surprising that European-influenced aesthetics should have resurfaced there in the 1940s – though transformed, of course, by the specific context of war-time and post-war Britain.

Madonna of the Seven Moons (1944) demonstrates this influence. The film is set in Italy. Phyllis Calvert plays Maddalena, a wealthy and saint-like Italian matron who was raped by a peasant when young, with the result that she now suffers from blackouts during which, transformed by her gypsy clothes into Rosanna, she escapes to the arms of her robber lover, played by Stewart Granger, who owns the Inn of the Seven Moons. Maddalena has a daughter (Patricia Roc) who has been educated in England, and who has returned home with modern ideas which precipitate Maddalena's present crisis. The scenes depicting Maddalena's other life as Rosanna are characterized by hyperbole in performance, costume, music and cinematography. Chiaroscuro lighting, exaggerated gesture, the use of superimposition and dissolves combine to create a world in which the expression of psychological and emotional states is predominant – indeed, a world in which expressivity itself is paramount. When Maddalena dresses in gypsy costume to leave her husband, her change of clothing is not motivated by the narrative, since neither her lover nor his family are gypsies, or even peasants. The gypsy costume functions primarily as an expression of Maddalena's desire for mobility and sexual freedom.

Many of the costume romances centre on identity crisis. Where the realist quality films privilege psychologically rounded, coherent, unified characters, the protagonists of the costume films are often deeply divided, caught in dramas of identity they sometimes do not survive (Maddalena/Rosanna dies at the end of *Madonna of the Seven Moons*, for example). If they successfully resolve the crisis, like Richard in *Caravan* (1946), the audience is often left with a sense of regret at what has been lost. Of course, it is possible to argue that these identity crises are somehow rendered 'safe' by being set in another time and place. However, their hostile reception by contemporary critics suggests otherwise. They addressed questions of national identity as directly as the consensus films, but they did so differently. Their much derided 'escapism' implied an unease with fixed boundaries of national identity, a desire to be someone else and elsewhere at a time when 'home', in official discourses at least, had acquired a particular resonance.

Audiences for these films were encouraged, through identification with British stars such as Stewart Granger, Margaret Lockwood, James Mason, Phyllis Calvert and others playing French, Italian or Spanish characters, to imagine themselves as Other, in this case as 'European'. The cycle's flouting of authenticity extended to the representation of national characteristics. Accents, costume and decor were as notoriously slippery in the depiction of geography as in the representation of period. In the realist films, there were some attempts to widen the scope of what constituted Britishness by incorporating regional characters into the narrative, and to soften chauvinism by reassessing national attitudes to our European allies (for example, Ealing Studios' *Johnny Frenchman*, 1945). It is also noticeable that European languages, particularly French, were spoken in British films of the time more frequently than they are today, and often without subtitles. British Europhobia was temporarily put to one side as the British imagined themselves overcoming cultural differences to a certain extent. To be British could also mean being European: national identity could be dual identity.

However, there were key differences between the contemporary realist films' treatment of this rapprochement and its depiction in the costume romances. In the realist films, British characters remain first and foremost British. Their values may be challenged, even modified by contact with other cultures, but this tolerance and flexibility is in any case seen as an essentially British quality. In the costume dramas, British identity is in crisis, seriously at risk of being swallowed up by the European Other. It is interesting, however, that this Other, and the qualities that are seen to make it Other, are given an unusual amount of space and value. The costume films deal in fantasies of loss of identity. They suggest that identity itself is fluid and unstable, like the costume genre itself, a hybrid state or form. And they suggest that national identity is not pure, but mixed.

Caravan, like *Madonna* directed by Arthur Crabtree, offers an example of this. Stewart Granger plays Richard, an impoverished writer of mixed parentage in that his doctor father married a gypsy. He is in love with an English woman, Oriana (Anne Crawford), from an aristocratic family whose debts put her at the mercy of the unscrupulous aristocrat Francis (Dennis Price) who, like Richard, has loved Oriana from childhood. Oriana and Richard plan to marry, but before this can happen Richard accepts a commission in Spain from a Spanish nobleman whose life he has saved. Francis secretly arranges for Richard to be killed in Spain, but he is saved by Rosal (Jean Kent), a gypsy dancer, who takes him to her mountain cave to recover. Richard has lost his memory and so lives as a Spanish gypsy with Rosal. An important part of his transformation is his change of costume. In the scene in which Richard declares his love for Rosal for the first time, he is dressed in Spanish matador garb and has to negotiate a dangerous quicksand in order to reach her.

Clearly this episode could partly be subsumed into parochial notions of national identity – it depicts an Englishman in peril. However, it is important to note that Richard's dalliance with his other self (he returns to his maternal roots) opens up space for desire and sensual pleasure absent from his life in England with Oriana. Of course, it is there that he returns in the end, but arguably at some cost: Rosal's tragic death, for one thing. She is a more vibrant, attractive character than Oriana, with a strong sense of pride in her gypsy origins. And it is Richard's superior knowledge of the foreign terrain, gained from his Spanish escapade, that enables him to destroy the villain Francis, who is a truly reprehensible example of Englishness: murderer, thief, rapist, coward and more besides. In other words, Richard's identity crisis, and by implication his mixed origins, are a positive force in cleansing Englishness and restoring equilibrium. This represents an interesting reversal of the principle of ethnic cleansing. *Caravan* offers a good example of what Sue Harper has called the symbolic costume narrative working against the script (Harper, 1983; 1994). In spite of the film's reaffirmation of Richard's Englishness on one level, Haffenden's designs emphasize the freedom and sensuality of Spanish dress in contrast to the restrictiveness and sobriety of Victorian English costume. It is also noticeable that Stewart Granger's Spanish clothes are distinctly feminized and sexualized, revealing his body in a way his English garb does not. There is no doubt that in returning home to England, Richard gives up a great deal.

Both *Madonna of the Seven Moons* and *Caravan* attach positive value to the itinerant gypsy spirit at the heart of the costume romances. The prominence of gypsies in popular literature and cinema of the 1930s and 1940s can, of course, be seen as a search for exoticism, and as a way of recognizing marginal groups in order to neutralize their threat to society. This is true in certain cases – in the Cineguild costume drama *Blanche Fury* (1947), for example, gypsies are seen as a dangerous, contaminating force. But there is more to the gypsy phenomenon than this. Gypsies are travellers who transgress boundaries of nation and property. They have little or no stake in national identity, and they are ethnically mixed. They are nomadic, which means that 'home', in the sense of a place to which they belong, is never more than a temporary dwelling. In the Gainsborough costume cycle, gypsies are depicted not as social outcasts, but as central figures in an essentially mobile society. Characters travel between home and abroad, between past and present and even, as in the case of *Jassy* (1947), in which Margaret Lockwood plays a gypsy woman, from the bottom to the top of the social ladder. Such an emphasis on mobility, particularly when it came to women, could prove troublesome to official agencies concerned with managing a difficult compromise between mobility and stability in wartime and post-war Britain (Lant, 1991).

The positive value attached to mixed identities in these British costume films did not last long. Soon after the war the optimism and forward-looking egalitarianism projected by most wartime films degenerated into introspective gloom, exemplified by the transition from the ebullient, colourful jingoism of Laurence Olivier's *Henry V* (1945) to the black-and-white melancholy of his *Hamlet* (1948). At the end of 1946, Sydney Box took over from Maurice Ostrer as head of Gainsborough, and the films subsequently produced by the studio manifested a darker tone. Significantly, Box was obsessed with authenticity, and his attempts to inject verisimilitude into the Gainsborough costume films and melodramas are documented. At the same time, the celebration of hybrid identities in the costume dramas came to an end: Europe became a site of xenophobic fears once more. This is illustrated by the film which is generally taken to mark the end of the Gainsborough costume cycle: *So Long at the Fair* (1950), directed by Terence Fisher and Anthony Darnborough. (The former went on to work for Hammer, where the British costume genre resurfaced in the late 1950s.)

In this film, the innocent English heroine, Vicky (Jean Simmons), visits Paris with her brother Johnny (David Tomlinson) in 1889, the year of the Paris Exposition – a peak time for French national identity. The lighting and decor present Paris as lushly decorative, almost to excess; Vicky is at first seduced by this colourful sensuality, but has to discover that it is all a facade. When her brother and his hotel room both disappear, she enlists the help of a young British painter (Dirk Bogarde) and together they break into Johnny's room, which has been sealed up, and through the plastered-over door into the hallway, effectively smashing through the deceptive veneer of Frenchness. In fact, Vicky's brother has contracted bubonic plague and has been spirited away by the hotel manageress to a nearby convent, a remarkably pessimistic view of the consequences of consorting with Europeans. *So Long at the Fair* returns to the realms of authentic, pure identities, supported by the search for truth which is also the search for verisimilitude. Rather than a positive celebration of fantasy, spectacle and anti-realism, it offers a paranoid vision of them as doomed and contaminated.

The Gainsborough costume romances are central to any discussion of national identity in 1940s British cinema. First, because they assert the feminine principle in history – not just in their narratives predicated on female desire as a motivating force in events, but in their overtly feminized 'look', which went against the grain of official demands for masculinized restraint. And second, because they celebrate an itinerant spirit in British cinema, an urge to move beyond fixed national boundaries to a more hybrid notion of national identity. The propensity for discourses around national identity to focus on officially sanctioned versions, important though they are, delivers a partial and misleading account of how national identity is constructed. In the fluctuating circumstances of 1940s Britain, when gender and class roles were in the process of radical revision, the achievement of consensus, if it happened at all, must have been particularly difficult. Spreading the investigative net wider not only produces a fuller historical picture, it transforms our perception of the object of study itself. The women who made up a large part of wartime cinema audiences enjoyed a wide range of competing and conflicting on-screen and off-screen representations and identifications. There is little to suggest that they identified solely or even primarily with the patriotic ideologies of restraint and self-sacrifice promoted by the realist films. Indeed, the popularity of the costume romances (Lant, 1991, pp. 231–3), with their emphasis on the instability of identity, implies that the formation of class, gender and nation should be perceived in terms of a constant process of oscillation between identities rather than the achievement of coherence, unity and settlement.

This paper has been delivered in a variety of forms and contexts since 1993. Thanks to all those who contributed to the many discussions that have fed into this version, which is still work in progress.

6

The Quality Film Adventure:
British Critics and the Cinema 1942–1948

John Ellis

English film production ... has been at the crossroads for so long
that it is in continual danger of dying there and being buried for a
suicide, with a stake through its middle.

> Michael Powell, *Penguin Film Review*
> (no. 1, August 1946, p. 107).

Powell wrote these words in the middle of what now appears to have
been the greatest period of British film production. The Rank empire
had created a film-making machine to rival that of any Hollywood
major. Buoyed up by massive box-office takings, British production was
creating a range of films which rivalled Hollywood's (Macnab, 1993).
There was everything from the war heroism of *The Way to the Stars*
(1945) to the historical fresco of *This Happy Breed* (1944); from
glorious melodramas like *The Wicked Lady* (1945) or *The Seventh Veil*
(1945) to the genre comedies of George Formby or Old Mother Riley;
assured musicals like *I Live in Grosvenor Square* (1945); trail-blazing
dramas like *Brief Encounter* (1945) and *The Rake's Progress* (1945).
British films suddenly seemed to have acquired a positive cultural
identity of their own. No longer were they patently inferior to
Hollywood.

Yet few saw these films as a necessary, mutually complementary
range of work. Each had their partisans, and from the cultural strength
of their support sprang the levels of budget that the films could attract.

Gainsborough's *Wicked Lady* had a lower budget and tighter schedule than David Lean's chaste housewife, even though *Brief Encounter* now seems constructed like a perfect melodrama. Many of the genre comedies, expecting no West End opening, were made as cheaply as possible. Only Michael Balcon, with top-line stars like Will Hay and George Formby, could think of giving genre comedy the budget of a modest A-feature.

Film critics played a crucial role during the period in defining many of these presuppositions. They identified a new spirit abroad in British films from 1942. They increasingly strove to define what that spirit was, and to promote it as the valid way forward for British cinema in general. They even coined a term for this spirit, 'the quality film'. Nowadays, the terms they used to define this desired object are at once familiar and bizarre, charged with meaning and strangely vacuous: 'truth', 'reality', 'logic', 'beauty'. They form a highly coherent set of aesthetic judgements, yet their true meaning is slipping away from us as we seek to reassess the films about which they made such confident judgements.

The critics themselves were only one force in the industry, and often felt themselves to be at odds with it. The critics wrote of 'the quality film'; the industry spoke of 'the prestige film'. The industry's definition is more financial: in terms of overall budget, predictable box-office components such as stars and source of the original story (play or book), or the event for which the film was destined. Ultimately, the term 'prestige film' meant 'an expensive film with which we can finally break into the mainstream American market'. This conception had an uncertain relation to that of quality, if any at all.

As a result, the critics became progressively disenchanted with British film-making as the decade drew to a close. 'Quality films' were proving more difficult to find, as were audiences willing to see them. *Brief Encounter* may have had a melodrama structure, but its emotional restraint struck many as laughable. After the crisis which hit the British industry in 1948, the critics began to seek their preferred form of cinema in more specialized outlets, offering foreign-language films.

The critics of the 1940s defined middle-class conceptions about cinema for decades to come. The critics had more success in influencing British tastes than perhaps they realized. Decades of film appreciation have maintained the divisions that they initiated. After all, it is comparatively recently that the Gainsborough melodramas or the output of Powell and Pressburger have found their proper place in criticism (see Christie, 1978b; Aspinall and Murphy, 1983; Christie, 1994; Harper, 1994; Cook elsewhere in this volume). Genre comedy still waits, despite the pioneering work of Marcia Landy (Landy, 1991).

Now that the approach of the critics of the 1940s is at last being superseded, it is time that they found their place in history. This chapter is an attempt to speak their language and, sympathetically, to reveal its presuppositions. It can be seen as a tribute to the importance of a group of British film critics in dividing British cinema into discrete departments. In doing so, they sealed the sense of superiority or inferiority of both individual film-makers and entire genres.

The method I have used is one of trying to reconstruct the discourse of the critics, term by term, using as far as possible particular enunciations drawn from writings of the period. It is a kind of attentive listening, trying to transcribe the various random comments and remarks of different individuals into the complete systematization that they were never given. The method is deliberately sympathetic rather than critical; no denunciation of the terms takes place as they are explicated.

I have taken the pronouncements of a certain group of critics in daily papers and periodicals on a selected series of mostly British films from the period 1942–1948. Fragments from these pieces of writing are then recombined and written out to demonstrate the system of the discourse. The critics who are given this treatment are those of the 'quality' daily or Sunday papers, together with those other papers which employed more radical critics at one time or another. The list of newspaper sources is thus: *News Chronicle, Daily Telegraph, The Times, Manchester Guardian, Reynolds News, Daily Mail, Daily Mirror, Daily Sketch, Evening News* (London), *Evening Standard* (London), *The Sunday Times, The Observer*, and the *Sunday Express*. A number of weekly magazines also appear as sources: *New Statesman, Spectator, Tribune, Time and Tide*, and *Our Time*. The critics identifiable by name are: Elspeth Grant, Simon Harcourt-Smith, Jympson Harman, C. A. Lejeune, Joan Lester, Fred Majdalany, Frank Mullally, Dilys Powell, E. Arnot Robertson, Stephen Watts, Noel Whitcomb, William Whitebait, Richard Winnington, and Basil Wright. The films were a randomly selected list of sixty British 'prestige' films produced between 1942 and

THE QUALITY FILM ADVENTURE

1949. The reviews were drawn from the British Film Institute micro-fiche collection, whose selectivity itself indicates a preference for this particular critical discourse: it is only towards the end of the period that the popular press critics and the *Daily Worker* (now *Morning Star*) begin to appear.

To this, I added the books of collected criticism by Richard Winnington (Rotha, 1947) and Caroline Lejeune (1947) and the more considered pieces of writing (some by the above critics themselves) which appeared in two cinema journals closely associated with the development of the conception of 'quality film': *Sight and Sound* and the *Penguin Film Review*.

During the war *Sight and Sound* was a dull educational journal, which changed in 1945 to become a substantial quarterly magazine of serious film criticism addressed to a wider audience than educators and film lecturers. The *Penguin Film Review* aimed to be a 'progressive review' of the cinema, publishing articles by critics and those working in the cinema, as well as reviews of world production. With a claimed readership of over 25,000, it ran sporadically for nine issues between August 1946 and May 1949, never attaining a regular publication pattern. These magazines provide a remarkable diversity of contributors and a remarkable consistency in writing, a sure indication that a common discursive system is being used.

The critics themselves recognized the originality of their project and the idea of the 'quality film' they were constituting. They saw it as different from traditional 'art cinema'. Crucially, 'the quality film' was something that they passionately hoped the wide public would come to recognize and appreciate. They hoped to change the nature of mass cinema in Britain.

Critics as contemporary historians

In 1942, the critics began to point out a fundamental change in British films made since the beginning of the war. The pre-war film showed 'the sunny side, the villas and shop-fronts of Filmlandia. There, everything was posed and gaudy, and the sham fascinated. But with war exerting its pressure, the glamour of day dreams faded, naturalism came into its own. The film fixed in reality no longer had to carry a rigidly unreal plot. *Next of Kin* [1942] like *One of Our Aircraft is Missing* [1941], is an admirable example of the new kind of English film, actual, thrilling, taking its tune from events'.[1] This movement continues: 'the number of good films about English life has been mounting up; *Millions Like Us* [1943], *The Demi-Paradise* [1943], quite recently have explored the unexplorable.'[2] The atmosphere is generally optimistic and ambitious comparisons are made: a 'section of *The Demi-Paradise* is the nearest thing ever to English René Clair.'[3] 'With *This Happy Breed* and *Millions Like Us* and *The Way Ahead* [1944], British films after the war should have their chance of becoming what we all should like them to be – English.'[4] The critic can now make a contribution by identifying the points of strength and weakness: 'the whole handling of the narrative [has grown] more authoritative. But the qualities of dialogue and narration have not always been matched by the quality of the plot-making.'[5]

Then, as victory is achieved in Europe, the first vindication for many critics of their growing faith in British films is provided by Olivier's *Henry V* (1945). 'If a flavour of smugness creeps into these notes this week you must be forbearing and think of me as a happy mother whose child whom the world deemed to be an idiot has at last proved himself the genius she always knew him to be. For those of us who love the cinema, and especially the English cinema, there have been moments lately when the flame burnt dim. ... Yet in spite of it all we kept faith, telling ourselves that cinema was an exciting and adult art and that one day English cinema would grow up. Well, the moment has come, our dream has happened'.[6] *Henry V* is one of a series of films from 1944–48 which are hailed as masterpieces of British cinema: the films, for instance, of 'Asquith, Carol Reed, Launder and Gilliat, the Boultings, Thorold Dickinson and David Lean among others are establishing a tradition of solid native skill'.[7]

Yet these films were produced as part of Rank's programme of 'prestige' films designed to 'break into the American market' by imitating Hollywood production values and expenditure patterns. And Rank is the dominant force in the industry at this time. 'I do not believe that the best British technicians, Mr Rank's or those of other producers, are temperamentally fitted to make "American" films. I do not even believe that it is necessary. The reception given in this country recently to true-blue British pictures by at least the better-class audiences suggests that the taste for this kind of thing can be spread throughout the British Isles. I think that it is much more likely that American audiences will cultivate an extra taste for essentially British films.'[8] 'The conscious critic grasped and protested that financial success lay in a direction contrary to the Hollywood path of lavishness and extravagance, that it was parallel to the utmost development of the poetic realism Britain had forged in documentaries and near-documentaries.'[9] Documentary versus extravagant entertainment defines the difference between quality and prestige films for most of the critics. Some reach further, trying to define, against their own taste, a low-cost domestic form of popular entertainment. 'Mr J. Arthur Rank's method of open attack on the American market by making the epic film to dazzle Americans will, I am certain, lead in the end to pleasing nobody and losing grasp of Britain's great moment. While *Caesar and Cleopatra* [1945] doesn't frighten Hollywood (if it does me), the success in Britain of *The Seventh Veil* and *The Captive Heart* [1946], and even of those Gainsborough horrors *The Wicked Lady*, *Madonna of the Seven Moons* [1944], and *Caravan* [1946], most emphatically does.'[10] Extravagance in the hopes of catching international attention does not guarantee financial success; but the development of a series of documentary-influenced or low-budget quality films for the home market (or even 'a nonsense of period so authentically Hollywood'[11] like *The Wicked Lady*) will provide a secure basis for further expansion.

At the end of 1945, there is *Brief Encounter*, everything that a feature film had never dared be before. At the end of the next year *Great Expectations* (1946) confirmed all the expectations of the Lean team: 'Surely the last doubter will see what we, who have been signalling the advance of British films, have been making all the fuss about.'[12] It is seen as 'the first big British film to have been made, a film that confidently sweeps our cloistered virtues into the open,'[13] vindicating 'an uncomfortable urge to overpraise British films, to wish them, almost, into realms of thought and feeling they inherit but never fully enter'.[13] It is soon followed by *Odd Man Out* (1946), which 'can be ranked with the best and most serious cinema of the Continent;'[14] 'more than a triumph for British films. It is an open proof that a film can satisfy every technical and 'highbrow' requirement, and still provide outstanding popular entertainment.'[15]

The critics agreed with Rank's policy of providing a great degree of freedom to creative units like Cineguild, Individual and The Archers.

However, they were not quite so keen on the results of this artistic freedom. Powell and Pressburger's company, The Archers, is the source of the most reviled films of the period, moving increasingly further 'away from the essential realism and true business of the British movie'[16] and producing *A Canterbury Tale* (1944), a reference point for a time for its violation of all the central tenets of quality. The policy also gives Lean and Reed 'the time and resource to become "prima donnas" [without which] they would have made rougher and possibly better films, certainly more'.[9] The disillusion with these two star directors becomes quite widespread with *The Third Man* (1949) and *Oliver Twist* (1948). With *Oliver Twist*, Lean 'fails for the first time in his career to move forwards with a new film, and Lean is of all the directors in England the most favoured and most free, the most answerable to himself'.[17]

By 1948, with the results of the economic crisis in the industry putting 'into supreme control over British production the chartered accountant,'[18] the critics' sense of doubt about British production becomes 'a sense of melancholia,'[19] a sense of unfulfilled promise. 'In the half dozen or so years of the war and soon after, British film-making at last showed itself able to compete on a professional footing with the best of other countries; but having demonstrated the potentiality, it has since then been far too largely restrained from putting the potentiality into solid effect by the pressing requirements of quantity militating against quality, by an excessive reliance upon the converted play and converted novel, and by an ingenuous belief that more money spent must necessarily mean more value received.'[20] In 1944, a critic compared himself to a proud mother; by 1948 the scene is one in which 'our critics have become too much like mothers who cannot see the faults of their own children'.[21]

Another explanation of the 'short history of disaster'[22] is that 'no producer has tried to grapple with the problems of peace. David Lean has contented himself with pretty comedies and treatments of Dickens. Anthony Asquith dallies with trifles like *While the Sun Shines* [1946] and *The Winslow Boy* [1948]. Michael Powell roams in the realms of fancy with *I Know Where I'm Going* [1945] and *Black Narcissus* [1947]. The Boultings waste their talents on *Fame is the Spur* [1947] and *Brighton Rock* [1947]. Carol Reed has the stern *Odd Man Out* to his credit and is now occupied with a mere murder story.'[23]

This murder story, by the way, turned out to be *The Third Man*, demonstrating how dangerous it is to rely on studio gossip as a critic ... or on hindsight as a historian. For the aim of this chapter is to excavate the preconceptions of the critics who experienced, collectively, this growing optimism followed by renewed despair. They were held together, first, by a common belief in humanity, or, as even the women amongst them were accustomed to write: mankind.

Human like oneself

A humanist conception of mankind is central to the critics' discourse, to their vision of film and its purpose.

Man is a universal, facing 'tremendous universal questions',[24] and speaking 'the human idiom in French, English or Turkish'.[25] Mankind is divided into nations or cultures which can produce considerable differences. 'We in Britain have been involved in six years of total war and we are now as remote in outlook from the citizenry of the MidWest of America as we are from that of the Fiji Islanders.'[26] Yet beyond these divisions of nation and culture there exist 'the human values of every situation, tragic, tense, grave or gay'[27] which 'identify man with man and place with place'.[28] We all share 'the human plight'.[29]

Mankind's basic nature is conceived according to the image of a graph, with one axis polarized around mind and heart, the other around surface and depth. This nature 'has to be trained to distinguish real and lasting values from poor and shoddy substitutes'.[30] The ability to discriminate between deep and surface values is the product of a definite 'balance between mind and heart',[31] between the two great faculties of man: his understanding head or force of intellect, and his passion, his emotion, his heart. The defeated peoples of Europe, for instance, are 'deeply concerned with war as with a passion which must be expressed to be purged',[32] moving deep emotion towards deep thought, avoiding 'shallow intellectual compromises'.[33] Again, it is to be remembered that 'without some ghost of a message from one human heart to another, no record, however factual, can be either truthful or complete'[34]: the head alone is not enough, one must be both 'intelligent and humane'.[35]

Man is prey to 'symptoms of a perverse and decadent imagination'[36] if this balance is not achieved. There will be a failure because this is part of the common lot of humanity, but man can be prepared for 'the moral dilemma which faces us and the man next door a dozen times in our lives',[37] and can face it courageously, without illusions. It is because of the universality of man and of the values that animate him that *man* can become *men*, 'real human beings'[38] with an 'individuality contrasting strongly with the rubber stamping'[39] process threatening to emerge in modern society. Each individual has their own 'way of looking at life',[33] and 'if you look closely enough into a person you discover his world'.[40] Individuality is not quirky, it is rather 'the trick of living one's life or doing one's work with an intense personal conviction, an utter singleness of purpose that is, as if one meant it, with all one's heart'.[41] What the individual should aspire to is a belief in precisely that which gives him his validity: 'a belief in man and the universal purpose of man'.[42]

The civilized man is capable of 'sympathetic, mutual understanding',[43] which can be produced by the film. He can be 'brought close into the feelings and lives of people',[44] can be brought to perceive 'not only the cause of conflict but the effects of it on human beings; all the facets of human behaviour and the amazing qualities of people at grips with life and forces beyond their control'.[45] The civilized, thinking man is able to respond to the 'human appeal or persuasion'[34] of others, to be 'ravaged'[46] by the 'agony of ordinary people caught in succeeding waves of misery, the sources of which are never clear to them'.[44]

Such a 'compassionate',[47] 'lucid; hopeful and clear-eyed'[48] audience can be reached by a film-maker who is not 'a propagandist but a passionately interested observer, a man with a point of view but no panacea, prejudices but no firm faith',[49] a man of 'pacifist acceptance and humanitarianism',[47] 'an adult mind'[50] capable of sensitivity to the 'insufficiently appreciated truth',[51] 'an affirmer of life [with a] passionate humanitarian conviction'.[52]

Light in the darkness

Cinema has a particularly important role to play as 'a medium of artistic expression and as a means of public information and education'.[53] It can at once 'entertain, inform, secure attention, touch emotions'.[54] It is propaganda and pleasure mixed: 'not only a new form of entertainment but a novel instrument for influencing the taste, mode of life and emotions of virtually unlimited numbers. Films are a new art.

Even more than that: by cinema a new sense through which to experience the visible world he lives in has been created for Man.'[55] However, this purpose has been largely betrayed. The dark cinema halls are filled with people used to murkier experiences. The problem with contemporary films is that 'in general, they are mere patterns of light and shade, mere noise to illuminate and warm a hall where you go as you might to a bar in search of oblivion on a strictly business basis.'[11] 'The certain glorious exceptions'[56] of the quality of film means that 'audiences are beginning to want and enjoy better screen stories; they are beginning to *think* in the luxurious hypnotic darkness of the cinema.'[57]

The means to make audiences think are 'realism, logic, truth',[8] but they 'must all be bent to the traditional requirements of drama and comedy, though they must never be renounced entirely. If we are interested in the use of the entertainment film as a means of cultural and educational enlightenment, we must not deprive it of its power to "take us out of ourselves". Therein lies the subtle influence of the film.'[8]

Popular cinema's 'job like that of the novel, is to tell a story entertainingly',[58] 'if the story is lacking, it is difficult to conjure up the film'.[5] In this context, film-makers are to be 'encouraged to make films about subjects which demand and deserve thought'.[57] It is no good, however, producing a 'well meaning bore',[59] like *Men of Two Worlds* (1946). It is rather a matter of finding a method that 'bridges the gap between talkies and life, between actors and human beings',[60] producing 'the dramatic link with real-life people and their problems'.[61] Film-makers should 'catch, in words and pictures, so many things that are penetratingly true'.[62] For instance, *Brief Encounter* catches 'the whole colour, the spring, the almost magical feeling of the discovery that someone's in love with you, that someone feels it's exciting to be with you; that is something so tenuous that it's never been put on the screen. And yet it's here.'[62] This fiction film is capable of inducing 'a feeling of closeness to the personality of each'[63] character, to present 'not an abstraction but a man',[50] through the affinity created between the audience and the film as an emotional experience. Issues present themselves through this affinity because the films 'reveal the individual in his own environment'.[40]

Organic unities

Film is a composite art, but unity is its aim. 'The perfect weaving of sound, movement and texture into a story creates an effect, through mind and heart, that no other medium could so quickly or so generally achieve.'[42] What is required is 'a film that has unity and sureness, one that never stumbles in confusion',[64] a film that is 'logical, well-shaped, cohesive'.[65] Unity is important because it creates or reveals (the discourse hesitates here) a sense of purpose, a coherent purpose that may or may not be linked to a controlling intelligence. Films that display the characteristics of unity 'move according to some sort of a design'.[10] They are therefore 'those that can be seen to possess a greater or lesser force of self-belief or purpose achieved'.[22] We can see a film that 'could so easily have been a vast agglomeration of visuals and sounds, and no more. But [the director] has used no sight, no noise, however brief, which is not germane to his overall purpose.'[66] Everything falls into place within 'the jigsaw facility of construction, the rounded completeness ... [as a result of] a pattern, a carefully composed pattern conceived in the mind of a deliberate artist'.[67] 'A seriousness ... makes the artist and the craftsman regard his work not simply as a means of entertaining or pleasing or instructing, but as a thing in itself both beautiful and important.'[14]

'The true essence of the cinema [is] the highlighting and wedding of detail to action.'[10] Elements do not appear in themselves, though 'the critic must identify the many separate elements that flow into a film'.[9] 'The test of all good technique is unobtrusive service.'[68] Thus, though acting is an element often remarked upon, a film of quality like *Went the Day Well?* (1942) owes some of its unity to the way in which 'no player detaches himself from the mosaic of village society'.[69] In the same way, *Millions Like Us* is admirable because 'background was not merely authentic scenery, it was integrated with the story. So was the humour which arose naturally out of situations, or characters, never sandwiched in as deliberate comic relief.'[70] And again, photography, dialogue, acting and settings can be integrated to produce a unified emotional effect: 'these scenes had a clipped documentary reality which related the broken accents of true love to the background of the film and gave them poignancy.'[71]

Even the most undisciplined of Britain's film-makers could achieve

THE QUALITY FILM ADVENTURE

this sense of unity: 'Powell and Pressburger have alighted upon a theme coincident with its inspirations and its ability and a story which arises naturally from that theme.'[72] Reactions to *The Red Shoes* (1948), however, were more typical. It left critics 'with a slightly dazed sense of returning from some strange exotic nether regions. This is caused by the mixture of styles I have mentioned and by the episodic nature of the story, but even more by the flamboyance of its spectacle, combined with the almost brutal insistence on backstage atmosphere.'[73]

What is desirable in a film is 'the unity, the logic and the force of a film as a connected entity'.[74] Unity has certain characteristics: flow, visual narrative, and tone which link together to form the harmonious whole.

Flow

Unity is neither static nor monotonous. It is realized as the film unfolds, and the habitual image for this process is that of a liquid flowing in a definite direction, smoothing over impediments, lubricating, carrying the audience along. The aim is to 'make a film flow visually'.[75] The flow sweeps up all the elements so that 'actors are carried along on the flow of [the] feeling which never misses a point or underlines a word'.[76] The quality film is 'sublimely conceived and wrought with an uninterrupted flow of camera logic'.[77] Flow produces the sensation of poetry. Once the unified direction and liquidity of the film is established, it can be seen that 'the screen is a running pattern':[78] flow is metrical and measured, there is a 'perfect shape [to] every sequence and [a] perfect rhythm, visual and aural, [to] the whole film'.[78] 'The rhythm of music and movement [applies] the poetry of mathematics to the practicality of drama.'[78] Flow is therefore poetic because it is periodized, rhythmic, and organized so that 'the screen sings';[79] it is logical because the poetic organization rests upon an overall purpose. Logic and poetry are the products and characteristics of flow. Flow is the mastery of one of the fundamentals of the film: movement.

The visual

The movement at the heart of the cinematic is visual movement. This is a new stress in film criticism, burlesqued by the older critic James Agate in *The Tatler* as the mark of the highbrow 'Dilysians', after Dilys Powell. He gleefully writes that 'his cherished colleague, who henceforth gives her name to this abstruse coterie, wrote a Sunday or two ago: "If the film has its own validity as an art it must affect us by its own methods, which are basically, though not exclusively, visual".'[80] The new critics of the 1940s have made a discovery: 'in the novel, plot, characterization and style are the three chief ingredients. Who can deny that style is what gives the book its flavour? So in the movie visual description, the poetry of the camera, makes the best banal or beautiful.'[71]

Yet, like the darkness of the cinema hall, the visual is as seductive as it is essential. It has to find its place in the patterned unit of the film. Otherwise 'visual eloquence becomes visual rhetoric, mere flowers of effect rather than active participation in the atmosphere and action of a story'.[81] A distinction has to be made between purely photographic qualities which produce seductive imagery only, and the more profound 'visual narrative, cinematic sense',[82] the creation of 'visual stories [which] make their main effects purely by visual images'.[5] Such moments of visual narration flow according to some overall design. 'The sheer visual pleasure they afford'[83] has its place in the unity of the film.

In a restrained tone

A favourite stylistic device is to list films for the purpose of comparison, characterizing their mood with well-chosen epithets: *Great Expectations* 'had romantic breadth', *Brief Encounter* 'its sad music', *Odd Man Out* 'its poetic slant on the human plight'.[29] The mood is described as though it were a voice: the voice of the film itself, speaking in warm tones, excitedly or dispassionately as the case may be. There are certain tones that the critics respond to, others that repel them, like 'uplift, and mock-simple, sermonising or instruction',[84] or the pointless hyperbole of most American films. The range of vocal colouring that most appeals to them is restrained, the voice carrying 'discretion, discrimination and taste'.[13] 'Wherein lies the greatness of the British fictional war film? Maybe our native instinct for understatement is the only way to balance the savagery of war. Maybe it's just simple sincerity.'[85] Sincerity is very close to restraint, 'the restraint which refuses to follow each emotion to saturation point'.[86] Such films speak with 'a simplicity which is most satisfying and in all [their] admirable restraint [they are] far more moving than any picture deliberately designed as a tearjerker'.[87]

Restraint is a matter of 'authenticity and understanding',[27] of a certain 'detachment'[51] in attitude where a film 'understates its message'[60] rather than being 'forced to be painfully obvious in subject matter and technique'.[28] The danger with a restrained attitude is that it might become lifeless: instead of an 'unsentimental warm-heartedness',[86] a bloodless corpse. Stage-bound acting tends to 'give our films the aetherial glow of anaemia.'[10] 'The success of Brief Encounter abroad was due ... to the warmth of feeling in the conception of character and acting in Celia Johnson's part. In too many even of our good films, foreign audiences feel the characters and the acting quite unexciting because the men are cold and the women brittle, conveying only the surface of human life and not its depths.'[88]

Restraint has another danger, too, that of precluding certain emotional attitudes and states from full consideration. The result is a film like Fanny by Gaslight (1944) which is 'aesthetically correct where it might have been passionate; there is a coldness in both its glitter and its shadow; a coldness for which, I believe, reluctance to admit true raffishness into the chaste precincts of contemporary cinema is to blame.'[89] This was a specific criticism of a quality production, however, not a call for more Gainsborough melodramas. Restraint in a film's attitude is generally the mark of its 'good taste and intelligence'.[12]

The truth of the real

The real is an absolute, the correlative of mankind. It exists outside films, beyond representation: the moral imperative for the quality film is that of representing the world correctly, avoiding 'misrepresentation of place and character for the sake of convention or the susceptibilities of romance'.[90] The real is therefore primarily a moral imperative, and it is often equated with truth itself: the two terms become interchangeable. Sunday Dinner for a Soldier (1944) is 'one of the truest pictures to come out of America, true in its unsentimental delineation of near poverty with all its simple hopes and joys'.[91] This conflation of terms can be taken even further to encompass other imperatives as well, when the critic is 'thinking of a quality in recent British films which can be most succinctly expressed as Truth. Alternatively it can be called Logic or Sincerity.'[8] The point at which a discourse slides into tautology of this order is the point at which its moral fulcrum operates. The discourse turns upon a term that is self-evidently true, necessary and comprehensible: the real. Films which show the real can be 'sordid, harsh, salty, alive. ... [It is] in the nature of things [that they] impart the documentary feel we crave for and miss in other films with ostensibly worthier objects. This quality contains the true essence of the cinema.'[10] It 'affirms the cinema as well as life'.[40]

The force of the absolute category 'the real' is vividly demonstrated by the critics' reception of Italian neo-realism. 'Rossellini's staccato use of the camera, his crude, unfinished portraits of the boy's family and general roughness of style, will no doubt jar on those who like their films fully explained, rounded and smooth.'[92] Neo-realism violates almost all the critics' carefully constructed criteria: 'it is episodic and sprawling, the photography is by no means good ... but it touches the mind and heart'[42] 'as no film within years has done'.[93]

The moral force of the category of the real is often turned against those who are seen to be selecting, concentrating on some morbid qualities to the exclusion of others. Hence 'those artists who work with a deliberate exclusion of beauty are sadly misinterpreting the temper of the people. The adulation of the spiv and all that goes with him is simply a pretence of the unfit and mannered minority, and the sooner his cult is expelled from the cinema the better for us all'.[94] Any film that eschews a representation of reality inevitably runs the risk of falling prey to 'a perverse and decadent imagination'.[36]

Concentrating the mind wonderfully

Cinema's relation to the real is not that of mirroring: it is a more subtle relation of 'making contact with the living world'[95] through a process of narrative construction. Unity describes the preferred form of this construction: it is linked to the real, but it does not ape the real. The problem with 'the genuine is [that it is] apt to sprawl. Artifice can concentrate in a single moment what the lazy eye and mind take hours to see and comprehend; and such concentration, after all, is half the art of narrative'.[96] The filmic narrative, properly handled, has 'the ability to combine absolute authenticity of background and character with the artificial movement forward of a prepared narrative.'[96] This 'realistic style [presents] life with an authenticity and understanding, heightened only by the intensity of the emotions revealed by the story and the acting required by them.'[27] 'Granted this, there is ... an extraordinary power in the drama of actuality, a power which no contrived thriller, with its characters "based on no living person" can ever achieve.'[97]

The powerful drama of actuality uses the concentration of the film form, with its unity, poetry, coherence of purpose and invisibility of technique, in order to go beyond it: to create an experience of the world, its people, its values. 'Anyone who has seen the Italian film *Roma Città Aperta* [1945] will agree that it has unforgettable realism. It does not need a very close examination of the film, however, to realize that so far from being "realistic" in the commonly held sense of the term, it is a rather "mannered" piece: it is a film in which the "art" is singularly ill-disguised. ... It is a pattern, a carefully composed pattern conceived in the mind of a deliberate artist. The result, on reflection, is real to a terrifying degree; frightening because with no conscious effort we find ourselves living again moments in the film. We have lived with the people in the film, we know them and when we recall the film we recall our own experience.'[67] Realism is a method of concentrating the real that can yield a shattering and salutary emotional experience. Realism, however, comes in a number of forms, which are understood in ways similar to those of André Bazin (Bazin, 1967, 1971).

Duplication

The surface level of realism is the duplication of the semblance of the real. It is the 'trick' of getting the right atmosphere, which is largely attributed to technical polish. So we have 'the effect of a film made in Berlin, though only the outside scenes, which are excellent, were photographed there. [So the director] can be congratulated on the realism of his back projection.'[98] This technical assurance has the effect of 'imbuing every studio shot ... with that feeling of absolute actuality'.[99] It can yield a particular form of visual pleasure which, properly handled, can contribute greatly to the overall impact of a film. For instance, *It Always Rains on Sunday* (1947) has 'an amused, a devoted attention to the tiny decorations of the everyday, to the chattering neighbour, the darts game and the black cat brushed with an exasperated gesture off the sofa head. These trifles mark the difference between the studio set and the room lived in; and an audience convinced of the realism of the scene it watches becomes submissive to the movement of the story'.[96]

Duplication of the external aspects of the real is often equated with background. This habitual term is the product of the separation into departments of character (the product of script and acting) and setting (the product of art direction, use of location). Background is thus the filmic equivalent of a backdrop before which the players perform. We see 'backgrounds like the pierrots on the beach before the war, the canteen dance, [which are] observed with a lucid eye'.[86] Yet to achieve a duplication of the surface of the real which can contribute to the overall unity of the film it is necessary to go beyond the implications of the term 'background', to dissolve it into the flow of the action. So with *Brighton Rock* 'what is particularly striking in the brilliant and horrible English piece is its handling of background. ... To the record of menace and split-second action [it] adds touches of grotesquerie, ironic pictorial comments which give features to the face of violence.'[100] An integrated background can provide a surface realism, features to the face. Deeper meanings are produced at another level.

Authenticity

Authenticity is a deeper level of realism. Beyond the convincing detail or background, it demands that the whole reality of the narrative be 'true to life'.[101] The absolutely authentic film is one in which 'there is never a moment ... when it does not feel like real life'.[102] Authenticity is a feeling induced in the spectator of closeness to events: 'the film [of the Berlin Olympiad] is a triumph, a complete use of the movie to describe a great event. The omnipresent cameras work at every speed from slow motion to normal and from every angle and distance to induce a feeling of closeness to the personality of each competitor. Style and character astonishingly come through.'[63] It is equally that of creating a plausible universe like 'the flurries, flounces, turmoils and sweat of that esoteric life behind the curtains of the ballet in the portrayal of which ... Messrs Powell and Pressburger touch better cinematography and better realism than in any other of their films ... You almost accept the Svengali-

Diagilev of Anton Walbrook ... the long shots of practising dancers, the snippets of dancing, the wit of Massine, the general truth of atmosphere.'[103]

There are two spheres in which authenticity is a crucial issue in British films: those of class and of sex. 'We are in our class consciousness unsuccessful at depicting the ordinary men and women of Britain in character, accent or behaviour.'[10] The problem is that ordinary people are caricatured, seen as generalizations rather than as individuals. 'The tradition of English life has imposed on its ruling classes a veneer of good manners and imperturbability which brilliantly conceals surface as well as temperamental individuality; to look at character thus becomes eccentric. The working and lower-middle classes have no such mask, and the temptation for the scriptwriter to exaggerate natural individuality until it turns to farce is clear.'[104] However, progress is made in producing authentic, recognizable working-class characters. In *Millions Like Us*, widely regarded as a landmark, the characters are perceived as 'connecting somewhere with reality'.[98] 'Nothing more clearly marks the coming-of-age of the British cinema than its treatment of ordinary working people, especially as minor characters or in the mass. The clowns of ten years ago first became the lay figures of sociological drama and then, with the war, patriotic heroes. In *Millions Like Us*, they are real human beings, and the British film has reached adult maturity.'[38] In fact, one correspondent panics before this intrusion: 'the continual accents with which the dialogue is delivered, though they are varied and represent different parts of Great Britain, tend to become monotonous. Surely it would not have detracted from the reality of the picture to have one character speaking the King's English ordinarily.'[105]

Sexuality is something that also presents problems for authenticity. 'With certain glorious exceptions, like *Brief Encounter*, blessedly adult, truthful and contemporary, everything to do with love in the cinema is early Victorian, adolescent at that'.[56] 'It is an extraordinary thing that the cinema, which is notoriously preoccupied with love, should so seldom manage to produce a really convincing love story.'[79] There is a prudery that prevents authenticity, which seems to centre in the portrayal of women's sexual feelings. 'To see [a female character in *Day of Wrath*, 1943] glow and grow smug and gay with fulfilment is to watch something that Hollywood doesn't understand: grown-up sex.'[106] This lack of authenticity in the portrayal of female sexuality is linked closely to the difficulties with class: 'most British women of the screen are suburbanised and simplified into nonentity.'[105]

Authenticity is deeper than surface or background as it is concerned to make the demands of narrative congruent with a convincing emotional register similar to that of real life. This gives the narrative the illusion of life itself. Yet though it is possible for a film to get by without total authenticity at all moments, authenticity is itself not the final level of realism. There is a further level which is attained only rarely, and can even lead to the violation of other canons of realism and unity: it is faithfulness to the very spirit of the real.

The spirit of reality

Authenticity can produce a convincing illusion, but this effect is not the final level of realism. The deeper levels are not necessarily self-evident to everyone, as the duplication of externals and the authenticity of the illusion are. 'The schizoid nature of the film lies ... precisely in the fact that it is equally capable of creative expressiveness and literal representation; and while the former can be extremely potent and is vastly attractive to the few, elementary representation gratifies the multitude, because it rests on a more primitive level of sensibility.'[107] This creative, expressive level is that of emotional truth: it is not just that of providing a convincing representation, but of giving the total emotional experience of people and events so that their truth shines from the screen, 'expressing the spirit of a country'[99] or of an individual. 'Art does not consist in repeating accurately what can be seen and heard around us. Art must try to conjure up, with the help of familiar symbols, things that are not perceptible to human eyes and ears. It must be a kind of second sight, what Baudelaire calls a "sorcellerie évocatoire". [The] feeling of absolute actuality'[108] is an exchange between spirits. It can even take place when other criteria of unity and realism are transgressed in various ways. *The Murderers are Amongst Us* (1947) 'carries a UFA heritage of camera angles, neurosis, senti-mentality and deviations into dim and fleshy cabarets. It is sombre, slow, intense, tragically moving and in common with the postwar Italian films as true as it can be to the surrounding reality.'[109] The UFA heritage breaks criteria of accuracy to external details, and Italian neo-realism some of the demands for a finished, rounded unity of narrative.

Yet both can reveal the spirit of the real. It is from this source that the impulse to aesthetic renewal comes.

The search for documentary

One term recurs in discussions of realism at this time. It is 'documentary', designating the source of the inspiration for the aesthetic renewal of British films during the war years. 'There was a time not so very long ago when England's films flowed along opposite sides of the street. Reality and fiction, the documentary and the feature – every film kept to one side or the other, and disastrous was the occasional attempt to cross over'.[110] It was during the war that the successful fusion took place, to the benefit of each form. For although documentary is the source of a precious impulsion towards the real, 'it has one characteristic that chills me. There is a detachment in much of its work, an almost scandalized mistrust of showmanship, an effort, it would seem, to avoid, not only melodramatics, but any form of human appeal or persuasion.'[34] 'The wedding of documentary and fiction'[71] provides the way out of the problem: the fictional narrative can provide the emotional charge necessary to provide an empathetic link with the real, 'for there could be no question that [a film like] *San Demetrio, London* [1943] "covered the ground", and pretty succinctly, thanks to an approach less impersonal than would at one time have been conceivable in documentary circles. If, by severe standards, this was fiction, then it was fiction with the realism uppermost; and adventure was reconstituted, as nearly as could be imagined to the real event.'[111] There even appears a tendency that would like to redefine the documentary itself, away from 'the didactic phase of documentary on themes of contemporary life. The individual, contrary to the Grierson tenet, becomes more and more important. He will be the core of the new documentary, whose aim will be to reach your mind not by giving a lecture but by telling a story.'[112] 'This new down to earth style of British documentary [would rely] on a central narrative and a stressing of human values and relations rather than on a series of images for their own sakes related to each other by montage and cutting (the old fancy style of documentary).'[113] Though documentary carries a definite charge of reality, it seems as though it can only reach the spirit of the real if it adopts the procedures of the fictional narrative.

Who makes films?

The discourse of the critics is highly coherent: ideas link together to constitute a definite object, the 'quality film'. Yet the critics have more of a problem in identifying who might be responsible for bringing together all the necessary elements into a unified, inspiring rendering of reality. The other arts teach that a single artist should be responsible. 'We can say that film technique is nearly advanced to the point at which the artist could control his medium wholly and bring it into the category of an art.'[28] But 'artist' has a very precise definition: 'the few, the inviolate artist [who] at the cost of comfortable popularity [pursues] the logic of his own nature. He [gives] us a work that in all its power and weakness is the emanation of a single and matured mind.'[114] Such an artist is Chaplin. More usually, the director is 'a strong personality [who] holds together [the] great number of people [that] may contribute towards the final achievement. Orson Welles is a creator of that temper; so is Noël Coward; Alfred Hitchcock is another; so is Preston Sturges. ...These men scrawl their signature across a film so boldly that no one can fail to read it.'[41] The derogatory tone is clear enough. Indeed, some are led to claim that the cinematic artist is incarnated 'not as a director or producer but as a writer who inscribes on paper, with a complete visual power of writing, the thing that will be put down on celluloid by craftsmen to the extent that in their individual spheres they are subservient to the film as a whole'.[28] 'The director is merely an executant in charge of a group of skilled technicians.'[115] Film may be an art, but the artist himself proves elusive.

Industry and audience

The critics have great problems with understanding the industry, and blame it for constantly underestimating the audience. They conceive film production along the lines of the factory in *Modern Times* (1936). 'The film takes shape, like an automobile on an assembly line, from the original ... to the final polish job.'[116] The whole process is 'big and vertical where it should have been small and horizontal'.[9] This industrial process of production means 'a bankruptcy of inspiration and the development of a blatant and monotonous insincerity'.[26]

'The present-day movie is forced to be painfully obvious in subject matter and technique because of the non-discriminatory methods of distribution and exhibition, but more because of the wholesale appeasement by the leading productive functionaries of box-office and business'.[28] And it is obvious that the notion of 'box-office' does not necessarily express the tastes of filmgoers. 'The hucksters of the cinema, the middlemen and the monopolists, have a lower set of values than the public whose pulse and pocket they have their fingers on and in.'[9]

During and immediately after the Second World War, the critics hope to influence the kinds of films available by raising the standards of audience expectation. 'They are doing a first-class job now in making people critically aware of the content of films. Because of their efforts fewer and fewer people go to the pictures in a purely escapist mood'.[57]

The main problem has been an 'imposition on the British character of foreign manners, talk and thought by films from overseas',[8] which in practice means America. The seemingly endless flow of 'puerile pulp, synthetic sex and Technicolor goo',[117] can be attributed to 'the fact that the average mental age of the American audience is round 15 years'.[118] 'It is well-known that Hollywood insures its enormous expenditure by aiming at the lowest common denominator, and that the mental age of Americans is lower than that of our own people.'[8] 'In British eyes [American films] lack quality and an adult approach.'[118]

'The long-suffering public far from knowing what it wants is ready to accept almost anything and make the best of it.'[119] 'The public is not so dim, not so lethargic, not so gullible as cinema believes. It is not a big baby that must be pampered and soothed to prevent it throwing porridge. Rather, it is a healthy adolescent, human, impressionable; but which needs a firm lead. It needs to be stimulated, too; it wants digging in the ribs, guidance, a sense of proportion and hope for the future.'[120] So the critic hopes to 'see the screen catch its audiences young – since they're bound to be in the cinema, anyway – with the idea that in the long run films like *The Overlanders* [1946] are more "fun" than glossy nonsense the audiences don't remember anything about the next day'.[121] The result will be threefold. First, an improvement in the quality of all pictures because 'only a demand from the people themselves can free the film aesthetically';[26] second, 'the attraction into the cinemas [of] that section of the public, a section traceable to no particular social stratum, whose faculties have not been atrophied by sentiment, and by self-pity';[120] third, that the cinema audiences will be 'aided by every possible means to the contemplation of such things as exist in beauty, strength and, above all, truth. Isn't this the way to eliminate the tawdry and the gimcrack, to destroy dishonest doctrine and banish ugliness and evil?'[122]

However, it was not to be. The critics found that their favoured films had difficult box-office careers in Britain. Disillusion with the popular audience set in at the same time as disillusion with British film production. Quality films, it seemed, could not be made for the mass audience.

Disillusion

The critics abandoned the universalist hopes that had motivated them during the war and immediately afterwards. 'Can one believe that, any more than *Henry V*, *Hamlet* [1948] will make cultural inroads on a mass consciousness? Most will miss the deeper meanings of the soliloquies and speeches, instinctively resist blank verse and fail to grasp a plot that however simplified is still more complex than a dozen of the obscurest whodunits.'[75]

This is merely the dissipation of the optimism of the 1945 General Election seen working itself out in a tiny section of the intelligentsia. Everywhere, British society was proving rather more impervious to good sense, good taste and good values than had been hoped. For the critics, it seemed that the good reception given to quality wartime pictures depended on the fact of war rather than the fact of quality.

The critics cast around for explanations and solutions. Then as now, youth took some of the blame. 'Economically, the middle stratum of cinema seems to be sold out to the adolescent wage-earner whose pay packet in America and Britain has increased considerably since the war. In Britain it is true that there is very little for the adolescent to buy but pictures, and demand creates supply in values and emotional responses. It is difficult to get by with maturer films in the face of such audiences, who will no more understand the last part of *Odd Man Out* than they seem capable of realising that the first part of *The Lost Weekend* [1945] was not another alcoholic comedy.'[37]

There had to be a solution, and it was found in the experience of British films in the American market. The critics had argued for several years that the quality film would reliably succeed in selected American cinemas, whereas Rank's prestige films would probably fail in the mass market. 'Thirty per cent of Americans economically and physically able to attend theatres make a habit of avoiding them. Amongst this potential audience of twenty five millions are the thousands who would wittingly go to see pictures of the calibre of *Henry V*, *Brief Encounter*, *The Welldigger's Daughter* [1946], *Les Enfants du Paradis* [1945], *The Informer* [1935], *The Long Voyage Home* [1940], or documentary films like *The River* [1951] and *A Diary for Timothy* [1945]. Experience has shown that the best way of handling such product in America is not necessarily to play it indiscriminately in the big houses, but to earmark definite neighbourhood theatres in the big cities, where sufficient support among the so-called "upper crust" is forthcoming for the pictures to run weeks and sometimes months.'[118]

When David Lean analysed the commercial career of *Brief Encounter*, he not only used terms drawn straight from the critics' discourse, he also put forward a solution to the problems of audience that was becoming increasingly popular. 'British films have got themselves into their present position on what audiences call their "reality". ... You will be wondering why in the light of all this, *Brief Encounter* did not "go" with this great new and enlightened British audience. I think the answer is that in this particular case we went too far; too far, that is, from box-office point of view. We defied all the rules of box-office success. A few years ago this would have been a recipe for box-office disaster, but this wasn't the case with *Brief Encounter*. The film did very well in this country in what are known as "the better-class halls", and is now having a similar success on a smaller scale, in New York.'[123]

Others argue that 'the ideal solution is to establish theatres of different character, some for Cocteau, others for Crosby',[118] 'because in Britain, by a slow process unperceived in Wardour Street, audiences are sorting themselves into several layers of film-consciousness.'[28]

Implicitly, it is acknowledged that the attempt to influence the mass cinema towards improved standards has failed. The renaissance of British films is deemed to have more or less passed, and mass cinema will fall back to its old pattern of monotonous entertainment with the occasional rare exception that the critic remarks upon enthusiastically. The strategy becomes one of trying to encourage the development of an expanding circuit of specialized cinemas building on the film society movement, rather than trying to raise the standards of commercial cinema as a whole. 'The Everyman [Cinema in Hampstead, London] is a light in the window of the future, for there should be such cinemas in every large area, developing the single film society audience into the multiple audiences of the general public necessary to support a permanent cinema.'[124] 'The peculiar strategic importance of the specialised cinema resides in the fact that it is not simply a place where good films in foreign languages are shown, but that it is the *only* channel through which creative and experimental work in the field of international film art is brought before the general public. It thereby performs a possibly slow but certainly constant and cumulative work of improving public taste with regard to *all* films which come before it, and thus enables the commercial film producer to take for granted a rising level of public taste.'[125] From the attempt to create a 'quality film' for the mass audience emerges the defence of the 'art cinema' of the 1950s.

The retreat into the specialized cinema arena is the first of a series of mutations that were to overtake the discourse that I have traced. First, the fundamental conundrum of the creative artist was resolved. The director became recognized as the creator. Specialized cinema films were categorized in terms of a set of known world authors: Bergman, Ray, Antonioni appear instead of the old categorization of 'this sensitive film from Sweden/India/Italy'. The marketing advantages of such a representation are obvious; to the critic they offered the possibility of coming to terms with the increasing formal experimentation of art-film directors without having to face the implications of this for their aesthetic. The formal difficulties were accounted for in terms of 'self-expression'.

In such circumstances, criticism could develop a native *auteur* theory, and it could also extend the concept of quality to the Hollywood film itself. Thus part of the project of *Sequence* and its writers who moved to *Sight and Sound* (for example, Gavin Lambert and Penelope Houston) was the evaluation of Hollywood genre films produced by recognized artists, with Lindsay Anderson, for example, writing on John Ford (subsequently published in book form: Anderson, 1981).

More recent developments seem to have been the erosion of a more general nature: the ideological bases of an overt humanism no longer exist in the way that the discourse of 1942–48 could assume. Instead the discourse of the 'quality film' has become more overtly aesthetic; the principal quality that is now stressed is that of experience for its own sake. Clarity (unity and realism) is no longer a principle requirement. Nowadays it almost seems that a film is more interesting because it is puzzling, because it is not self-evident at first viewing. Allied to the direct and personal nature of the experience is a stress on the sensual aspects of the film. These no longer have to be subservient to a wider design, an overall unity. This points perhaps to the way in which the subjectivity of the experiencing, witnessing audience has become the central term for newspaper critics, rather than an aesthetic of unity and reality based upon a proselytizing humanism.

Notes
The research for this article was conducted largely by reference to the British Film Institute's collection of periodical material recorded on microfiche. All the sources quoted can be traced through the BFI Library either through publication or title of film referred to. In the notes below, the following abbreviations have been used: (authors) AV: Arthur Vesselo; CAL: C. A. Lejeune; DP: Dilys Powell; RM: Roger Manvell; RW: Richard Winnington; WW: William Whitebait; (periodicals) NC: News Chronicle; Obs: Observer; NS: New Statesman; PFR: Penguin Film Review; ST: Sunday Times; SS: Sight and Sound. (The Penguin Film Review is available as a reprint published by the Scholar Press, London 1977. The dates of individual numbers referred to are no. 1, August 1946; no. 2, January 1947; no. 3, August 1947; no. 4, October 1947; no. 5, January 1948; no. 6, April 1948. Other publications: CHL: Chestnuts in Her Lap (Lejeune, 1947).

1. Anon, Spectator, 5 April 1946.
2. WW, NS, 27 May 1944.
3. WW, NS, 27 November 1943.
4. WW, NS, 21 October 1944.
5. DP, ST, 9 September 1945.
6. WW, on Henry V, NS, November 1945.
7. Humphrey Swingler, Our Time, October 1946.
8. Jympson Harman, SS, Spring 1946, p. 5.
9. RW, NC, 27 December 1947.
10. RW, PFR, no. l, p. 33.
11. Simon Harcourt-Smith, Tribune, 23 November 1945.
12. Stephen Watts, Sunday Express, 15 December 1946.
13. RW, NC, 11 December 1946.
14. DP, Britain Today, April 1947.
15. Noel Whitcomb, Daily Mirror, 3 January 1947.
16. RW, NC, 2 November 1946.
17. RW, NC, 23 June 1948.
18. RW, NC, 22 May 1952.
19. RW, on Fighting Lady, NC, March 1948.
20. AV, SS, Winter 1948, p. 182.
21. RM, PFR, no. 5, p. 10.
22. RW, NC, 6 December 1948.
23. Jympson Harman, Evening News, 1 April 1948.
24. RW, NC, 30 July 1949.
25. RW, NC, 3 January 1948.
26. RW, PFR, no. 1, p. 27.
27. RM, PFR, no. 6, p. 122.
28. RW, Harper's, May 1948.
29. RW, NC, 22 November 1947.
30. Editorial, PFR, no. 3, p. 7.
31. Fred Majdalany, on The Third Man, Daily Mail, September 1949.
32 RM, PFR, no. 4, p. 12.

33. CAL, *Obs*, 3 October 1948.
34. CAL, on *Target for Tonight*, CHL, p. 83.
35. RW, *PFR*, no. 1, p. 29.
36. RM, *SS*, Spring 1946, p. 27.
37. RM, *PFR*, no. 3, p. 14.
38. 'DS', *Manchester Guardian*, 28 December 1943.
39. RM, *SS*, Spring 1946, p. 24.
40. RW, *NC*, 24 February 1948.
41. CAL, on *Night of the Opera* revival, *CHL*, p. 168.
42. RW, *NC*, 18 September 1943.
43. Sir Stafford Cripps quoted by H. H. Wollenberg, *SS*, Autumn 1947.
44. RW, on *Bicycle Thieves*, *NC*, January 1950.
45. Pat Jackson, *PFR*, no. 3, p. 85.
46. RW, *NC*, 23 November 1946.
47. RW, *PFR*, no. 1, p. 30.
48. RW, *NC*, 27 July 1946.
49. Clifford Leach, *PFR*, no. 6, p. 102.
50. DP on *Citizen Kane*, *ST*, October 1941.
51. RW, *NC*, 25 October 1947.
52. RW, *NC*, 24 April 1948.
53. Editorial, *PFR*, no. 1, p. 7.
54. RW, *NC*, 11 April 1949.
55. Anthony Asquith, *PFR*, no. 1, p. 49.
56. E Arnot Robertson, *PFR*, no. 3, p. 32.
57. John Sherman, *PFR*, no. 6, p. 87.
58. RW (1947), in Rotha, 1947.
59. RW, *NC*, 29 July 1946.
60. WW, *NC*, 29 July 1945.
61. Frank Mullally, on *A Matter of Life and Death*, Tribune 1944.
62. CAL, *Obs*, 29 November 1945.
63. RW, *NC*, 7 February 1948.
64. RW, *NC*, 25 November 1944.
65. RW, *NC*, 7 February 1949.
66. Basil Wright, *Spectator*, 7 February 1947.
67. AV, *SS*, Spring 1948, p. 23.
68. CAL, on *Passionate Friends*, *Obs*, January 1949.
69. DP, *ST*, 1 November 1944.
70. Catherine de la Roche, *SS*, Autumn 1946, p. 94.
71. RW (1947), in Rotha, 1947.
72. Anon, *Time and Tide*, 31 July 1948.
73. Joan Lester, *Reynolds News*, 25 July 1948.
74. AV, *SS*, Spring 1947, p. 40.
75. RW, on *Hamlet*, *NC*, May 1948.
76. WW, *NS*, 27 May 1944.
77. RW, *NC*, 24 April 1948.
78. CAL, on *Henry V*, *CHL*, p. 135.
79. CAL, on *Millions Like Us*, *CHL*, p. 99.
80. Agate, 1946, p. 215.
81. RM, *PFR*, no. 5, January 1948, p. 11.
82. DP, *ST*, 3 November 1946.
83. RW, *NC*, 23 June 1945.
84. RW, *NC*, 13 April 1948.
85. RW, *NC*, 9 June 1945.
86. RW, *NC*, 9 October 1943.
87. Elspeth Grant, *Daily Sketch*, 8 June 1945.
88. RM, *PFR*, no. 4, p. 15.
89. DP, *ST*, 7 May 1944.
90. RM, *PFR*, no. 2, p. 95.
91. RW, *PFR*, no. 1, p. 31.
92. RW, *NC*, 18 April 1949.
93. RW, *NC*, 4 December 1943.
94. CAL, *Obs*, 30 November 1947.
95. RW, *NC*, 29 March 1948.
96. DP, *ST*, 30 November 1947.
97. AV, *SS*, Spring 1949, p. 49.
98. RW, *NC*, 3 August 1948.
99. Matthew Norgate, *PFR*, no. 6, p. 14.
100. DP, *ST*, 9 January 1948.
101. WW, *NS*, 21 October 1944.
102. E. Arnot Robertson, *Daily Mail*, 23 November 1945.
103. RW, *NC*, 26 July 1948.
104. DP, *ST*, 29 September 1942.
105. RW, *NC*, 22 November 1947.
106. RW, *NC*, 23 November 1946.
107. J. Gassner, *PFR*, no. 3, p. 25.
108. CAL, on *This Happy Breed*, CHL, p. 117.
109. RW, *NC*, 7 April 1948.
110. WW, *NS*, 23 May 1942.
111. WW, *NS*, 9 December 1944.
112. RW, *NC*, 14 February 1948.
113. RW, on *The Overlanders*, *NC*, September 1946.

114. RW, *NC*, 8 November 1947.
115. A. L. Vargas, *SS*, Winter 1947.
116. Martin Field, *PFR*, no. 6, p. 32.
117. Anon, *Evening Standard*, 30
    September 1948.
118. Jan Read, *PFR*, no. 5, p. 68.
119. Thomas Taig, *PFR*, no. 5, p. 32.
120. D. A. Yerrill, *SS*, Winter 1947/8,
    p. l53.

121. E. Arnot Robertson, *PFR*, no. 3,
    p. 35.
122. Keith F. Bean, *SS*, Winter 1944/5,
    p. 38.
123. David Lean, *PFR*, no. 4, p. 31.
124. RM, *SS*, Spring 1947, p. 36.
125. Elizabeth M. Harris, *PFR*, no. 6,
    p. 85.

7

From *Holiday Camp* to High Camp: Women in British Feature Films, 1945–1951

Sue Harper

The post-war settlement in Britain entailed a return to traditional family values. The war had provided a watershed in most women's sexual and work experience, but many of the old class antagonisms remained unaddressed. There is ample evidence to suggest that, in the immediate post-war period, the population desired a return to an improved domestic sphere, and was resistant to state enterprises such as British Restaurants and community laundries. These may have been expedient in wartime, but were widely felt to provide facilities inferior to the privacy of home. Indeed, after 1948 the post-war Labour government did not significantly extend the incursions of the state into domestic life (Fielding, Thompson and Tiratsoo, 1995).

It is arguable that wartime social changes were neither permanent nor deep-rooted. The liberalization in sexual behaviour, which had been widely noted during the war, did not generate a new radicalism in sexual politics. The central ground of both the feminist and the anti-feminist cause was captured by conservatives, and this had a complicating effect on the disposition of class and gender loyalties.

How does film culture deal with such issues? In the under-researched field of sexual politics during Attlee's Governments, it would be tempting to argue that film gave straightforward access to reality. However, this would be fatally reflectionist. The cinema always produces imagery which is at a tangent from history: it makes symbolic readings of it. Class or gender interests rarely appear straightforwardly in film texts, and they are usually displaced, complicated or disguised. In my opinion, cinema's most important function is to provide a site for the restatement and the questioning of notions of the sacred and the profane, the pure and the dangerous; it does not even begin to approximate real life (Harper, 1994). During World War II, changes in women's experience were dealt with extremely selectively by the film industry. Official anxieties about women's employment were filtered through films such as *Millions Like Us* (1943) which laundered contemporary problems. Other films backed by the Ministry of Information (MoI), such as *The Gentle Sex* (1943) and *The Demi-Paradise* (1943), only ratified those women who were dutiful and chaste. Studios and production companies had differing styles of gender representation too, and it is quite feasible to describe an 'Ealing Woman' or an 'Archers Woman'. Commercial films which contained more liberated images of women, such as *The Wicked Lady* (1945), *Great Day* (1945) or even the Gert and Daisy films, had two things in common: they avoided realistic modes of representation, and they circumvented the social power of the middle class, on a symbolic level. It remains to be seen whether similar patterns inform post-war film culture (see also Aspinall, 1983).

First, though, the question of the gender of the film-maker should be addressed. The *Kinematograph Yearbook* for the war and post-war periods reveals important contrasts. During the war, female workers tended to specialize in traditionally feminine areas of continuity and costume design, and increasing numbers of women worked in Art Departments; Gainsborough also constituted a limited space for female scriptwriters. In the post-war period, it became possible for Muriel Box (initially through her husband Sydney) to develop as a producer; later both Wendy Toye and Betty Box (Sydney's sister) directed films. It would, of course, be sentimental to assume an automatic fit between the sex of the originator and the politics of a film. For example, Betty Box produced *Miranda* (1947), *Here Come the Huggetts* (1948) and *So Long at the Fair* (1950). But one would search in vain for evidence of what would now be recognized as a feminist sensibility behind these films. *Miranda* dealt with a mermaid whose voracious sexual appetite and fishy smell put her beyond the pale of bourgeois society and constituted a threat to 'normal' females. The business of *Here Come the Huggetts* was to humiliate and neutralize the lively adolescent played by

Diana Dors. And the heroine of *So Long at the Fair* was the object of a conspiracy to keep her in virginal innocence, which was signalled by hiding a key, papering over a door, and concealing a room; these may be read as metaphors for the repression of heterosexual female desire. Muriel Box did not express a radical position in the sexual politics of the films she produced. In addition, male film-makers did not automatically endorse patriarchal practices, and they produced some films which could be categorized as feminist. Of course, when analysing patterns of gender representation, it is folly to scrabble through films and apportion praise or blame for their 'positive' or 'negative' attitudes to women. Such an approach is ahistorical, since it attempts to rescue texts and belabour those which got things wrong, politically speaking. Rather, we need to categorize films according to their production context and visual style, and relate them where possible to contemporary debates about representation and stereotypes.

First of all, we need to consider the attitude of the Government to film producers in the post-war period. During the war, the MoI had maintained its belief in the persuasive power of films about contemporary life. It gradually lost confidence in the efficacy of history as a means of propaganda, and it attempted to discourage commercial film-makers from deploying the past. Jack Holmes, the Ministry documentarist, argued:

> I don't know that history as such interests cinema audiences much, unless it is a bastard kind of dress-up story of some picturesque characters, with all the historical effects suitably distorted and with plenty of love-life thrown in for extra seasoning. Most people can easily be made interested in contemporary life.[1]

This 'bastard' kind of history was then, and continued to be regarded as, a female prerogative, and as such, of course, was of minimal status. The MoI always displayed a certain puritanism in its attitudes to popular film, and after the war the Central Office of Information (CoI) maintained this tendency, but with an additional depressing gloss. Staff there were not wholly convinced of the new Government's policies, and some felt that 'the whole country is not behind the present methods of tackling the aftermath ... every audience has a large proportion of cynics, doubters, the bored and the frankly antagonistic.'[2] Clearly, there were some continuities between the pre-1945 and post-1945 bureaucracies; many government employees working under Attlee's administration were no less elitist than before. The CoI had little energy for their task; and what they had was squandered in wresting residual film work away from the British Council.

So the only post-war Government film body displayed a contempt for the mass audience and indifference towards its female side. Producers received little useful guidance there; and the Board of Trade was if anything less helpful, since it thought that 'most of the people engaged in the industry are rogues of one kind or another.'[3] The Board was riven by conflicting schools of thought. One championed the producer Filippo del Giudice and his brand of quality film:

> *Henry V* [1944] was the only film which is really bringing substantial sums from America to the British film producers. ... it is *no use* sending to America the films of the mass product type based on a stereotyped formula of entertainment.[4]

Another influential caucus petitioned on behalf of Alexander Korda (head of London Films), arguing that he was a better businessman than his fellow-producers Michael Balcon or Sydney Box.[5] The President of the Board of Trade until late 1947, Sir Stafford Cripps, chose J. Arthur Rank as his favourite.[6] Conflicting Board interests, therefore, obscured its influence, and there is little evidence to suggest that the Board of Trade had any concern for films which might picture or appeal to the female population. For the Board of Trade, women were merely potential consumers, as evidenced by its support for Herbert Wilcox's fashion epic, *Maytime in Mayfair* (1947).[7]

The British Film Producers' Association (BFPA) was in a tense relationship with Attlee's Government. When the 1948 Cinematograph Films Act eliminated the distributors' quota in order to conform to the new GATT requirements (the General Agreement on Tariffs and Trade), a whole tranche of cheap films could no longer be made, and this exacerbated bad feeling. In addition, the industry was assailed by rising costs, and the BFPA entirely blamed the Government for the debacle of the Ad Valorem Tax, a swingeing surcharge imposed by the Board of Trade on film imports, which provoked an embargo from the American film industry. The Association's Export Committee was particularly hostile: 'little is to be expected from the Board of Trade.'[8] Film producers in the post-war period were not naturally inclined to perceive the advantages of socialism, especially when they thought it was being administered in a maladroit fashion. And so their Executive Council wasted energy in acrimonious debate, instead of formulating a policy; its minutes suggest a querulous truculence about Government misalliances, but no coherent plan.

The producers were in combative mood with the British Board of Film Censors (BBFC) too. Their wartime relationship had been conciliatory; under conditions of national emergency the censorship behests of Government (largely organized by the MoI) had been obeyed. But if we check the post-war advice of the BBFC against the completed films, it seems that the producers had been stricken with mass deafness. Project after project bore no sign of the censors' intervention; the Gainsborough melodramas were particularly flagrant in this regard. Clearly the BBFC reverted to its old standards on sexual matters, but the producers decided to follow their noses in the prediction of mass taste and the pursuit of profit.

The post-war film industry, therefore, was in a hostile relationship to a number of Government bodies, and we can conclude that general film output in no sense reflected or even approximated Labour's sense of reality. Only one film (*The Chance of a Lifetime*, 1950) can be interpreted as a mouthpiece of Government views. Otherwise, a vacuum in official policy on film content met with no coherent challenge from the industry. Economic crises in the film industry and producers' alienation from bureaucratic institutions meant that competition shook loose a range of approaches. An overview of film production will provide a motley confusion in the area of gender relations. A woman could appear as a sex-crazed spinster (*A Man About the House*, 1947), as dignified labour (*Esther Waters*, 1947), as a robot (*The Perfect Woman*, 1949), as a statue (*Latin Quarter*, 1945), as a shipwrecked bigamist (*Piccadilly Incident*, 1946), as a witch (*Jassy*, 1947), as a Republican heroine (*Odd Man Out*, 1946), or as a fur-lined sleeping bag (*Scott of the Antarctic*, 1948). Let us attempt to delineate some pattern, firstly by categorizing films according to their producer or production company. The producer in post-war Britain was usually the one who, in the last instance, orchestrated the different authors at work on a film, and the one whose cultural competence and definitions of normality informed the whole text (Harper, 1994). Of course, a canny producer would monitor and respond to changes in audience taste.

Let us first consider the post-war work of Herbert Wilcox. He had, of course, been successful in the 1930s with films like *Nell Gwyn* (1934) and *Victoria the Great* (1937). Wilcox combined class and gender arguments in his earlier work, and he possessed an outstanding sense of the anxieties of a conservative group plunged into radical change. This trajectory was continued in his post-war career. Films in which women played a key role were *Piccadilly Incident* (1946), *The Courtneys of Curzon Street* (1947), *Spring in Park Lane* (1948), *Elizabeth of Ladymead* (1949), *Maytime in Mayfair* (1949), *Odette* (1950) and *The Lady With the Lamp* (1951). In all these films, the female lead was combative and inventive, but was finally returned to a status quo which she herself had reinvigorated.

The Courtneys of Curzon Street, which was the biggest box-office success of its year, dealt with the marriage of an Irish maidservant (Anna Neagle) to an aristocrat (Michael Wilding). Visually, the film was competent if unremarkable, Neagle's accent was erratic, and Wilding connoted nobility by wearing his shoulders up round his ears. In spite of these drawbacks, the film was a hit because of the arrangement of sexual and class values. It welded the aristocracy to the working class with the glue of sexual desire and popular song. The Courtney marriage was structured in such a way that the husband remained romantically passionate, and the wife magically unwrinkled; it was thus a film of lyrical improbabilities, in which class tensions were resolved by love and art, but without changing social composition or gender stereotypes. In a display of fancy footwork, the studio publicity material presented the film as both escapist and patriotic.

Wilcox had discovered a potent mix for the post-war period, and he used the same ingredients for *Spring in Park Lane*, which again was the top moneymaker of its year, according to *Kinematograph Weekly*. Here Neagle, arrayed in sumptuous frocks, was wooed while waltzing by her impoverished butler, who was an aristocrat in disguise. Class mobility was the ostensible theme, while the status quo was endorsed with a new vigour. The heroine's bounciness concealed her conventionality, and the whole transaction was bound together by music. Wilcox had a unique ability to express a view that appeared as commonsense reformism, but which was in fact a comforting retrospection. *Elizabeth of Ladymead*, too, appeared in the *Kinematograph Weekly* listings, and is particularly interesting for our purposes. It dealt with four wives from the same family from the Crimean and Boer wars, and from both World Wars, and showed the difficulties experienced when war encouraged female independence. Wilcox modulated changes in women's experience in such a way that they could be recuperated within a rhetoric of democracy and straightforward sexual difference. The script suggested that each woman's struggle for autonomy showed the modern heroine that 'our past shapes our futures, and that what women have battled for is the right to a say in that future'. Significantly, that 'say' was usually minimal, and the only wife to be placed beyond the pale had become a promiscuous flapper. But perhaps the sight of the staid Neagle in libidinous *déshabillé* prevented the willing suspension of disbelief. Certainly the *Daily Mail* critic thought so; he had, on 24 December 1948, 'quite irresistibly the feeling of a small boy who has accidentally caught his governess undressing'.

None of Wilcox's other films of the period departed significantly from this formula. His hyperactive heroines were pegged down beneath a tarpaulin of old beliefs. Wilcox's films indirectly evoked a world of residual class and gender values, and they implicitly suggested that middle-class insecurity could be assuaged by making a small and temporary settlement with the new ways.

Alexander Korda was a different case. He too had had a successful pre-war and wartime career with such films as *The Scarlet Pimpernel* (1935) and *Lady Hamilton* (1941). These combined a sensuous visual texture with an attention to female autonomy; Korda also inculcated the audience with the desirability of class confidence (Harper, 1994). The learning of an aristocratic code was possible for all, and both social and sexual crises could be resolved by creating a symbolic union between the landed and the working classes, excluding the middle class. But in the post-war period, Korda lost his way. To be sure, London Films was the production company for some films relevant to our topic, such as *Mine Own Executioner* (1947) and *Gone to Earth* (1950), but Korda took no part in their production process and he cannot be construed as their author. The post-war films in which Korda was personally involved were *Anna Karenina* (1947), *An Ideal Husband* (1948), *Bonnie Prince Charlie* (1948), and *The Elusive Pimpernel* (1950). Only *Anna Karenina* was mentioned in the popularity listings, although Korda told the Board of Trade that it only made £65,000.[9]

How did Korda deploy women in these films? The style of *Anna*

Karenina was extremely mannered, and the visual texture, though dense, suggested joylessness. The final script omitted most of the Levin story, and thus threw greater weight on to the Anna/Vronsky relationship. Anna was clearly meant to experience sexual pleasure ('I should feel ashamed, but I don't'), whereas Tolstoy's heroine did not; and the film did not permit their illegitimate child to survive, thus simplifying matters. All this should have led to a more erotic version of the novel. But Anna was portrayed throughout as a beautiful victim, whose chief significance in life was to be looked at rather than to feel; and so the jealousies and suicide seemed merely the result of undignified feminine whim, and woman's passion looked like a tableau from Madame Tussaud's.

The problem was that, with *Anna Karenina*, Korda was aiming at the international market, and he now lacked the sure touch which had caused him earlier to deploy key historical topoi in British culture. *An Ideal Husband* was cast in the same mould. The *mise-en-scène* was remarkably sumptuous, but it was also static. The female protagonists appeared in such a way as to augment, rather then reduce, their stereo-typicality, and no insight was offered into their interior life. The whole was, the *Sunday Graphic* suggested in a preview on 16 November 1947, 'a spectacle for jaded housewives'. *Bonnie Prince Charlie* was beset by production and scripting problems, such that Korda ordered another battle every time he ran out of script pages, and he was unable to deploy history in a fruitful way. And *The Elusive Pimpernel* was inferior when compared with the 1930s *Pimpernel* films. To be sure, Sir Percy negoti-ated his way through various class discourses, as before; but the female leads were less vigorous and complex.

We can conclude that Korda's early preoccupations with aristocratic symbolism and female pleasure had lost their allure, and that he was in-strumental in producing images of women which were passive and petulant. Korda may well have been a favourite at the Treasury and, to some extent, at the Board of Trade.[10] But the sexual politics of his films were flaccid, and this was the result of his loosening grasp on key cultural patterns.

The third major producer of the period, Michael Balcon, is a more clear-cut case. He had been more enthusiastic about the MoI than his fellow-producers, and held much more overtly patriotic views. Balcon had experimented with an early form of unit production at Gaumont-

British in the 1930s, and he had encouraged favoured individuals so long as they concurred with his world-view. Balcon's arrangements at Ealing were similar; a small creative elite and a large administrative staff followed his intellectual leadership, and little autonomy was granted to separate studio units. This management philosophy accounted for the intellectual conservatism of Ealing's output. Balcon thought that national identity could be straightforwardly expressed in films. As Head of Production at Ealing in the wartime and post-war period he was responsible for a body of films which attempted two things: a taxonomy of the middle class, and the virtual eradication of sexually active females.

Ealing's output in the post-war years has a clear pattern. There is only one film which deals with female autonomy: *The Loves of Joanna Godden* (1947). The original novel by Sheila Kaye-Smith dealt with a vigorous woman farmer who courageously decided not to marry the father of her child, and it ended with a celebration of female independence. But the film insisted on the social pressures impinging on the heroine, who was forced to conform; and the script evoked the desirability of traditional sexual roles, arguing that Joanna was 'a mare who ain't never been properly broke in, and she wants a strong man to do it'. Painterly as the film's visual texture was, its tone was one of elegiac regret for a past in which women knew their place.

An Ealing film which foregrounded a female protagonist differently was *Frieda* (1947). Here the German heroine was the victim of her husband, brother, and British class society. Her only means of self-expression was in self-sacrifice; firstly in a sexless marriage to save a soldier, and secondly in a suicide attempt to avoid confrontation. Frieda clearly symbolized 'womanly' virtues: timidity, blondeness, dependence, passivity. Indeed in all Ealing films of the period, women who were sexually as well as socially active were by implication predatory. *Pink String and Sealing Wax* (1945) was an interesting example of this. The script instructed that Pearl, who was evil and sexual, should have 'a hard loveliness, and the essential coarseness of her nature is always in danger of breaking through'. A revealing aside on the *mise-en-scène* noted that 'she is sitting on a pile of dirty underwear and old corsets'. A frisson of sexual disgust was prompted, which was absent from the original play.

This pattern was repeated in *It Always Rains on Sunday* (1947) and

Saraband for Dead Lovers (1948). The heroines in these films were fatally split. Rose in *It Always Rains* could not unite her past blonde self with her present dark appearance, and was torn between being a wife who mutters 'haddock' and a mistress with her head in the gas oven. *Saraband* contained two heroines: one was a vapid beauty who dared not consummate her desire (Joan Greenwood), and the other was an ageing harridan who felt desire but was too decayed to inspire it (Flora Robson). In a significant scene Robson, made grotesque by measles and calamine, confessed to her young lover from behind a screen that 'I love you, but I shan't be a woman for much longer'.

So many Ealing films offered a horrid set of alternatives to the female audience. The only ratified conditions were virginity or respectable con-jugality. Any departure from these norms met with severe punishment, and this held good for Ealing films by a range of directors, set in a variety of historical periods and dealing with all classes. The most extreme example is *Scott of the Antarctic* (1948), which was a major prestige production and a Royal Command Performance film. *Scott* could be interpreted as a paean to male bonding, from which the female presence was forcibly expunged. The script constructed male identity as a speechless but inexorable yearning towards one's own kind; at the end 'Scott looks affectionately at his companions. Then he moves so as to be alongside Wilson, and he throws his left arm over Wilson's shoulder.' But verbal expressivity was taboo; for a key speech, 'emotion should be washed out of his voice'. Moreover, the utmost unease was evinced about women. One of the heroes could see 'the place where the letter's going to, I mean, where she is; but her face is always misty.' And the female body was presented as a source of anxiety. In a key scene, Ponting delivered a music-hall rhyming monologue. The one selected was about the difficulties of wriggling into his fur sleeping bag: 'so the fur side is the outside and the skin side is the inside.' This could be read as a covert metaphor for female genitalia. They were the site of danger and distaste, if the manner of the verse's delivery and of the explorers' sniggering response is taken into account. *Scott* dealt with a wasteland in which bourgeois heroism could be defined, and which was mercifully cleansed of female mess.

All Balcon's films attempted a celebration of some aspect of middle-class culture, and this was attended by a profound misogyny. This is not an inevitable combination by any means; as I shall show, Cineguild had similar cultural politics, but different sexual attitudes. Balcon's own type of production control led to a body of films which constituted an ambitious attempt to locate the whole middle class at the centre of the cultural debate, and to define that class as male. A strong contrast can be drawn with Gainsborough studios, which had different production values, and which was oriented towards women and the working class.

Gainsborough slanted its melodrama output uncompromisingly towards women, and cared little for the critical opprobrium which attended its efforts. The studio was directly owned by J. Arthur Rank, and until late 1946 it was run by Maurice Ostrer, Ted Black and R. J. Minney. Under their aegis some highly profitable 'woman's films' were made in wartime, such as *The Man in Grey* (1943), *Love Story* (1944) and *Madonna of the Seven Moons* (1944). All these films were visually flamboyant, and deployed a cheap but effective form of expressionism; they contained heroines who engaged actively in their own destinies.

This pattern was repeated in the post-war period by the same production team. *The Wicked Lady* (1945), *Caravan* (1946) and *The Magic Bow* (1946) were all phenomenally successful. All these films contained females who risked everything for emotional fulfilment. The women failed, finally; but the films suggested, in a high Romantic manner, that real life became an anticlimax once fantasy had been totally achieved. These films also implicitly placed a high value on popular culture; consider the Tyburn scene in *The Wicked Lady*, and the gypsy wedding in *Caravan*. And Paganini in *The Magic Bow* was energetically recuperated as a proletarian whose artistry was freed from polite constraints. So these films, produced under the Ostrer/Minney partnership, offered a powerful form of identification to their female viewers. They invited them into a country in which males were constructed as the object of female desire, in which hitherto forbidden modes of wilfulness and self-gratification were permitted, and in which women were firmly welded to a vigorous popular culture.

Minney and the others had a sure sense of mass taste, and the studio was tightly organized in order to produce non-realist melodramas. But when Rank appointed Sydney Box as Head of Production in late 1946, everything changed. Together with his wife Muriel and his sister Betty who came with him, he had become convinced that realist methods were more appropriate for the post-war period, and it is significant that in all his later films there is an almost exclusive interest in contemporary life.

Consider, for example, *Holiday Camp* (1947) and *When the Bough Breaks* (1947). The first was produced by Sydney and the second by Betty Box, but they share common themes and methods. *Holiday Camp*, displaying in the opening sequences some of the conventions of the newsreel style, was concerned with the miseries of female celibacy. The film dealt ostensibly with changes in working-class leisure; but its real business was to find a husband for the Huggetts' daughter and a step-father for her child. This central tale was flanked by those of a wise but unfulfilled spinster, an unmarried mother, and a plain and sexually voracious fool who was summarily murdered. *When the Bough Breaks* dealt with the essential respectability of an unmarried mother who was a bigamist's victim; motherhood, and its most appropriate social arrangement, preoccupied the film, whose sexual morality and class politics were conservative.

An important change in nuance gradually appeared in Gainsborough films from late 1947. Consider *Dear Murderer* (1947), *Easy Money* (1948) and *Snowbound* (1948). Each of these was thoroughly informed by the notion of female guilt. *Dear Murderer* began by analysing the obsessive jealousy of a betrayed and murderous husband; in a remarkable travelling shot, the wife was seen looking in three different mirrors, and the film pivoted round at that point so that the real site of guilt seemed to be her vanity and sexual hunger. In *Easy Money*, the females were easier prey to cupidity and absurdity than the males. And in *Snowbound*, the answer to the film's riddle was held by a female aristocrat, who died rather than tell the secret and assuage the audience's and the protagonists' curiosity.

We can conclude that Gainsborough shifted from being a studio which celebrated female desire to one which repressed it; this was probably the result of changes in the production team and philosophy. I have already suggested that the gender of Muriel and Betty Box was not at that stage a visible influence in their work. Arguably, it is the shared preoccupations evinced by all the Boxes which account for the shift in studio output. For further proof, we should consider some non-Gainsborough films produced by the Boxes in this period; *The Seventh Veil* (1945), *Daybreak* (1946), *The Upturned Glass* (1947) and *Good-Time Girl* (1948). All these films took female weakness or guilt as their leitmotif. The first presented the split between the heroine's artistic creativity and sexual desire as a deep-seated neurosis; the last argued that the sexually active female was essentially inclined to crime. There was a clear consistency in the Boxes' work over the whole period.

Gainsborough was owned directly by Rank; but there were several other production companies under the umbrella of his Independent Producers Ltd., each with different sexual politics. Two Cities, for example, was run until 1947 by Filippo del Giudice, who was influential in the development of the 'quality film'. Del Giudice had had enormous financial support from Rank for *In Which We Serve* (1942) and from the MoI and Rank for *Henry V* (1944). Increasingly, he felt that the quality film required different marketing and distribution techniques since the audience it appealed to was irredeemably different from the mass audience, while films which pleased or foregrounded women were rigorously excluded from his canon:

> The masses are unfortunately more inclined to enjoy a *Wicked Lady* than one of our pieces of art which have brought such a credit to the British film industry. ... my contention is that if we make a film comparable to Cartier's jewels, we ought to sell it only in specialised shops like Cartier's.[11]

Del Giudice's puritanism was combined with an insistence that those concerned with profit could never produce great art. There were those in Government who were prepared to take Del Giudice on his own terms; Harold Wilson, then President of the Board of Trade, was advised that he should 'consider Del's films as a reserve for British film art and treat them as you would treat the Old Vic, for pride and prestige of the country'.[12] But it was a pride and prestige in which women played no part.

Two Cities began to experience managerial problems after the war, probably because of del Giudice's growing hostility to Rank. The films he produced there before he left to found Pilgrim Pictures were of interest, however. *Beware of Pity* (1946) dealt with a crippled girl who fell in love with an insensitive chucklehead, and the position offered to the female audience was one of helpless misery. *Carnival* (1946) was carelessly scripted, and the idiom coarsely handled; the dour farmer hero killed his ballerina wife, saying 'I am the prey of a woman who has surrendered to the foul dictates of the flesh and the devil.' This film, like many Two Cities productions, quoted high culture but in a very maladroit way; and the same held good for *Hungry Hill* (1947). This was a family saga which Two Cities presented as superior to Gains-borough bodice-rippers; Margaret Lockwood was presented in the publicity material 'not as a wicked lady, but as girl, wife and mother'. For the decor, 'extensive research was necessary to ensure that every-thing was in period.' This combination of historical accuracy with a disregard for scripting also afflicted *Vice Versa* (1948), in which every-one was playing in the Crummles style. The failure to control script material was also evident in *The Mark of Cain* (1948). This was a stab at melodrama, which failed artistically because all the people working on the film despised the genre and its aficionados. The publicity material contained what must be history's most downbeat account of adultery: 'Discouraged by her husband's lack of appreciation, Sarah makes Richard her confidant.'

Hamlet (1948) was the last Two Cities film to be made under del Giudice's aegis. It was a critical and box-office success, which owed much to its elaborate pre-release publicity. *Hamlet* was made and marketed in such a way as to encourage audiences with a modicum of elite cultural competence to feel confident about high art. However, Olivier depoliticized the play by excising Fortinbras, Rozencrantz and Guildenstern; and his film foregrounded the misogynistic aspects of the play. The direction of the Gertrude/Hamlet relationship forced an Oedipal interpretation, and the Hamlet/Ophelia scenes were unusually full of sexual loathing. So the status conferred by *Hamlet* was of a special type.

Del Giudice's attempt to inject high cultural values into cinema had a high cost in the post-war period, with the possible exception of *Hamlet*. He produced films in which females were dangerous without being interesting, which may have been the result of trusting wilful and inex-perienced personnel. Two Cities was also responsible for *Odd Man Out* (1947) and *Fame is the Spur* (1947). But del Giudice could not control these films, because Carol Reed was the producer as well as director of the first, as the Boulting brothers were of the second. Interestingly, both these films contained female protagonists with some autonomy and psychological complexity; the heroine of the first appropriated a gun, and in the second, the heroine's feminism was a serious complication.

The subsequent history of Two Cities was not edifying, as far as the representation of women went. Joseph Somlo supervised a series of low-status vehicles in which females played decorative roles, such as *The*

Weaker Sex (1948) and *The Perfect Woman* (1949). Any attempt at high seriousness had been abandoned. In the poster for *Trottie True* (1949), the frilly skirts of the Gaiety Girl filled the frame, and her legs were spread at right angles.

We can conclude so far that, within the Rank empire, different types of production control had a clear but unpredictable effect on images of women. Much depended on the cultural theories endorsed by the producer, and on his (or her) ability to enforce those on the studio floor. Cineguild played a distinctive role. It too operated under Independent Producers Ltd., and was formed by Anthony Havelock-Allen and Ronald Neame, to produce Noel Coward's *This Happy Breed* (1944). Havelock-Allen was a contentious personality who was opposed to any union involvement in artistic matters, and thought that 'films which were artistically and culturally of the highest importance were made by producers not conditioned by the needs and notions of the front office of a major company'.[13] David Lean was in agreement with such cultural politics. The most interesting Cineguild proponent was Ronald Neame, who had considerable intellectual ambition and rejoiced in his reputation as an 'art-house' director. In *Kinematograph Weekly* on 18 December 1947, he applied to the cinema Bevin's remark about Britain's artisanal excellence:

We have never been able to compete with Americans in mass-producing articles. But when it comes to hand-made articles, everyone turns to Britain. ... Let our films also be good hand-made articles, each individual and special in its own way.

These views are of the greatest interest. Cineguild clearly exemplified an Art for Art's Sake position far more rigorous than that of Powell and Pressburger's The Archers. And traditionally it has always been part of aestheticism's repertoire to insist on the *ambiguity* of the artefact; consider the attitude of John Keats, William Morris or Oscar Wilde to the art object. For them, its multifaceted nature was not obscured but enhanced by its craft origins. Art's meaning was infinite because the conditions of its production contradicted the procedures of industrial capital.

Cineguild was firmly rooted within this aesthetic. But for Neame and his colleagues, the complex cluster of feelings about the art object was displaced on to the female psyche. All the heroines in Cineguild films were characterized by ambiguity, either in their motives or in their morality. Like a great painting, they were mysterious and endlessly significant. In *Brief Encounter* (1945), Laura Jesson combined the 'good' and 'bad' woman within one body; but her self-knowledge was minimal, and her limited capacity for pleasure inhibited knowledge by others. *Great Expectations* (1946) was masterly in its recuperation of Victorian realism, and the power of its visual compositions owed much to the glacial composure of Estella. The film reinterpreted the novel so as to intensify her unfathomable qualities, and this was also the case with *Blanche Fury* (1948). This film had scripting problems, and the different extant versions indicate that it was the concealment, rather than the display, of the heroine's motives that was intended. The final film encouraged the audience to identify with its unfathomable protagonist by using distorted point-of-view shots and privileged flash-backs. *The Passionate Friends* (1949) also celebrated the indecisiveness of the adulterous heroine, whose charm resided in her inability to conceal duplicity. But the most striking example of all was *Madeleine* (1950). This dealt with the case of a woman tried for poisoning her lover; the court's verdict of 'not proven' dominated the film, and Lean's direction sat on the fence, morally speaking. Cineguild's publicity material was preoccupied with the conflicting legal evidence, and the whole film stressed the impossibility of either approval or blame.

Cineguild, then, expressed a unique configuration of elements. The late Romantic inheritance was nuanced there so as to insist on the irrelevance of morality when contemplating the desired mystery; the chief enigma was woman, rather than a work of art. But elsewhere in Rank's empire other film-makers were also freed from financial con-straints, and they proposed a different sexual politics in the post-war period. The Archers, Powell and Pressburger's production company under Rank's umbrella, made *A Matter of Life and Death* (1946), *Black Narcissus* (1948) and *The Red Shoes* (1948). Great care is required in interpreting these films, as a vulgar feminist analysis would find ample evidence of sexist perfidy in them, particularly in the last. One can imagine a reading of *The Red Shoes* which argued that the film endorsed the excision of those females who aspired to the status of artists, and that the blood on the ballet shoes symbolized the authors' desire that women return to an essential, menstrual femininity. But such an interpretation would severely underestimate the complexity of Powell and Pressburger's sexual politics.

Rank provided The Archers with freedom from financial anxiety and artistic interference, and allowed them to develop a coherent position on the key social roles of eroticism and elite groups. For Powell and Pressburger, females were not passive bearers of tradition but key speakers of it. Nor were they sacrificial victims; the heroine's tear, and her willing step upon the staircase in *A Matter of Life and Death*, symbolized her high place in the chivalric order. Archers films of this period celebrated an eroticism in which the woman was (of course) *secunda inter pares*, but without which social groups must falter. *Black Narcissus* should be interpreted as a sustained meditation upon female sexuality. It argued seductively that female desire was robust, and would surface in inimical conditions. Three scenes in particular instance this. An early shot juxtaposed Mr Dean and Angu Ayah against a mural in the erstwhile harem. Closer scrutiny revealed this as a faded erotic fresco, and Ayah exchanged a marvellously tolerant, conspiratorial glance with Dean; old and malodorous as she was, she remembered enough to facilitate others' pleasure. A second telling scene showed Kanchi, before the arrival of the Young General, dancing alone; self-appeasing, self-delighting, the curves of her body complementing the architecture. Thirdly, the denouement between Sister Ruth and Mr. Dean demonstrated the fatal effects of repressed desire; red hysteria followed her declaration of love, and his blunt 'I don't love anyone'. The scene presented them both as emotionally crippled.

Black Narcissus argued that elite groups which outlawed desire could not survive, and that sexual repression was as dangerous for females as for males. *The Red Shoes* extended the debate into the constitution of the artistic temperament. It did not argue that women had to choose between marriage and a career, but that domesticity was inimical to any creative drive. Both sexes inside the artistic coterie had love affairs; what excluded them from it was domesticity. In *The Red Shoes* it was family life, with its suffocatingly mean horizons, which rang the death knell of creativity. The film's sexual politics were thus bohemian.

Rank, then, had a salutary influence on The Archers. His masterly inactivity left them free to pursue a radical sexual and cultural politics, albeit firmly located within organic conservatism. However, once Rank began to experience severe financial difficulties in 1947, he interfered more, via his acolyte John Davis, and Powell and Pressburger sought fresh support. But this inhibited them politically. The production difficulties of *Gone to Earth* (1950) are well known, but the film was nonetheless a masterpiece, in which Heckroth's sets provided a fairy-like insubstantiality. The heroine, Hazel Woodus (Jennifer Jones), expressed an eroticism acutely in conflict with convention, and the scenario contained a very intelligent interpretation of Mary Webb's novel. But the film's expression of sexual radicalism was hampered by pre-production and post-production constraints, and it was a box-office failure. Clearly, Powell and Pressburger were more likely to win critical and audience approval when their films were part of a recognizable trajectory, and when they had total artistic control.

Other smaller companies produced significant films under Rank's aegis. Wessex Films, for example, headed by Ian Dalrymple, produced *Esther Waters* in 1948, which dealt unflinchingly with the privations of an unmarried mother. The film was an innovative attempt to create a visual correlative of literary naturalism; Esther was excluded, through her illiteracy and religiosity, from the world of racing jargon and upper-class idiolect, but this was conveyed visually, via composition within the frame and editing patterns. The problem was that 1890s literary naturalism, from which the film drew its sustenance, was an avant-garde phenomenon never fully assimilated into British cultural life. The film had a visual patina of reference to the documentary movement, which was predictable considering Dalrymple's former career as head of the Crown Film Unit. But the time was out of joint for such a style. Moreover, *Esther Waters'* extreme sexual and social determinism made it a depressing experience. So although it *could* be recuperated within a feminist canon, *Esther Waters* stood no chance at the box office because of its miserabilism and the naturalist aroma of its style.

Launder and Gilliat's Individual Pictures, too, was relieved of some financial strain by the Rank umbrella. But their company had little to say about women. *I See a Dark Stranger* (1946) displayed women as an amusing but fallible diversion, and they had no significant role in *Captain Boycott* (1947). It was only after Launder and Gilliat left Rank that they developed a coherent cinematic role for women, and this was, significantly, a comic one; *The Happiest Days of Your Life* (1950) and the later St Trinian's films located women as the site and cause of anarchy.

Rank's effect on types of gender representation, therefore, was extremely complex, largely because of his *laissez-faire* methods.

Gainsborough's output shifted from libidinous freewheelers to downtrodden conformists with Rank's appointment of Sydney Box. Two Cities suffered from del Giudice's elitism and lack of control on the studio floor, while Cineguild pursued a consistent but idiosyncratic 'art house' trajectory in which females played the dominant symbolic role. Rank's support permitted The Archers to co-opt females into a coherent debate about eroticism and elite culture. Other smaller production companies produced innovatory but unpopular films, or used Rank's support as a temporary stopgap in preparation for their final position on the role of women. On this issue, there was clearly a sharp divide between Rank-backed producers and the big independents. Wilcox, Korda and Balcon developed more consistent links between their theories of class and of gender, and their post-war work displayed clear debts to their wartime and pre-war work. All three had a more integrated approach.

However, if we wish to attempt a comprehensive map of the role of women in British film culture of the period, other production companies, and especially the smaller independents and the American companies, must be taken into account. Anatole de Grunwald was a producer at the Associated British Picture Corporation (ABPC) during the late 1940s, and he held high-art views very similar to del Giudice's. However, it is extremely difficult to discern any pattern in the films he produced at ABPC. To be sure, women were the pivot of the plots of *While the Sun Shines* (1947), *Bond Street* (1948) and *Portrait of Clare* (1950). But there was no consonance of approach. Indeed the company appeared markedly hamfisted; the poster for the last film showed a giant female with three male homunculi in her hand, which was highly inappropriate for the taste of the period.

British National, headed by Louis H. Jackson, had a different profile. During the war, it had produced low-budget films with minimal profit and no discernible class position, and this was repeated in the post-war period. The company still failed to capitalize on its settings, with one important difference: all its films contained a female who caused nothing but trouble. *The Laughing Lady* (1946), *Woman to Woman* (1946), *Green Fingers* (1947) and *No Room at the Inn* (1948) had female leads who ran the gamut from petulance to outright villainy. But British National's treatments lacked flair, and made no important intervention in the field.

The smaller British production companies said nothing of interest on sexual politics. Butcher's, John Corfield and Acquila all deployed errant females in their films; but there were insufficient similarities or parallels to be significant. One fact is clear: small outfits needed the support of larger ones if they were to take risks with their subject matter. Examples are *A Man About the House*, which was produced by British Lion in 1947, and *Mine Own Executioner*, made by London/Harefield in the same year. The first was produced by old Gainsborough hand Ted Black, and directed by Leslie Arliss, who had directed many blockbusters there. Korda was involved also. *A Man About the House* was a box-office success, largely because of the frank way it dealt with sexual repression, and because of the visual pleasures of the Italian setting. The publicity material suggested that the local colour be stressed as the background to 'the kindling of the fire of love in the sex-starved Agnes'. The emotional texture of the film was intense, and it insisted throughout that women of a certain age could not only experience desire, but could (and should) achieve pleasure. *Mine Own Executioner* was radical also, but too much so for profitability. It dealt with a therapist unsuccessfully treating a psychopath; the latter killed his own wife, and the doctor began to take on the patient's ailment. It was not a case of guilt by association. Rather, the film engaged with the whole paradigm of male sadism and female masochism, and drew some remarkable conclusions about the complicity of psychoanalysis in the repression of females. But such a film could not be made by risking small, private capital; it relied upon the support of Korda's company.

Finally, we should turn to British-based but American-owned companies. In general, these were in retreat in the post-war years, largely because of the hostile attitude of the Board of Trade and the Ad Valorem tax furore. The American companies made a markedly different use of female roles; their films contained heroines who were abrasive, acquisitive and ruthless, but none of these films appeared in the *Kinematograph Weekly* popularity listings. Consider *The Idol of Paris* (1948) and *So Evil My Love* (1948). *The Idol of Paris* was made for Warner Bros and directed by Leslie Arliss, and it dealt with the colourful life of a ragman's daughter who became a famous courtesan and fought a duel with whips against her rival for the favours of Napoleon III. On the face of it, the film should have succeeded, since Arliss made it with R. J. Minney and Maurice Ostrer, and it was billed as 'by the team which made *The Wicked Lady*'. But the heroine's rapacious personality was inconsistently constructed, since she was supposedly still a virgin; no audience could suspend that amount of disbelief, since her performance displayed that bemused abstraction which always betokens sexual excess. The company clearly lost its nerve, and produced a film which was internally incoherent; its sublimely tacky qualities almost made it a camp masterpiece.

So Evil My Love had different problems. It was made for Paramount, and dealt with a missionary's widow who became a wicked lady, and it had impressive support; Sir Robert Vansittart loaned his country estate for exterior shots, and Edith Head designed the costumes. But the script was subdued, and its assertion that 'evil is as universal as love' lacked conviction. Moreover the film's art director was Tom Morahan, whose work had always been realist; so the visual texture nowhere approached the melodramatic subject matter. Another American-financed image of female villainy, therefore, was artistically misjudged. American production companies appeared to lack the cultural nous to combine gender issues with class elements, and did not concoct the rich brew produced by British companies. The Americans were also clearly informed by changing cultural patterns in their own country, which they attempted to duplicate in their British work.

If there were no limitations of space, a survey of changing audience and gender taste in the period would also have been included here. Such work would be able to address the complex relationship between producers, authorial desires, and audience responses. But I have demonstrated the range and complexity of cinematic representations of women in the period, and shown that the film industry was alienated from the Labour Government's policies. I have argued that images of women were constructed along lines laid down by the producer, and that the most coherent and often the most popular films made intimate connections between gender and class politics. But such films were never predicated on a reflection of real events; the relationships they made between gender and class elements drew from, and remained on, a symbolic rather than an actual level.

What is remarkable about post-war film output, in terms of the representation of women, is its variety. During World War II, the MoI was profoundly influential on patterns of film production, and all films made during that period exhibited what we may call a 'can-do' mentality. That is to say, wartime films expressed an optimism and an energy about (or on behalf of) subordinate groups such as women; the films argued implicitly that women could rise to the occasion of war, and could obtain confidence by assimilating and transforming the discourses of other marginal groups.

After 1945, all that changed. The film industry was, during the years of the Labour Government, essentially a seller's market. Its interests were commercial, and producers nuanced their representations of women according to their own instincts about what would sell. Because of the acute nature of the cultural and social resettlement, post-war producers were in the grip of conflicting currents of feeling. On the one hand, they felt joyfully liberated from the controls of the MoI; on the other hand, they appear to have been unsure about what kind of gender representations were most appropriate. They simply tried anything on, to see if it would fit.

After about 1951, the film industry shifted from a seller's to a buyer's market. There were changes in leisure patterns and audience composition, such that cinemagoing was no longer the nation's principal leisure activity. Cinema exhibition had to respond to the changing market place. Instead of giving the public a supply-led service, it had to become demand-led. This had a dramatic effect on patterns of gender representation in film. There are sharp distinctions to be drawn between images of women in films of the late 1940s and those of the 1950s. But a detailed analysis of those distinctions must wait for another day.

Notes

1. PRO (Public Record Office, Kew) BW 4/40, Holmes to Bundy, 18 August 1944.
2. PRO INF 12/564, memo from Forman, dated 1947. See also PRO INF 12/562, COI memo, 25 January 1947.
3. PRO BT 64/2366. This is an undated memo, probably to Wilson from one of his aides, if we take into account its place in the file.
4. PRO BT 64/2366, Board of Trade memo, 4 May 1948.
5. PRO BT 64/4139, Board of Trade memo, 24 March 1946.
6. PRO BT 64/4139, memo from the President, 19 November 1945.
7. See Hansard, vol. 476, 1950; *Daily Graphic*, 21 February 1949; and an interview with the actor Peter Graves, in S. Kochberg (1990), *The London Films of Herbert Wilcox*, MA thesis, Polytechnic of Central London.
8. Minutes of the BFPA Export Committee, 16 July 1946.

9. PRO BT 64/2366, memo of a Board meeting on 7 July 1947.
10. PRO BT 64/2366, memo from Eady to Somervell, 19 April 1949. See also a note from an unnamed Treasury official, dated 15 June 1948, arguing that Korda should be supported because 'he is not excluding other people's talents'.

11. Letter from del Giudice to Bernard Miles, 12 November 1947, in the Bernard Miles Papers, British Film Institute Library.
12. PRO BT 64/2366, memo from Nicholas to Wilson, 10 June 1948, marked 'Private'.
13. PRO BT 64/2366, letter from Havelock-Allen to the Board of Trade, 28 February 1948.

8

Victim: Text as Context

Andy Medhurst

The relation of text to context is decisively important to a theoretical and critical construction of the cinema/ideology relation.
(Klinger, 1984, p. 44)

Locating the text specifically lays it open to question. It also encourages us to perceive it on the level of everyday political strategy, which is where our own interventions must be conceived.
(Sinfield, 1983, p. 93)

Preface (1995)

The text which follows was published in *Screen* in 1984. Much has happened since, but it is a piece of writing which I am still mostly in agreement with, and which has achieved a certain currency in other people's footnotes and reading lists (the only way academics can ever genuinely gauge whether their work has any impact), so I think it earns its place in this book. At the risk of self-indulgence, I want to preface this reprint by spending a few lines reflecting on it with the benefit of a decade's hindsight.

For an aspiring Film Studies academic in the mid-1980s, to be published in *Screen* was to make the big time. It was the pre-eminent journal in the field, and its appearance on your CV was a boost like no other. The problem I faced was that my approach to the study of cinema was significantly out of step with the tradition that *Screen* so magisterially and glacially embodied. Its commitment throughout the

1970s to ostentatiously dense and difficult writing, to the hermetic intricacies of textual formalism and (most of all) to the new fundamentalism of Lacanian psychoanalysis was hard to square with my tendencies towards linguistic accessibility and a critical practice that wanted to evaluate films in terms of their social impact and cultural contexts. True, in 1982 a major shake-up in the editorial personnel had made the journal significantly more readable and open-minded, but I still felt largely excluded. When invited, by Christine Geraghty, to submit an article based on my University of East Anglia post-graduate dissertation on homosexuality and British cinema, I felt flattered and excited, but still daunted and fearful. What could a person like me have to say to a publication like that?

The answer was simple: when in doubt, lash out. The substantial part of the article, its consideration of *Victim*, was preceded by a rather intemperate polemic that wildly cudgelled what I thought of as the *Screen* legacy and in particular those who seemed to be trying to extend the less endearing aspects of those methodologies into the study of British cinema (which was, a few pioneer books and articles aside, still a massively neglected topic in film academia). Those sections of the original article have not worn well, and hence are not reprinted below, though readers interested in the micro-minutiae of the history of British film culture can of course seek out the original version should they have nothing better to do.

As things turned out, I needn't have worried. The zealous, monastic excesses of the old-style *Screen* are now as much a part of critical history as the literary musings of Sir Arthur Quiller-Couch, and the study of cinema, British or otherwise, is today a market-place of competing voices. The approach argued for below, that films need to be carefully located in the cultural and historical circumstances of their moment of production, is now a commonplace, however reckless an assertion it seemed at the time. Traces of that sense of recklessness are still discernible in the rhetorical tone of the article – in its defence I can only say that it, like *Victim*, is very much a text of its times.

Introduction

In the struggle to establish itself as a distinct and dynamic body of knowledge, film theory in the 1970s made enormous gains. It achieved a radical break from the varieties of crude determinism and lavish aestheticism that occupied positions of dominance, but, as in any struggle, there were also losses. Most regrettable among these was any sense of the film text as social object. In order to gain more rigorous insights into their internal workings, texts were wrenched out of history, given autonomy, cast adrift from context into a sea of significatory interplay which need never be referred back to the historical specificities of the moment of production.

In the belief that no reputable study of a text can be made without a detailed consideration of its cultural, historical and social contexts, I want to use a British film as a case study in proving the necessity of looking beyond the confines of the text itself. The film I shall be looking at is *Victim* (1961), the first British film to centre its narrative around male homosexuality, and I want to consider it in relation to two broad problematics: conceptualizations of homosexuality, and British film culture's general attitudes to sexuality at that time.

Situating *Victim*: Conceptualization of homosexuality

Victim is not a film that makes us dig very deep to unearth an ideological project; it is a film with a specific social intention, as its producer, Michael Relph, wrote:

> The film puts forward the same point of view as the Wolfenden Committee, that the law should be changed. ... The film shows that homosexuality may be found in otherwise completely responsible citizens in every strata of society. (Letter to *Films and Filming*, May 1961, p. 3)

The Wolfenden Report was published in 1957, and recommended the partial decriminalization of male homosexual acts (Wolfenden, 1957); the law was eventually changed in 1967. *Victim* was explicitly conceived of as part of a public debate on homosexuality which had been going on since the early 1950s. This had been instigated by the Burgess and Maclean scandal in 1951, when the two spies who had fled from Britain to Moscow were revealed to be homosexual. The scandal established a parallel between sexual and political deviance which was one of the central tenets of the ideologies informing the Cold War. In the United States, the virulent paranoia of McCarthyism insisted on this connection to the extent that the government officially forbade the employment of 'Homosexuals and other Sex Perverts' (Weeks, 1979, p. 160; my historical generalizations about this period are greatly indebted to Weeks' invaluable book). (In May 1982, Margaret Thatcher issued a directive banning the employment of homosexuals in the British Diplomatic Service – old Cold War ideologies for the new Cold War.) Homosexuality was 'exposed' by the popular press, led by the *Sunday Pictorial*'s series called 'Evil Men'. There were a number of sensational trials, some involving public figures, and it was one of these (the trial of Lord Montagu, Michael Pitt-Rivers and Peter Wildeblood) that was a major catalyst in the setting up of the Wolfenden Committee.

The Montagu trial has a particular importance as an index of the prevalent constructions of homosexuality. Debate centred not on the morality or immorality of homosexual practices, but on whether the basis of the law forbidding them was in any way just – was it the function of the legal system to prohibit individually chosen behaviour? As Peter Wildeblood recalls in his autobiography (Wildeblood, 1957), he and his co-defendants received a great deal of public sympathy, with sympathy being the operative word. Homosexuality was conceptualized as a disease which was incurable – thus its sufferers could not 'help' the way they were. This theory, offensive as it now seems, was at least a step forward from the hatred of homosexuality expressed by organized religions. Discourses of illness and treatment thus replaced those of sin and damnation. A leading advocate of the disease theory stated that:

> The homosexual is not just a man with a wicked or perverse wish to behave differently from others. He is not someone offered the loveliness of women and by sheer cussedness spurning it; he is ill inasmuch as a dwarf is ill because he has never developed. (Allen, 1958, p. 34)

The same writer comes to this perfectly sincere conclusion:

> Possibly the greatest importance of homosexuality is that it causes so much unhappiness. If happiness is of any value (and the writer regards it as having the greatest human importance) then homosexuality should be eliminated by every means in our power. (Allen, 1958, p. 54)

The fact that such unhappiness might be due to the social situation of homosexuals rather than their sexuality lies entirely outside this writer's vision. That the idea of a contented homosexual is anathema to him is shown by his typology of deviants, in which Type 3 is the 'homosexual in whom inversion is accepted as part of his personality. ... One must accept that Type 3 is too ill, too grossly deviated and lacks the urge to be cured' (Allen, 1958, p. 73).

The Wolfenden Report rejected the idea of homosexuality as a disease, but saw it as 'a state or condition' (Wolfenden, 1957, p. 11). The law ought to be changed, argued the Report, because other, equally repugnant, forms of behaviour were not proscribed by the criminal law: to penalize homosexuality alone was unfair. Wolfenden was in no way a validation of the homosexual option, but a logical, utilitarian acknowledgement of an injustice that should be rectified. The nuclear family was still written of as 'the basic unit of society' (Wolfenden, 1957, p. 22), leaving homosexuality as an unfortunate, implicitly inferior condition.

Much of the debate that followed Wolfenden aspired to some kind of sociology, and homosexuals were transformed from laboratory specimens into statistics. Books about the homosexual subculture began to appear, blending charts and tables with prurient reports from intrepid sociologists who ventured into gay clubs and pubs. Their conclusions tended to show little advance on the disease theory:

> Society should help (but not force) its citizens to live a full and happy family life. ... It is worth making an effort to try to bring this about ... since there are many who are not completely homosexual but may be deflected from normal heterosexual pursuits or at least may be hampered by homosexuality. ... On the other hand, those who are true homosexuals should be advised and helped to live with their social underdevelopment as a handicapped minority without any false glamour and yet without victimisation. (Hauser, 1962, p. 25)

Others were compassionately post-Wolfenden:

> The present social and legal methods of dealing with the problem are irrational and tend to create more social evils than they remedy. This emotional hostility affects many thousands of individuals and reflects upon the community as a whole. (Westwood, 1960, p. 198)

These quotations ought to indicate the range of heterosexual notions of homosexuality; what remains to be examined is how homosexuals saw themselves.

Obviously a marginalized social group only constructs a self-image as a result of dissatisfaction with the images of it constructed by others, and those imposed images continue to set the parameters. The homosexual self-image of the 1950s, then, was entirely bounded by heterosexual paradigms. Even Peter Wildeblood can only see his sexuality in these terms:

> I am no more proud of my condition than I would be of having a glass eye or a hare lip. On the other hand, I am no more ashamed of it than I would be of being colour-blind or of writing with my left hand. ... I am attracted towards men in the way in which most men are attracted towards women. I am aware that many people, luckier than myself, will read this statement with incredulity and perhaps with derision; but it is the simple truth. ... I know that it cannot ever be entirely accepted by the rest of the community and I do not ask that it should. ... If it were possible for me to become like them I should do so. (Wildeblood, 1957, p. 8)

Despite the anger, or more likely sadness, that such words are liable to produce in any modern gay reader, it must be remembered that in the context of 1955 an autobiography containing the phrase 'I am a homosexual' was a major intervention. Wildeblood's book also contains a number of remarks echoed or even repeated in *Victim*. Henry the barber's 'Tell them there's no magic cure for how we are' comes from page 185 of Wildeblood, while Calloway's quotation from Oscar Wilde about 'the rage of Caliban seeing his own face reflected in the glass' also appears in Wildeblood. Most importantly, there is the crucial exchange between Melville Farr and his wife:

> Farr: I believe that if I go into court as myself I can draw attention to the fault in the existing law.

> Laura: Knowing it will destroy you utterly?

> Farr: Yes.

This is not at all dissimilar to the way Wildeblood describes his reasons for openly declaring his sexuality in court:

I could see what I must do. ... I would be the first homosexual to tell what it felt like to be an exile in one's own country. I might destroy myself, but perhaps I could help others. (Wildeblood, 1957, p. 59)

Before handing out labels like 'progressive' or 'reactionary' to a text (and if that smacks of evaluation, all I can say is that non-evaluative analysis is a self-deluding myth unhelpfully fostered by certain critical tendencies), it must be precisely situated within the circulating discourses, the flux of ideas (to borrow Richard Dyer's useful phrase [Dyer, 1979, p. 36]) informing its moment of production. *Victim* is a point of intersection, a site of confluence between two such fluxes. One of these is the contemporary range of constructions of homosexuality, as indicated above, and the other is the contemporary range of positions on sexuality taken up within British film culture. This latter topic is clearly immense and intensely problematic. As a way of illuminating the issues involved without losing myself in textual micro-analysis, I want to look briefly at the critical reception of *Victim* in the context of the ideological stances and value-systems mobilized at that point in history by dominant critical discourses. What attitudes did those discourses adopt towards sexuality?

Situating *Victim*: Sexuality and British film culture

Charles Barr, with characteristic accuracy, has written of Ealing films' 'suppression of a dark world' (Barr, 1977, p. 76) as being a major structuring force in those particular texts, and this perception can be extended across the whole range of post-World War II British film production. This suppression, this clamping down of desire, can be seen at work in films as varied as *Brief Encounter* (1945), *The Dam Busters* (1955), and *The Belles of St. Trinian's* (1954). However, the relentlessly middlebrow parlour game that goes under the name of British film criticism (in newspapers and non-specialist magazines) can never perceive the presence of sexuality in texts unless it is made blatant, discussed and/or enacted on screen. In the context of film criticism in the late 1950s and early 1960s, this is made plain in the adulation given to the social realist, angry-young-men films, like *Saturday Night and Sunday Morning* (1960).

The treatment of sexual matters in these films played a crucial part in their being acclaimed as some kind of artistic renaissance. Key words in the discourse of acclamation were 'maturity' ('When will British films grow up?', asked an impatient critic in 1958 [Whitebait, 1958, p. 11]) and 'frankness'. Thus the sight of June Ritchie's naked back in *A Kind of Loving* (1962) was seen as a step forward, even a breakthrough, in the quest for a 'relevant' and 'contemporary' national cinema. Obviously this attitude has its roots in the omnipresent hegemony of 'realism' that still dominated conceptions of cinema in Britain at that time, and that hegemony also helps to explain the hostility towards certain other areas of film production expressed by the same critics who rushed to welcome the naturalistic impetus. Furthermore, when one reads that hostility through a perspective of sexuality, all sorts of things fall into place.

The two specific areas of film production that I am referring to are the Hammer and *Carry On* films. Both were major commercial successes, both were dismissed or attacked by contemporary critics, and both are centrally concerned with sexuality. Hammer's early horror films are clearly informed by displaced eroticism, and the *Carry On* comedies base their humour on a contempt for bourgeois propriety and a grinning awareness of desire. The critical consensus, with its prescriptive commitment to a narrowly realist aesthetic serving as the vehicle for a vapidly liberal social awareness, could not be expected to cope with either coded sexual fantasies or dirty jokes – any film which dealt with sexuality outside a fundamentally moralistic framework was simply not acceptable.

One more, now infamous, case should be mentioned here. The critical reception of *Peeping Tom* (1960) crystallizes the attitudes I have been sketching. Michael Powell's films had long been distrusted by the critical consensus, principally through their (clearly interdependent) stress on visual excess and eroticism (*Black Narcissus* is probably the best welding of the two). That distrust became, with the release of *Peeping Tom*, genuine ostracism. The critical reaction was nothing short of hysteria, a fascinating case study of the psychopathology of the English middle classes, and it centred precisely on the text's implications regarding sexuality and cinema. The film flushed the dormant puritanism of the critical consensus into the open, with, for example, the *Daily Worker* accusing it of 'befouling the screen', and hurling adjectives like 'perverted', 'debased', 'diseased', 'pornographic' and 'depraved' (see Christie, 1978, pp. 55–6).

How can *Victim* be placed in such a context? Its very choice of topic puts it in some ways under the rubric of 'frankness', but its visual and narrative modes are those of melodrama, not social naturalism. It can in fact be linked to a series of earlier 'problem pictures' which had dealt with issues like racism (*Sapphire*, 1959, made by the same team responsible for *Victim*, and its twin in many respects) and juvenile crime.[1] The people involved in its production ensured that it was seen as part of the 'old school' of British film-making rather than as part of the supposed renaissance. Its use of the thriller genre is explained by the dominant notion of homosexuality as a social issue, a problem that had to be discussed rather than depicted; but since audiences would not pay to watch a discussion, the issues are mediated through generic codes. (The two 1960 films about Oscar Wilde utilized codes of costume drama and fictional biography to similar ends.)

Many reviews remarked upon this use of genre, with the *Monthly Film Bulletin* claiming that the film 'dressed up ... male inversion in a cleverly designed Crime Club dust-jacket' (*Monthly Film Bulletin*, October 1961, p. 141). The notices were of course determined by each writer's attitude to homosexuality, and these range across the variety discussed above. Some were openly hostile: 'Make private association lawful, it pleads, and blackmail will cease. But will homosexuality?' (*Sunday Telegraph*, 3 September 1961) The most anti-homosexual review of all came when the film opened in the United States:

Everybody in the picture who disapproves of homosexuality turns out to be an ass, a dolt, or a sadist. Nowhere does the film suggest that homosexuality is a serious (but often curable) neurosis that attacks the biological basis of life itself. 'I can't help the way I am,' says one of the sodomites in this movie. 'Nature played me a dirty trick.' And the scriptwriters ... accept this sick-silly self-delusion as a medical fact. (*Time*, 23 February 1962)

Most British reviewers were more informed by the debates around Wolfenden, and took up a position of liberal concern: 'it does invite a compassionate consideration of this particular form of human bondage', wrote the reviewer for *The Times* (30 August 1961), while the *Daily Worker*'s critic was struck by 'a serious and sympathetic study of men in the grip of a compulsion beyond their control. ... a sobering picture of the way homosexual inclinations make a permanent nightmare of private lives' (2 September 1961).

The critical consensus could be summarized as regarding *Victim* as a well-intentioned piece of special pleading, successful in making its social point, but in the process of doing so becoming schematized and propagandist and therefore aesthetically unsatisfactory. Two particular points shared by almost every review are firstly a direct reference to Wolfenden, and secondly specific praise for the acting. According to the *Monthly Film Bulletin*, despite the plot's 'glibness', 'The performances ... have a definite passion ... a dignity, a sobriety, an impression of really caring' (October 1961, p. 141).

The use of the word 'passion' sits rather uneasily in this context, and potentially opens up another way of reading the film. Dignity, sobriety, caring, compassion, sympathy – reviews which use words like these are clearly situated in a post-Wolfenden ideology, connoting a tone of self-congratulatory benevolence to one's unfortunate inferiors, but 'passion' is a term of a different order, an index of a different code. An opposition of dignity/passion could usefully be employed as a way into the text, for if *Victim* holds to the former, stays within the bounds of liberal tolerance asked for by Peter Wildeblood and granted by Wolfenden, then its only real interest is as a piece of cultural history. If, however, it transgresses so as to incorporate passion, refute sobriety and expose sympathy as oppressive condescension, it might still have a use in terms of modern gay politics. Michael Relph's remarks indicate the intention behind the making of the film, and that intention would seem to have succeeded in terms of critical reception, but I would argue (and hope to show in the next section) that *Victim*'s moments of passion, as the *Monthly Film Bulletin*'s reviewer unwittingly described them, subvert the hegemonic drive to dignity and tolerance and hint at what could be called a genuinely gay discourse, a discourse of homosexual desire.

The affirmation of homosexual desire is, of course, exactly what the opponents of Wolfenden feared would happen if the laws on homosexuality were altered. By its mobilization of concepts of compassion and tolerance, Wolfenden (and *Victim*) attempted the balancing act of advocating legal change without being seen to 'approve of' homosexuality. Even as the 1967 Sexual Offences Act was passing into law, belatedly implementing Wolfenden's proposals, Lord Arran, one of its strongest parliamentary advocates, showed his trepidation over the possible consequences in a speech in the House of Lords:

> I ask one thing, and I ask it earnestly. I ask those who have, as it were, been in bondage and for whom the prison doors are now open to show their thanks by comporting themselves quietly and with dignity. ... Any form of ostentatious behaviour now or in the future, any form of public flaunting, would be utterly distasteful and would, I believe, make the sponsors of the Bill regret that they have done what they have done. (Quoted in Hyde, 1970, p. 274)

Locked doors, continence, and humble gratitude – these were what was expected of homosexuals after 1967. As Tom Robinson's song 'Glad to be Gay' acidly put it, 'The Buggers are legal now, what more are they after?'

What we were after, and what we are still after, depended on precisely what the liberal heterosexual consensus was so afraid of – ostentation, flaunting, coming out. I base my belief in the comparative radicalism of *Victim* in the view that it is a film that, against the grain, advocates coming out. I don't want to offer a long and detailed analysis, as my methodological intentions in writing this article are founded on providing the necessary socio-cultural and historical information that would make an informed reading possible – in other words, I don't want to set up my reading as anything unique or special. Given the knowledge of the relevant debates and discourses, I think my conclusions would seem fairly standard.[2] Instead, I want to indicate those moments in the text when the maintenance of its inscribed liberalism fails, and when what I see as the discourse of homosexual desire (an acknowledgement of which is the prerequisite for any notion of gay politics) emerges.

Reading *Victim*: an indictment of repression

Film analysis which attempts to tease out strands of meaning other than those signalled by textual mechanisms is usually compelled to locate contradictory elements of narrative and/or *mise-en-scène*, but with *Victim* this is especially difficult to do. Since the film was made primarily for extra-textual reasons, consciously to effect social change, it is in many ways propaganda, and as such is particularly careful at sewing together its various threads. Richard Dyer has already mapped out the intricacy with which every character and incident is bound tightly into the central narrative drive, but there still remain, as he says, 'hints of strain' (Dyer, 1993, p. 102). If we want to identify where that strain is greatest, in terms of the liberal problematic being exposed and questioned, we must look at two adjacent scenes – Farr's 'confession' to Laura, and his visit to Mandrake's flat. It is here that the containment of desire breaks down.

In the 'confession' scene, Laura forces her husband to tell her the truth about his relationship with Jack Barrett. As she pleads 'Tell me everything, I want to know', it is easy to read her as the heterosexual audience inscribed into the text, with 'everything' meaning the physical details of homosexual love – so that Laura's desire for narrative elucidation becomes a kind of prurience. (The motif of the photograph which is the source of the blackmail and thus of the whole narrative, but which we are never allowed to see, serves a similar function of instigating a double-edged desire.) Farr's reply is that 'I stopped seeing him because I wanted him. Do you understand, because I wanted him.' Simply writing those words cannot convey the strength of Dirk Bogarde's delivery of them, and thus it is here that my reading is liable to slip into helpless subjectivism, for until we have some adequate account of film acting beyond the loose and impressionistic, it is impossible to pin down precisely how or why it is this exchange that shatters *Victim*'s carefully tolerant project. It is the moment when irresistible sexual desire finds, literally, its voice. It is tempting to make grand claims for this instant in this text, since it is desire that British cinema fought so long to suppress, and here it becomes unanswerable, the text's project irreparable. In a heterosexual context the directness of these words, their deeper resonances, would be striking enough; as the unleashing of homosexual desire it borders on the revolutionary. Except, of course, that the film must now put all its efforts into the unravelling of the complex thriller plot, in an attempt to bury the radical break in the seductions of the hermeneutic resolution. Before that, however, there is the second of the two crucial scenes.

Here Farr is confronted by three other homosexuals who are also blackmail victims, and they attempt to dissuade him from continuing his search to find the blackmailer. They mention Farr's own homosexuality, at which point he tries one last piece of self-denial:

Farr: I may share your instincts, but I've always resisted them.

Mandrake: Yes, that's what cost young Stainer his life.

This refers to an incident some years previously when Farr's attempts at denying his sexuality had ended in his lover's suicide. Thus the link between repression and death, which has already been hinted at in Jack Barrett's suicide, is made explicit. The film becomes an indictment of repression, an attack on the refusal to acknowledge the desire that Farr/Bogarde has in the previous scene finally affirmed. As if to underline the centrality of this moment, the film flares into the one moment of violence in an otherwise very wordy text, as Farr punches Mandrake to the ground. This single assertion of physicality confirms the sudden presence of sexual desire, here displaced into aggression. The subsequent narrative twists cannot hope to erase what has gone before. The ending's move towards repositioning Farr as the bearer of timid Wolfendenism, its attempted recuperative strategy, seems both unworthy and risible.

I have chosen to stress the escape of desire into the text as its most important feature, and have insisted that the narrative resolution fails to achieve any convincing degree of closure. It might be useful to mention one of the more insidious ways in which the ideologies governing the text construct notions of sexuality. This returns us to the liberal reformists' fear of ostentation and flaunting, by which we can assume they mean camp.

I use camp in a purely descriptive sense, as designating the attitudinal and conversational theatricalized male femininity adopted by many gay men as a mixture of defensive parody and calculated shock tactics (it may also be a potent weapon of subverting ascribed gender roles, but that is a difficult question I don't have the space to deal with). A major feature of the liberal tolerance of homosexuality centred around Wolfenden is its hostility to camp, which, given camp's inherent snubbing of codes of dignity and restraint, is hardly surprising. What is perhaps odd, and not a little unnerving, is the eagerness with which those few homosexuals who found a public voice as part of those debates sought to join the condemnation of their more flamboyant comrades. Peter Wildeblood was at great pains to differentiate himself, as a man labouring under a 'tragic disability', from 'the effeminate creatures who love to make an exhibition of themselves' (Wildeblood, 1957, p. 13). This tendency to court heterosexual approval by striving to project a 'normal' appearance is even more strongly shown in a 1950s novel called *The Heart in Exile*, where the suit-wearing, professional-classes homosexual narrator attacks

> pansies. ... I try hard to be understanding, but I shudder from them. It is not only that they give the game away, but it is my experience that such people are usually unintelligent, verbose, neurotic and generally tiresome ... full of either self-pity or of that peculiar parody of self-righteousness which would be ridiculous if it were not so pathetic. ... Nature has been unkind to them and they try to restore the balance through the easier and less efficient of two ways. Instead of physical exercise, which could help, they resort to plucked eyebrows and an excessive application of the wrong shade of rouge. (Garland, 1961, pp. 47–8)

Since *Victim*'s project depends on securing heterosexual audience sympathy (and nothing more), it must take pains to ensure all its homosexual characters are impeccably non-ostentatious. There is one slightly camp man, perhaps in the interests of social verisimilitude, but that is Mickie, whose involvement in the sub-plot of writing fraudulent begging letters removes him from the sphere of the pitiable into that of the reprehensible (in terms of narrative logic, at least; I find him among the most sympathetic characters, which may well have something to do with his campness). More importantly, there was a scene in the shooting script which did not reach the screen, in which Jack Barrett's friend Eddy is said to speak with 'a faint "camp" note in his voice'. Clearly the negative feelings campness was assumed to evoke in the heterosexual audience could not be risked. One of the prejudices *Victim* so stoically sets out to answer is the equation between male homosexuality and (to use the word which in itself contains a wealth of cultural/ideological meaning) effeminacy. Until *Victim*, after all, audiences were likely to have seen homosexuality on screen purely in terms of stereotyped queens, most often in comedies or as comic relief (on homosexuality and comedy, especially television comedy, see Medhurst and Tuck, 1982). The text positions its assumed audience so that it will nod in agreement with Inspector Harris' talk of 'little people' and 'unfortunate devils', and comfort itself with the patronizing remarks made by Frank to his wife about Jack Barrett – 'I feel sorry for him. He's very lonely deep inside. He hasn't got what you and I have got.'

So, the ideological project of *Victim* is clear enough, but I hope I have shown that it is still possible to snatch moments of radicalism from the text, moments which could still be of particular use to gay spectators.

Afterword (1995)

There is one last point I want to make, which returns me to the personal and political impetus behind the dissertation whence the article originated. I chose to write about homosexuality and British cinema because of my own involvement, in however limited and local a way, in gay politics. *Victim* struck me then as a key point in the social and cultural history of British homosexuals, and it is my articulation of this (even though it is couched in what in these queer days looks like frightfully naive sexual politics) that remains for me the most important aspect of the article. What I never expected to happen is that the film would seem just as relevant and compelling a decade later. Its moving evocation of its social moment, the sense of claustrophobic fear felt by homosexual men of that generation leavened by the earliest glimmerings of that passionate resistance which would fully flourish much later, still works, despite its occasional lapses into generic cliché and stylistic stiltedness. Students to whom I show the film (and there are cynical friends who claim that I have never taught a course that I didn't manage to squeeze *Victim* on to somewhere) almost invariably find it rich, involving and remarkable. That's particularly and gratifyingly true of non-heterosexual students, who may, as I did back in 1982, initially expect to find nothing more than a cosy, clumsy period piece but instead find themselves looking at a film which still has something meaningful to say to them about queer history, about Englishness and about homophobia. The 'confession' scene is justly celebrated above as the crux of the film, but if anything its power as one of the most electrifying moments in British cinema history has grown and deepened for me over the years (I'm still awash with goose-pimples even after seeing it a thousand times), and if this article did nothing else, it helped to bring that moment, in all its shattering intensity and with all its radical import, to the attention of a wider audience.

Notes

1. Director Basil Dearden and producer Michael Relph collaborated on many films, including *The Blue Lamp* (1950) and *The League of Gentlemen* (1960), as well as *Victim* and *Sapphire*. See Dyer, 1993, and Hill, 1986, for further information on the 1950s 'problem picture'. I would like to acknowledge here how influential Dyer's article (first published in 1977) has been on my work, however our conclusions may differ.

2. Although, of course, not closed to dispute, Dyer, 1993, reads the film in a different way, and Weeks still sees it as the 'archetypal liberal "pity" film of the period' (Weeks, 1979, p. 174).

9

Space, Place, Spectacle: Landscape and Townscape in the 'Kitchen Sink' Film

Andrew Higson

It was what was called the 'kitchen sink school', rather unkindly, I think, because the remarkable thing about *The Loneliness of the Long Distance Runner* and *A Taste of Honey* etc. is not that they treat working-class people, working-class problems, but that they have a very poetic view of them. It's not at all a strictly realistic view. It's very much a romantic view, and that's what attracted me to them, I think. (The cinematographer, Walter Lassally, quoted in White, 1974, p. 61)

I think it is nicer to create a romantic atmosphere (just so long as it isn't schmaltzy) than to create a strictly documentary realist one. (Lassally in White, 1974, p. 62)

Today people talk about a New Realism – a realistic realism, and that would mostly seem to cover swearing, talking about contraceptives, two people just up to the moment of sexual intercourse and That Long Shot of Our Town from That Hill. (Krish, 1963, p. 14)

I want to investigate what is at stake in these three quotations, which comment on the New Wave cycle of British 'realist' films, from *Room at the Top* (Jack Clayton, 1958) to *This Sporting Life* (Lindsay Anderson, 1963). More specifically, I want to look at a range of landscape and townscape shots in these films and tease out some of the apparently contradictory meanings and pleasures they offer the spectator, relating these to the ways in which the films were discussed at the time by reviewers and critics. For reasons of space and convenience most of my examples will be taken from *Saturday Night and Sunday Morning* (Karel Reisz, 1960) and *A Taste of Honey* (Tony Richardson, 1961). I will also refer back to the documentary movement of the 1930s and 1940s, from which the New Wave films inherit certain of their realist attributes – or what the film critics of the period saw as realist. For the term 'realism' is used because it is the key term in that discourse mobilized by contemporary critics and film historians alike to validate these 'quality' films as the most worthy aspects of British film-making.

Landscape and townscape shots – that is, expansive shots of rural or urban scenery – must at one level construct a *narrative space* in which the protagonists of the drama can perform the various actions of the plot. Narratives require space in which they can unfold. But because the British New Wave films are promoted as realist, landscape and townscape shots must always be much more than neutral narrative spaces. Each of these location shots demands also to be read as a real historical *place* which can authenticate the fiction. There remains a tension between the demands of narrative and the demands of realism, however, with the narrative compulsion of the film working continually to transform place once more back into space. This tension can be transcended when landscape and townscape shots are incorporated into and as the movements of the narration itself. In these cases, place becomes a signifier of character, a metaphor for the state of mind of the protagonists, in the well-worn conventions of the naturalist tradition. There is a further way in which these shots can be read, however, and it seems again to cut against narrative meaning and flow. For the shots can also be read as *spectacle*, as a visually pleasurable lure to the spectator's eye. This is particularly the case with That Long Shot of Our Town from That Hill, which, as the third quotation above indicates, so rapidly becomes an iconographic cliché of this cycle of films.

Across this network of effects is a series of tensions which are brought out in the above quotations: the tension between the drabness of the settings (the 'kitchen sink') and their 'poetic' quality; between 'documentary realism' and 'romantic atmosphere'; between social problem and pleasurable spectacle. All novelistic forms have to accommodate both narration and description, both narrative movement to a new and different space and time and the repetitive description of a single moment in space and time. In cinema, the image can of course both narrate and describe at the same time. Even so, there remains a tension between these two processes. Although the narrative system of a film struggles to fix the meaning of an image, there is always *more* than the narrative can hold in place. As Stephen Heath puts it, 'Narrative never exhausts the image. ... Narrative can never contain the whole film which permanently exceeds its fictions' (Heath, 1975, p. 10).

The ambivalence, the potential redundancy of the image, this 'something more', is rarely wasted in the classical Hollywood film. While *mise-en-scène* is predominantly organized in the interests of clinching narrative significance, it is also developed as something fascinating in itself, a source of visual pleasure, a spectacle. The pull between narration and description is thus partly transformed into the pull between narrative and spectacle. The experience of narrative is in part the feeling that something is missing from each image we are offered. Since the whole story is not yet complete, since this particular image cannot tell us the whole story, we want to move on, to explore further, to see the next image, and the next, until we have found what was missing and the story is complete. With spectacle, on the other hand, the spectator is confronted with an image which is so fascinating that it seems complete, with nothing missing. Consequently, the desire to move on, to see the next image, is much less urgent (Ellis, 1982).

British cinema, particularly 'realist' cinema, is not usually noted for its visual pleasure – hence the derogatory label 'kitchen sink' films. But clearly, at the same time, the image does still hold the eye – thus Lassally's notions of 'poetry' and 'romantic atmosphere'. In an attempt to understand how the same films can yield such diverse readings, I will move through a discussion of the ways in which these films were taken up as realist to an exploration of some of the visual pleasures they seem to offer. First, then, there is the idea of realism as mobilized by contemporary critics when discussing the British New Wave films. Claims for realism are invariably multivalent, and certainly there are a number of conflicting assumptions underlying the claims for the 'kitchen sink' films as realist. These different assumptions produce at least three versions of the visual in relation to such films, three ways of making sense of the image: the visual as 'iconography', the visual as extraneous and obtrusive 'style', and the visual as 'poetry'.

Initially, however, it is important to recognize that part of the realist claim for these films is that they are no different from the classical Hollywood film. A film like *Saturday Night and Sunday Morning* is still a narrative film which aims to achieve the conventional verisimilitude of classical cinema. Its style is more or less unobtrusive, subordinated to the primary function of the text, which is to tell a self-contained, coherent and credible story. As in the classical film, *re*presentation masquerades as presentation, the fictional diegesis as the real world. The spectator is invited to attend to the unfolding of the story, not to the way in which it is told. As Colin MacCabe once put it, when trying to understand the realism of the classical film: 'The real is not articulated; *it is.*' (MacCabe, 1974, p. 12). Indeed, in the discourse of the contemporary critics, the processes of narration employed by British New Wave films are noticed and commented upon only when they seem problematic, or uneconomic. Thus one critic, commenting on the adaptation of *A Taste of Honey* from Shelagh Delaney's play, could write: 'Taking a calm, level view, Richardson has straightened out and imparted narrative to his wry original' (Stonier, 1961, p. 196). The means by which a series of events and characters are presented to the spectator are otherwise taken for granted.

But this realism of the classical film has never been enough for certain strands of British film culture; there have always been other, more clearly argued, claims for the realism of the British 'quality' film as *different* from Hollywood's 'melodramatic fantasies'. First of all, there is a claim for a *surface realism*, an iconography which authentically reproduces the visual and aural surfaces of the 'British way of life'. The 'authenticity' of place and character, for instance, is achieved by breaking some of the studio conventions of classical cinema – by shooting on location in actual British landscapes, for instance, and by using unknown, or unglamorous or non-professional performers.

As such, surface realism involves a fetishization of certain iconographic details, rather than their incorporation into a 'fuller' sense of *mise-en-scène* as one of the means by which the film narrates its fictions. We are thus confronted with the spectacle of the real, as distinct from its narrativization. But an authentic iconography in itself is not enough for the apologists of such films, and invariably there is a second claim for the realism of the British 'quality' film as distinct from 'Hollywood'. This we can name *moral realism*, in that it involves a moral commitment to a particular set of social problems and solutions, a particular social formation. Inevitably, the claim for moral realism is in part bound up with the claim for surface realism – there is a moral thrust to the iconographic commitment to the representation of 'ordinary people'. But the claim for moral realism also involves a particular construction of the social in terms of 'universal human values'. It is that same demand voiced by the documentarists of the 1930s that films should show *the dignity of the working man*.

The concern for factual accuracy is thus gathered up in the desire for moral truth, focused on the figure in the landscape. A concern for personal relations and human values invests the landscape with a greater sense of moral urgency and a more compelling sense of human sympathy, while the real historical landscape, local and concrete, legitimates and authenticates this moral universe. It is almost an implicit acknowledgement that narrative film is precisely *fiction*, and that it must therefore be made as credible and plausible as possible, by rooting the drama in history. This is something of an intensification of the strategies used in the classical film to make plausible an entirely imaginary world.

The moral force of this regime of representation is really a reworking of the sociological, propagandist strand in the documentary movement of the 1930s (Higson, 1986; and 1995a, pp. 176ff.) With its rhetoric of social responsibility, of education and instruction, and its resistance to the more self-consciously aesthetic strand in the movement, it has left a residual sense of the *aesthetic*, the *stylistic*, as a problem in British film culture. Hence the sense of the visual as no more than an iconography, and *mise-en-scène* as a neutral vehicle for this 'content'. Hence also the construction of visual style as only self-conscious stylization, as something extraneous, something tacked on to the 'organic text'.

But within the Griersonian discourses of the 1930s, there was always also an undertow running against the most ardently voiced educative sociologistic strand, which sought to acknowledge and foreground the aesthetic work of the text. This we may call the discourse of poetic realism: it involves a more perfect conjunction of surface realism and moral realism, a conjunction which in fact *transcends* ordinariness, which makes the ordinary strange, beautiful – *poetic*. By the time of the 'kitchen sink' films, as can be seen from the quotations from Walter Lassally at the beginning of this chapter, the term documentary realism is now assigned to the more prosaic renderings of surface realism and moral realism. And it is no accident that, for the New Wave film-makers, the most favoured of the documentarists was Humphrey Jennings, described by Lindsay Anderson as 'the only real poet the British cinema has yet produced' (Anderson, 1954). Significantly, Anderson's own film *This Sporting Life* was widely praised for its poetic qualities by British reviewers.

The strand of poetic realism in British film culture opens the door to a (guarded) valorization of a self-conscious style in British 'realist' films (as in the case of the critical response to *This Sporting Life* and, to a lesser extent, *A Taste of Honey*). At the same time, it also allows a (guarded) inscription of the artist in filmic discourse: the poetic film is a film of personal vision which foregrounds the work of the director. The Romantic tendency is held in check by the continuing demand for moral commitment, but there inevitably remains a tension here between the sociological and the aesthetic, the moral and the poetic.

The rest of this chapter will consider this tension in relation to the use of landscape and townscape shots in the 'kitchen sink' films. As already suggested, there is a general sense in which these films take place in actual locations in the urban-industrial areas of the Midlands and the North of England. But there is also a particular shot of the city to which these films insistently and obsessively return: it is That Long Shot of Our Town from That Hill, a shot which lures the eye across the vast empty space of a townscape (the view from the bus stop outside Joe Lampton's lodgings in *Room at the Top*; the view from the parapet outside Nottingham castle in *Saturday Night and Sunday Morning*; the view from the hilltop park in *A Kind of Loving*, 1962; the view from the kitchen window of the flat rented by Jo's mother in *A Taste of Honey*; the view from above the quarry which Colin and his friends visit in *The Loneliness of the Long Distance Runner*, 1962, and so on). In what sense can this set of images be incorporated into the narrative space of the film? Although these images are coded as spectacular, they can still be clawed back into the narrative system of the films according to a logic of point-of-view shots and establishing shots. They each offer a general shot of the city, establishing, economically, the overall space in which the action takes place.

For instance, at the beginning of the 'Sunday morning' section of *Saturday Night and Sunday Morning* (between the fight in which Arthur Seaton gets beaten up by the two soldiers, and his girlfriend

Doreen visiting him at home in bed), a series of three shots move from a spectacular townscape (a view not seen before in the film) taken from a high camera position, dissolving to a high angle long shot of the backyards of two rows of terraced houses (which *could* be the back of Arthur's house), and finally cutting to an interior shot of Arthur lying in bed. At one level, this is an absolutely classical movement from the general to the particular within a scene. The first of the three shots is in this sense a conventional establishing shot, a form of the master shot. The movement from one image to the next rapidly impregnates the space, after each transition, with increasing narrative significance and dramatic purpose, until finally the individual is placed in his environment, the figure in the landscape. A logic of narrative motivation thus defines the space for the purposes of the fiction. At this narrative level, the initial townscape is not displayed simply to be looked at, but is caught up in a fiction which holds it in place.

Earlier in the same film, Arthur Seaton meets Brenda, with whom he is having an adulterous affair, on the parapet in front of Nottingham Castle. Behind them is a 'magnificent' view across the city, which, while it is at one level displayed as spectacle, is at the same time literally a backdrop to the action. Further, as the scene progresses, the view is increasingly integrated into the system of looks which make up the scene (as Peter Wollen puts it, 'protagonists appropriate the places they are "in"' (Wollen, 1980, p. 25)). The scene opens with the camera panning on Brenda's movement as she walks up to Arthur. Effortlessly, the view is offered to us as part of the narrative: 'I was just looking at the lovely view,' says Arthur (and indeed the view is spectacular, despite the chimneys, smoke and railway yards). 'Better come down to earth then, hadn't yer,' replies Brenda, calling Arthur, the spectacular view, and the film spectator back into the narrative, to confront the problems which face the protagonists (she brings news of a failed abortion). Clearly, then, space is being *used* narratively, it is being psychologized, since Arthur's position outside and above the problems of the city metaphorically represents his state of mind.

This sense of space being used up would seem to be precisely what David Bordwell and Kristin Thompson have in mind in the following discussion of the classical film:

In the classical paradigm, the system for constructing space (the 'continuity style') has as its aim the subordination of spatial (and temporal) structures to the logic of the narrative, especially to the cause/effect chain. Negatively, the space is presented so as not to distract attention from the dominant action; positively, the space is 'used up' by the presentation of narratively important settings, character traits ('psychology') or other causal agents. Space as *space* is rendered subordinate to space as a *site for action*. (Bordwell and Thompson, 1976, p. 42)

However, the narrative system of a film is never as simple as Bordwell and Thompson's formalism would allow: there is always an undertow of meanings pulling against the flow of the narrative, always more than the narrative can use, whether it is in the form of the spectacular, or in the form of descriptively authentic detail. In the case of the latter, the novelistic demand for a certain accumulation of 'realistic detail' transforms narrative space into a *real historical place*, much of the detail of which is structurally redundant to the narrative (compare Barthes, 1978). For example, at a simple level, a film such as *Saturday Night and Sunday Morning* is a classic melodrama of individual desire regulated by censorial social relations and responsibilities. There is no structural necessity for the films to be set in the Midlands of England or to be shot on location. The machinery of criticism, promotion and selling, and the dominant historical memory of these films, endlessly stresses the detail of location, but this detail is a product of moral demands rather than structural (narrative) demands.

Narratively, such films are about an individual's efforts to fulfil a wish or a series of wishes. (*Room at the Top*, for instance, was advertised as 'A savage story of lust and ambition'.) Morally, however, the significance of the film is not so much its story as the *reality* of its events. This emphasis on *place* in – or against – the narrative historicizes the narrative, shifting it away from the particular to a more general level of concern. But at the same time, place is used up by the narrative at a metaphorical level, as a 'geography of the mind'. This metaphorical work then turns the historical back on to the discursive, the psychological, the individual.

To return to the three shots which open the 'Sunday morning' section of *Saturday Night and Sunday Morning*: the initial townscape is on the screen long enough (thirteen seconds) for the spectator to scan this real place, to make some sense of the city as a city, to notice details of movement (a trail of smoke or steam), perhaps to examine the extent to which the landscape has been worked over and transformed by industrial labour under capitalism. It is a place with a history which might possibly be read off the image. But at the same time, the narrative always returns to make a *particular* sense of this multiplication of detail, to *psychologize* rather than *historicize* the space, to marshal it into a representation of a state of mind. It is a new day, the sun is shining, the urban-industrial image seems peaceful, stable, there are no immediate signs of work, of struggle: exactly – Arthur Seaton has turned over a new leaf in his life, and the geography, the *mise-en-scène*, is a sign of this change.

The townscape shot thus exists as a descriptive shot, a temporally unmarked space: this is a city (this is the city where Arthur Seaton lives). But it is also narrational, it is gathered up narratively and articulated now temporally: narrative *contains* descriptive sequences. The individual image is caught up in a sequence of images which establish both an abstract or metaphorical time (the narrative sense of 'Sunday morning') and a specific time (the time when Arthur Seaton receives a visit from Doreen). The 'useless details' (Barthes, 1978, p. 131) which fill out the view and which produce a 'realistic effect' are thus also use*ful*; they are absorbed by the narrative and used up.

But clearly there is a tension in the image, a tension which is intensified by the moral demand that the spectator *investigate* the image, almost against the grain of the narrative. This moral obligation depends upon an empiricist ontology of the photographic image inscribed in the Griersonian discourses of the documentary ideal. This ideal institutes a particular mode of looking as observation, a belief that we can *see the real*, in images which document the social condition of the people who inhabit the landscape. It institutes at the same time a particular status of the image as denotative, as referential: 'Walter Lassally's photography [in *A Taste of Honey*], at times purposely rough and imperfect, has an immediate, direct sense of reality' (Boleslaw Sulik, *Tribune*, 22 September 1961). Place becomes a 'sign of reality': the implication is that it speaks a history, a memory. But access to this history always seems blocked. There is a resistance, for instance, to the representation of industrial (or indeed domestic) labour, obviously a major factor in the condition of the city (even in *Saturday Night and*

Sunday Morning, we really only see Arthur at the factory just as he is about to *finish* work, or have a break). The landscape seems empty, except for the dominant *psychology* in the foreground, a psychology which is always much more the product of personal relations than economic relations. The fascination is with a *moral* landscape, hence the resistance to a historical reading of the landscape, at least in the dominant critical discourse of the period.

The form of this fascination becomes clearer if we look at some of the contemporary reviews of *A Taste of Honey*, which describe the landscape in essentially emotional and aesthetic language:

> At last to one's delight, Tony Richardson's direction fulfils the poetic promise and avoids the technical pitfalls of *Look Back In Anger* [1959] and *The Entertainer* [1960]. ... The film's real heroes are Mr Richardson and his masterly cameraman Walter Lassally, who between them have caught Manchester's canal threaded hinterland to a misty, moisty, smoky nicety. And they have found unforced poetry ... among the mist, the moisture, and the smoke. (Paul Dehn, *Daily Herald*, 15 September 1961)
>
> [*A Taste of Honey*] is memorable ... for the air of naturalness with which the words have, so to speak, been taken out of a small stage set and put into the large, drab, yet picturesque hurly-burly of a Northern industrial town. (Unsigned review, *Guardian*, 16 September 1961)
>
> Richardson has used the place and its objects as he uses people, moodily, lovingly, bringing beauty out of squalor. (Isabel Quigly, *Spectator*, 22 September 1961)

What becomes clear from this critical response is the extent to which the film's *mise-en-scène* of the city is organized in terms of aesthetic pleasure, visual pleasure – or at least this is how these critics choose to read the images. But if, as spectators, we read the images in this way, we can feel secure in our admiring gaze since the images can also be read in terms of the morality of their commitment to a particular subject matter. The beautiful tragedy (the 'beauty out of squalor') of these images serves to elicit our sympathy for a particular social condition, and our gaze is thus authorized (indeed we should note that the gaze is precisely *authored* by 'Mr Richardson and his masterly cameraman'). For the London-based critics, films like *A Taste of Honey* are a magic journey to the exotic working-class places of the Midlands and the 'distant' North:[1] this is the Mass Observation tradition of 'an anthropology of our own people'. The otherness of the place and the people is potentially threatening, dangerously strange. But the images are also beautiful, picturesque: the poetic in British film culture is both beautiful and strange. The self-conscious aestheticization of the landscape erases the danger, the traces of the otherness, rendering it an exotic and spectacular landscape like so many other landscapes with which 'we' are familiar.

This order of shots is of course already familiar from the documentary movement, which has always since the 1930s tended to aestheticize work and the working class, poverty and struggle – indeed has aestheticized struggle out of the image. Slums, in this tradition, become seductive, fascinating: *vide*, for instance, the street shots in *Housing Problems* (1935) – if we are visually fascinated by these images, we can at the same time rest assured that our gaze is morally sanctioned.

The demand for moral realism is only completed when an individual consciousness centres our attention, a psychologically complex character who can develop morally, but who can also be developed narratively according to the 'universal human values' of bourgeois subjectivity. Some more comments from contemporary reviews of *A Taste of Honey* can help to illustrate this point. First, Paul Dehn in the *Daily Herald* again: 'Solely concerned with one another, [the protagonists] make us deeply concerned for them.' Secondly, the *Spectator* again: 'You cannot and are not meant to draw any social conclusions, only human ones.' It should be clear that in these and earlier comments aesthetic and psychological concerns continually block access to the social and the historical. But this immediately raises the problem of the relationship between character and environment, between the protagonists of the fiction and the real historical conditions of the place which they inhabit. If we turn to the contemporary reviews again, we find a naturalist argument for the relationship of character and environment. First, there is the question of authenticity, interest, commitment (the comments are again from reviews of *A Taste of Honey*):

The point of this brilliantly directed film is that it really does take us to Salford, steep us in such a town's way of life, and make us take a far deeper interest in the characters ... than we could do in the play. (Alan Dent, *Sunday Telegraph*, 17 September 1961)

Secondly, there is the naturalism of the figure in the city, as in this further extract from the *Spectator* review:

> It is hard to imagine, if you never saw it on the stage, how it was ever anything but a film. Alleys, docks, churchyards, shopping streets, backyards, the canal, the sky, the weather, ships and buses and prams are all so intrinsic a part of its speech and action that it hardly seems they could have existed on their own between four stage walls. This, of course, is what a film ought to make you feel: that it was conceived in cinematic terms ... [with] people seen not isolated and spotlit but belonging to a background that explains, enriches and illustrates them; objects and places seen as part of what happens, not props for the action, but integral parts of it.

David Robinson's review in the *Financial Times* follows a similar line:

> Shooting largely on location [Richardson's] great achievement is to convey the fusion of people and environment. The characters are part of the landscape, as the landscape is part of them. ... this is in no small degree due to Walter Lassally's masterly photography of a land of smog and wet pavements, of lanes and factory chimneys and filth-throttled canals. (15 September 1961)

This relationship of landscape and character is in effect psychological: it is not just that the character is *in* the landscape, but that the landscape becomes part of the character. Indeed, it is not enough simply to place the character in a *real* city – that reality must be used up by the character as a state of mind. It must be psychologized into a point of view, a subjective consciousness. There is in these films a narrative distinction made between the country and the city. Arthur in *Saturday Night and Sunday Morning*, Jo in *A Taste of Honey*, and Colin in *The Loneliness of the Long Distance Runner* are all metaphorically imprisoned in the 'squalid' city, and long for the 'freedom' and 'open space' of the countryside. As such the landscapes do not so much refer to real places outside the text as produce meaning *at the level of representation*, in terms of a system of differences: urban/rural, imprisonment/escape, the mass/the individual, social structure/ bohemian fantasy, deferral of pleasure/wish fulfilment, the everyday/ romance. At the same time there is a meaningful intertextuality: in comparison with films from different genres and different national cinemas, there is a further set of binary oppositions: location/ studio, contemporary/past (or futuristic), English/ international, poverty/wealth (also textually marked in *Room at the Top*).

If we focus on the country/city distinction, there are three sets of shots which need to be taken into account in these films: shots *within* the city, where we see the protagonist actually in the street; shots of predominantly rural settings; and That Long Shot of Our Town from That Hill – a sort of in-between stage, where we are outside and above the city, but where the city is itself prominent within the frame.

The city-dwelling protagonists of *A Taste of Honey, Room at the Top, The Loneliness of the Long Distance Runner* and *This Sporting Life* all go on trips into the countryside. In each case, the countryside is invested with a sense of romance, a sense of escape from the drudgery of everyday life in the city, a sense of what might have been (if only things had turned out differently). These semi-romantic rural scenes are in a sense a reprise of similar scenes in some of the melodramas of everyday life of the 1940s. For example, *Love on the Dole* (1941), *Millions Like Us* (1943) and *It Always Rains on Sunday* (1947) all contain scenes where major characters are seen enjoying a temporary romantic idyll in a rural setting. The scenes function very similarly to those rural scenes in the later 'kitchen sink' films.

In all these scenes there is also, finally, a curtailment of pleasure, a refusal to allow the individual to remain in this 'natural state' of wish fulfilment. Either the pleasure of the country is tainted by the memory of the city, and the necessity to return to it, or the problems of the city return to the figure in the country. Thus Jo and Alice in *Room at the Top* stay for a while at an idyllic cottage in the country, but know that they must eventually return to the city to face the consequences of their adultery; Frank Machin, in *This Sporting Life*, takes Mrs Hammond and her children out to the country in his new Jaguar, but almost as soon as she shows some unexpected happiness, we are returned to the city and the roar of the crowd at the sports stadium; Colin and his friends in *The Loneliness of the Long Distance Runner* are shown having a wonderful time at Skegness until their money runs out and they are forced to return to the city, feeling bitter and argumentative. In *A Taste of Honey*, Jo, Geoff and a group of children (symbols of hope, the future) make a temporary escape from the city into the rolling hills outside. But the romance of the scene is an impossible one because Geoff is gay, and his unexpected advances to Jo on the hilltop are resisted as 'abnormal' in the context of their existing relationship (Jo has earlier defined Geoff as 'like a big sister'). What is perhaps most memorable about the scene is its visual pleasure: the breathtaking rural landscape falling away behind them, the framing and the lighting of the shot.

In *Saturday Night and Sunday Morning*, there are two scenes at either end of the narrative where Arthur Seaton and his cousin Bert fish beside the canal. The published script describes it as 'a scene of utter tranquillity' (Taylor, 1974, p. 281) but it is much more complex than this: they are in a 'rural' setting, and hence by convention a tranquil one. But the signs of the city are still very evident. It is a canal (man-made), not a river; it is a very bleak, desolate place, and the factories are not far away. The two men are caught between country and city, just as Arthur and Doreen are in the final scene of the film when they look down from a grassy hilltop to a half-built housing estate.

In each case, there is both a literal narrative motivation for the images of the rural (the protagonists do visit the countryside) and a metaphoric narrative motivation. In the latter case, the rural setting as a site of pleasure represents the fantasy wish-fulfilment of the figure in the city (the individual who desires to escape). For these films are in part about the entrapment of the individual, who attempts to create his or her own space, and hence identity. This identity is very much defined in terms of escape, but it is an escape structured in relation to the individual: it is not open to a whole class (as Terry Lovell suggests elsewhere in this collection, it is the escape of the scholarship boy). The dominant social theme of these films is the upward class mobility of the working-class male youth, articulated at the same time as a sexual mobility. Where such mobility is blocked, there is a drift into a fantasy world (as in *Billy Liar*).

As such the 'kitchen sink' films are less about the conditions of the industrial working class and their collective class consciousness, than they are about the attempts of individuals to escape from those conditions and that consciousness, associated as they are with an older generation irredeemably tainted by mass culture. (Indeed, class difference has been displaced by generation difference as the basis for the organization of consciousness and conflict in these films.) These films define individuality in terms of escape from the mass, the class, and class consciousness, into an individual consciousness.

As Raymond Williams has shown, this way of dramatizing the experiences of the urban working classes can be traced back to naturalist writing about the figure in the city in the late nineteenth century:

> the sense of the great city was now, in many minds, so overwhelming, that its people were often seen in a single way: as a crowd, as 'masses', or as a 'workforce'. ... Under the stress of this experience the problem of the individual and society acquired ... a new and bitter dimension. The individual was the person who must escape, or try to escape, from this repulsive and degrading mass. (Williams, 1973, p. 222)

In developing this tradition of representation, the British New Wave film engages with a psychological realism somewhat different from that of the classical Hollywood film, which tends to define characters in terms of action (for masculinity), or passion and/or the body (for femininity). But it is also the characteristic propensity of melodrama to internalize and psychologize ideological problems and conflicts (in this case it is an internalization of the problems of a class under specific historical conditions). These two modes of representation are held together in an attribution of *bourgeois* subjectivity to the working class, once more rendering their otherness safe. The urban working-class 'mass' becomes the individual feeling subject, sincere and meaningful, defined in terms of personal (not economic) relations and 'universal' human values, and with a familiar psychic investment (the two aims of Freud's family romance, eroticism and ambition [Freud, 1977]).

The subject who desires to escape becomes the victim in the city, a situation which the spectator is encouraged to respond to in a very particular way. It is the same response noted by Williams in relation to the naturalist literature of the late nineteenth century: 'an insistence on human sympathy just because the obstacles, the contradictions, the mysteries are so clearly seen' (Williams, 1973, p. 234). This way of reading the narrative is encouraged by the particular images of the figure in the city, and, perhaps most acutely, by the shots which stand between the country and the city. The power of these images is their capacity to represent both the extent to which the protagonist is trapped within the city and the intensity with which he or she desires to escape.

Thus a scene early in *A Taste of Honey* opens with one of those shots from outside and above the city, looking across the city. The shot is retrospectively motivated as Jo's point of view: there is a cut to a second shot which shows her looking out of the kitchen window (at her mother's flat). The marking of this point of view is entirely absent from the initial townscape. In the metonymy of these two shots, Jo seems to be presented to the spectator as precisely imprisoned within the city but desiring to get outside it. The first shot, although *of* the city, is outside and above it, and effectively represents the position which Jo desires. The second shows her as a small figure in the frame, in the literal kitchen sink *mise-en-scène* (battered old cooker, pans, the actual sink and draining board – all intentionally drab and uninviting), fixed behind the bars of the window looking out from an 'imaginary' vantage point, the figure of what might be, if only ...

Unable to escape permanently from the city (caught as she is in a circle of personal relationships), Jo subsequently attempts to create her own space within the city, moving into a huge, ramshackle, barn-like room which she transforms into a privatized, individualized space. The montage sequences which deal with the transformation represent a celebration of this appropriation of space.

Surface realism and moral realism (which we can now recognize as a form of psychological realism) work over the text of classical narrative realism to produce a compelling sense of the urban figure as part of and produced by the city. Space and place together are absorbed metaphorically into the weave of the narration. But this organic fusion of character and environment is troubled by the spectacular construction of the townscape shot. The problem is essentially one of the form of the gaze offered to the spectator, and the status of the points of view constructed. The city, apparently a place of poverty and squalor, becomes photogenic and dramatic. In becoming the spectacular object of a diegetic and spectatorial gaze – something precisely 'to-be-looked-at' – it is emptied of socio-historical signification in a process of romanticization, aestheticization (even humanization). This production of the city *as image* undercuts the moral sanction which authorizes our gaze at it, and at the same time tends to *separate* the protagonist from the space which defines it.

This is a problem noticed by those critics of the period who were less bound to a moral vision which might validate the gaze – and which, indeed, might validate the whole cycle of 'realist' films. For it is at this same period, in the early 1960s, that the *auteurism* of *Cahiers du Cinéma* finds a voice in British film culture in the form of the magazine *Movie*. Here, iconography is incorporated into a fuller sense of *mise-en-scène*, and a more structural (rather than moral) conceptualization of the 'organic' relationship between protagonist and setting. The concern of the *Movie* writers is predominantly aesthetic, the problem of the relationship between character and environment worked through at the level of narrative and *mise-en-scène*; no longer is it a worry about authentically historicizing the characters:

> Richardson, Reisz, Schlesinger and Clayton are weakest exactly where their ambitions demand strength: in the integration of characters with background. Because of this weakness, they are constantly obliged to 'establish' place with inserted shots which serve only to strengthen our conviction that the setting, though 'real', has no organic connection with the characters. So Richardson tarts up *A Taste of Honey* with his street games. And Schlesinger [director of *A Kind of Loving*] landscape mongers in the most inept fashion. (Perkins, 1962, p. 5; see also Graham, 1963)

This line of criticism underlines the weakness of the narrative motivation of those cityscapes discussed in *Saturday Night and Sunday Morning* and *A Taste of Honey*; the problem is the extent to which a simple iconography (the Pub, the Street, the Fairground, the Canal, etc.) is used to establish the moral authenticity, the 'reality', of a place. They stand in the text as conventional 'signs of reality', unable to be fully absorbed into the narrative action (see Elsaesser, 1972, p. 5, also Keiller, 1982). In the case of the scene on the castle parapet in *Saturday Night and Sunday Morning*, for instance, there is no necessary narrative reason for the meeting to take place here, and dialogue references and point-of-view shots can only weakly use the place for the drama. It is in effect a form of cultural tourism.

What is at stake in this 'problem' of the disjunction of character and place is the uncertainty, the potential incoherence of point of view. The 'kitchen sink' films posit, as their organizing consciousness, the point of view of the central character inhabiting a 'full' environment. This organizing consciousness is established by the narrative centrality of the characters, by the use of optical point-of-view shots, and by various forms of interior monologue (spoken in voice-over in *Saturday Night and Sunday Morning*; visualized in flashbacks in *The Loneliness of the Long Distance Runner* and *This Sporting Life*, and in daydreams in *Billy Liar* – and, in a different way, in *A Taste of Honey*).

Any film which, like these 'kitchen sink' films, works more or less within Hollywood's classical system of narrative construction risks a lack of fit between the 'subjective' looks of characters within the diegesis, and the 'omniscient' look of the camera (and spectator) from outside it. The classical film generally attempts to give the impression of there being a match, a perfect fit, between the looks of individual characters within the world of the fiction and the look of the camera at this performance. Thus we are encouraged to empathize with the characters rather than to be aware of the camera and the way in which it presents those characters to us. But there are always certain shots which seem to trouble this sense of a perfect fit. They seem to draw attention to the fact that we are watching a film, and that the story-teller views things from a particular perspective.

It is this ostentation which problematizes the vision of the 'kitchen sink' films. The overwhelming 'visibility' of certain shots precisely as *views through a camera* troubles the coherence of a film which is organized around the point of view of the central protagonist. Hence the sense of doubt which lingers over the status of That Long Shot of Our Town from That Hill. The problem can only finally be contained by a naive *auteurism* ('Mr Richardson and his masterly cameraman Walter Lassally') and the 'transcendentalism' of poetic realism, which, as I have already suggested, rests somewhat uneasily alongside the otherwise empiricist ontology of the photographic image.

This instability of point of view, and the 'visibility' of an authored, enunciative look, exist in a particular form in the 'kitchen sink' film. It is the problem of the irreconcilability between an 'internal' point of view of the figure in the city, the working-class victim (which corresponds to those shots *within* the city), and the 'external' point of view from outside and above the city, the look of the master-cameraman, the sympathetic gaze of the bourgeoisie (which corresponds to That Long Shot of Our Town from That Hill). It is at the same time the gap between a moral commitment (a desire for sociological and historical knowledge) and an authorial mastery of aesthetics (a love of spectacle, a desire for cinema). Poetic realism as a loosely articulated discourse can only struggle to hold the two ends together, to produce a coherent point of view.

We can also relate this dichotomy to the split in the documentary movement between those instructional films which stand back from their subject matter and offer a public, social gaze at a place, a process, a people; and, on the other hand, the story documentary which begins to individuate characters within the diegesis, to emphasize psychological realism, and to offer a private, personal look from the point of view of an individual member of 'the people', from within the place that he or she inhabits (Higson, 1986; 1995a, pp. 176ff.).

The spectator of the 'kitchen sink' film is in a privileged position, privy both to the interior monologue of the figure in the city, and to the master-shot, the all-embracing view of the city from the outside. This position of visual mastery is also a position of class authority, which relates back to the authority of the voice-over in an instructional documentary such as *Housing Problems*, where the middle-class professional, the expert, guides our view of the working class as victims of slum housing. It is a position of mastery to which the working-class protagonist of the 'kitchen sink' film has only a limited access: it is, as we have seen, the position to which the victim-who-desires-to-escape aspires.

It is only from a class position outside the city that the city can appear beautiful. The reviewer for *The Times*, 'the top people's newspaper', for instance, writes: 'What strikes the spectator about a film like *Saturday Night and Sunday Morning* or *Room at the Top* is not so much the drabness of the backgrounds as their astonishing pictorial quality.' (24 April 1961). That pictorialism can only really be achieved by placing the camera in the room at the top of the hill; that is, in the house which belongs to the factory owner in *Room at the Top*, and which overlooks the factories and the old working-class housing below. It is perhaps not so strange that the Victorian city should seem visually pleasurable from a certain class perspective. Nicholas Taylor, for instance, has shown that the public and industrial buildings of the Victorian period were designed according to the aesthetics of the Sublime, inspiring 'the strongest emotions' of awe, terror, astonishment, magnitude (Taylor, 1973).

Significantly, the formal categories of the Sublime, as defined by Taylor, correspond in most respects to the formal categories of the spectacular image in the 'kitchen sink' films. We can then suggest that it is only by standing outside the city and reconstructing a Sublime vision (as in the 'kitchen sink' films) that the city can become once more visually pleasurable.[2]

To its inhabitants, however, the city can only be a problem: for the victim who desires to escape, there could be no other view. And indeed, Nina Hibbin, reviewer for the Communist Party newspaper, the *Daily Worker* (although in most other respects within the dominant moral discourse of British film criticism), adopts a position of identification with the urban working-class figure and produces at times a quite different reading of the 'kitchen sink' films from that found in the pages of *The Times*. *A Taste of Honey*, she writes, 'was filmed entirely on location, and the camera searches out grimly and bleakly the crumbling exteriors of the Manchester slums with their broken down buildings humped up each side of a dirty backwater canal' (16 October 1961).

The victim in the city and the masterly cameraman; the ambiguity of the image and the authority of the look; the city as problem and the city as spectacle: it is only in the discourse of poetic realism that the difference can be held together. It is only the figure of the author which can accommodate both a moral fascination with otherness and a strange but beautiful imagery. A simple visual pleasure in the images of the city would on its own be reprehensible: lacking a moral validation, the sadism involved in looking at the victim in the city, captured in the masterly photography, would be revealed.

That Long Shot of Our Town from That Hill involves an external point of view, the voyeurism of one class looking at another (or the scholarship boy observing the class he left behind, as Lovell suggests elsewhere in this collection); to read the shot in this way is to identify with a position outside and above the city. The actual perspective of this shot draws heavily upon a very conventional aesthetic of spectacle. It is an aesthetic which organizes space in a very particular way, and which depends upon the camera 'as the point of a sure and centrally embracing view' (Heath, 1981, p. 30), offering the spectator a highly privileged vantage point. As Steve Neale suggests, the spectacular image is a very intense and self-reflexive form of representation which seems almost designed 'to stress, to *display*, the visibility of the visible', and to catch – and hold – the eye of the spectator (Neale, 1979, pp. 66–7).

That Long Shot of Our Town from That Hill, its 'camerawork beguiling the eye' (William Whitebait, *New Statesman*, 15 October 1961), is organized precisely as spectacle. The way in which the image is framed, its extreme compositional contrast, its grand spatial scale, and its clarity of vision are all characteristic constituents of the spectacular image (see Neale, 1979, pp. 63–86).[3] The framing of That Long Shot characteristically requires a very high camera position (That Hill ...) with an undifferentiated mass of houses, factories, chimneys and so forth falling away from the point of vision. Sometimes this point is marked in the frame – the edge of a street, a window sill, a castle parapet – thus setting up an extreme contrast between the security and specificity of the point of vision and the awful vastness and generality of the city below. At other times, the point of vision is unmarked in the field of vision, underlining the sense of an omniscient shot (it is almost an aerial shot, although it is always static). In both cases the *scope* of the vision, the (near) perfection of the vantage point, is stressed: spectator and cameraman are masters of the world below.

Although the camera position itself is high, the angle of the shot remains level, and characteristically a half to two-thirds of the frame consists of sky. Obviously spatial scale, framing and composition cannot easily be distinguished, but we can note, in addition, a certain monumentality of the view, particularly in terms of the distance of the vision, the depth of field. The image manages at the same time to be both overwhelmingly full (the almost infinite scope of the vision ...), and disturbingly empty (it is, after all, just an image, which we can do no more than look at). This ambivalence of the spectacle is stressed further in the relation between the clarity and the obscurity of the view. There is always a certain haziness to the long shot – whether it is a mist, or smog, or clouds, or factory smoke. This haziness masks the image, but in so doing suggests both the infinity of the space, and the (im)-possibility of the gaze encompassing the infinite.

On the one hand, the spectator is placed at the 'perfect' vantage point, a position of visual mastery, offering the possibility of gazing at the infinite; on the other, this mastery is continually headed off by the reassertion of narrative movement, and the interruption of our gaze by the gaze of another. The spectacle is, finally, caught up in the system of looks which traverse and perhaps even construct the diegesis of the film. It is no longer *our* vision, but the vision of a narrative protagonist, or the space of their actions. As we have seen, certain of Those Long Shots already have an edge within the field of vision: they mark the vantage point as within the space of the film. This marking encourages the spectator once more to become involved in the unfolding of the narrative – and thus to establish the vision as once more *finite*.

The initially unmarked shots are more disturbing: they seem to offer a perfect, omniscient view, both in terms of class position and authority, and in terms of the aesthetics of spectacle. The view is offered initially for the spectator alone – as in the first shot of the 'kitchen window' sequence in *A Taste of Honey*, and the first shot of the 'Sunday morning' sequence in *Saturday Night and Sunday Morning*. In both cases, the shots seem at first unmotivated – and their occupation of screen time seems inordinately long. The shots can only be narratively motivated in retrospect, as we have seen, and even then they characteristically reside behind moments of narrative pause, or minor incident, or inconsequentiality. But still, the narrative does, finally, muster up a use for an image that runs the risk of being a gratuitous spectacle; it does finally insist on the flaw in the vision, and provide a metonymic narrative reading of the image in order to fill the empty, infinite space of the spectacle, or at least turn attention away from it.

To be caught up in the unfolding of a narrative is generally to be caught in an anxious, precipitous frame of mind. We want to know what is going to happen next, and so, in a narrative film, we want the images to be subordinated to the flow of the narrative, to assist in its unfolding. But when the image is coded in terms of the spectacular, we are more likely to be fascinated by the image itself, as image. The weak enigmas, and the episodic structure of the 'kitchen sink' films, however, allow narrative curiosity to be displaced by a documentary inquisitiveness, a demand for the knowledge-effect of a documentary mode of observation (see Kuhn, 1978, pp. 71–83). The curiosity is less in the causal movement of the narrative than in the conditions of a particular place at a particular time, as experienced by a particular individual, consciousness, state of mind. It is a humanist fascination with a particular social condition, which is in the end a fascination with a generalized 'human condition'.

The problem for the 'kitchen sink' films is that the documentary ideal requires a quite different mode of observation from that brought into play by the spectacular, as Steve Neale argues:

Spectacle is content neither with simply rendering visible the observable, nor with inscribing the spectating subject simply in position as observer. It is much more concerned with the processes of rendering visible and looking themselves. What counts in spectacle is not the visible as guarantee of veracity (of truth, of reality) but rather the visible as mask, as lure. What counts is not the instance of looking as observation, but rather as fascinated gaze. (Neale, 1979, p. 85)

The *moralism* of the realist discourse in British film culture must on the one hand be able to accommodate a *repression* of the fascination, the visual pleasure, of the imagery, in an ontology which allows the image of a place to articulate an unmediated history of that place. On the other hand, this discourse must be able to *acknowledge* the visual pleasure of the spectacular in terms of the 'beauty' of the strange, the other. Poetic realism at once represents *and transcends* the ordinary, the mundane, the *uninteresting*. And it also produces the working-class figure as 'the victim in the city', who elicits sympathy from the morally committed spectator: 'A sordid tale? Somehow it is not. Somehow [*A Taste of Honey*] is touching, uplifting, heartwrenching and very funny in turns.' (Leonard Mosley, *Daily Express*, 15 October 1961)

As we have already noted, the 'kitchen sink' films are in many ways comparable to the naturalist writing of the late nineteenth century, which, as Raymond Williams notes, is

a way of seeing which has been praised for its naturalism and its apparent exclusion of self-conscious authorial commentary. The real point is that the 'commentary' is now completely incorporated; it is part of a whole way of seeing, at a 'sociological' distance. (Williams, 1973, p. 226)

The same is true of the 'kitchen sink' films, with the rider that That Long Shot is a betrayal of authorship (and a betrayal of the class position of that authority as outside the city and the consciousness of its inhabitants). The distance in That Long Shot, between the vantage point of the spectator and the city as the object of the gaze, is at the same time a representation of the distance between the classes. From the class outside the city, the city is unknowable, impenetrable. But in constructing the shot as spectacular, the distance is disavowed; the impenetrability of the real living city is transformed into a surface, a representation, an image which does not need to be penetrated, but which can be gazed at in fascination precisely as image.

Townscape and landscape: space, place, spectacle ... The terms indicate the imbalance of the 'kitchen sink' films as they try to hold together the documentary ideal and a desire for cinema. It is a risk which disturbs the whole tradition of British 'realist' film-making and it is perhaps only in some 'independent' films of the 1980s that the question has been seriously confronted of how cinema might investigate a landscape historically.[4]

Notes

1. 'Place implies memory, reverie ... the imaginary. ... Place also implies displacement, being elsewhere, being a stranger. Films are like imaginary journeys; the cinema is a magic means of transport to distant places. Places are functions of narrative (actions must take place somehow) yet the fascination of film is often with the places themselves.' (Wollen, 1980, p.25)

2. I am indebted to Mick Eaton for pointing out to me the relevance of this argument.

3. Much of my subsequent argument depends on a reading of Neale's article.

4. A number of articles have broached this theme, for instance, Gibbons, 1983; Watney, 1983; Clarke, 1982; and Aspinall and Merck, 1982. A key film in this respect is *Darkest England* (Mick Eaton, 1984), which in part explores the idea of a moral landscape as the background to narrative, in relation to the Victorian industrial city.

10

Landscapes and Stories
in 1960s British Realism

Terry Lovell

... lives lived out on the borderlands, lives for which the central
interpretive devices of the culture don't quite work.

Carolyn Steedman, *Landscape for a Good Woman*
(Steedman, 1986, p. 5)

In *Landscape for a Good Woman*, Carolyn Steedman tells of her
working-mother's life and death, and of her 1950s girlhood. Her book
is a landmark in feminist theorizings of autobiography and personal
writing. Once written, such personal stories may provide publicly available terms in which others may order their own lives and experiences.
Or they may be simply re-mapped onto existing narratives. The story-
teller may push the reader towards preferred readings of the tale. But
twentieth-century theories of language have taught us how writing may
escape the interpretive control of even those who tell their own story,
especially as it is transposed into another medium.

In this article I want to look at the fictional story told by Shelagh
Delaney in her play, *A Taste of Honey* (Delaney, 1959), as it was
transposed into film. The play was produced by Joan Littlewood at the
Theatre Royal, Stratford in 1958, one year after the publication of
Richard Hoggart's *The Uses of Literacy* (Hoggart, 1957). Littlewood's
work was based on improvisation and collaborative work with the
playwright, and the written text of *A Taste of Honey* is a transcript of
the Theatre Royal production. It was associated with the 'angry young

men' plays of 1950s theatre, and was adapted for the cinema by Tony Richardson in 1960, along with a number of other plays and novels with working-class settings. The intellectual content of Delaney's play and Richardson's film was epitomized by Richard Hoggart's book, which came to define the moment. It will be necessary, first, to take a look at this context and at the 'structure of feeling' which Hoggart's work shared with many of these novels and plays, and at the ways in which that structure of feeling was articulated in the film adaptations of the British New Wave, and in the early episodes of *Coronation Street* (Granada 1960–).

The Moment of the uses of literacy

Hoggart drew on his own remembered past to sketch a 'landscape with figures', the traditional Northern working-class community, and to tell the story of its transformation under the impact of affluence and mass culture. *The Uses of Literacy* was an enormously influential text. It has never been out of print. The 1950s had seen a number of sociological ethnographies of the traditional working-class community (see Dennis, Henriques and Slaughter, 1956; Young and Willmott, 1957). But it was Hoggart's book, along with the work of the man whose name was closely linked with his at that time, Raymond Williams, which inspired many young men and women, especially politically engaged adults returning to higher education as mature students, to embark on the study of sociology in the early 1960s. Asked why they had chosen sociology, such students were more likely to cite the influence of *The Uses of Literacy* or *Culture and Society* (Williams, 1958) than any professional sociological text.

Hoggart's book coincided with the cultural and political flowering of the New Left in the late 1950s. Hoggart's and Williams' writings were founding texts for the New Left, and for the discipline of Cultural Studies which emerged at this period, to gain a footing in higher education with the founding of the Centre for Contemporary Cultural Studies at the University of Birmingham in 1964 under the directorship of Richard Hoggart.

The 1950s had seen a cycle of plays and novels which took working-class subjects – the plays of the 'Angry Young Men', and the novels of men such as Alan Sillitoe, Stan Barstow and David Storey. These works provided the sources for the film adaptations of the British New Wave. The 'structure of feeling' common to many of these works has been defined by Alan Lovell as 'a sympathetic interest in working-class communities, [combined with] unease about the quality of leisure in urban society' (Lovell, 1972, p.52). The analysis of industrial capitalism on which this 'structure of feeling' drew had its roots in developments which had already attracted comment in the 1930s. A number of writers had observed the emergence of newer forms of working-class life, centred not in the older industrial communities of the North and the West, and on those heavy industries which were most badly affected by the Depression, such as coal, iron and steel, and ship-building, but in the Midlands and the South, clustered around newer light industries whose workers were protected from the ravages of unemployment. J. B. Priestley identified this new England which he discovered on his English journey of 1934:

> the England of arterial and by-pass roads, of filling stations and factories that look like exhibition buildings, of giant cinemas and dance-halls and cafes, bungalows with tiny garages, cocktail bars, Woolworths, motor-coaches, wireless, hiking, factory girls look-ing like actresses, greyhound racing and dirt tracks, swimming pools, and everything given away for cigarette coupons.
> (Priestley, 1934, p. 375)

Where the older working class had been defined in terms of production and work relations, the terms of Priestley's observations of the new were typical in their focus on leisure and consumption.

In the 1930s the theme of the new Americanized consumer culture had taken second place to the problem of mass poverty and unemployment. In the 1950s there was a widespread consensus that such primary poverty was a thing of the past, and concern among left intellectuals shifted to the effects that working-class 'affluence' and an Americanized mass culture might have on traditional working-class communities and politics. Traditional working-class culture, as charac-terized by writers such as Hoggart, was forged out of material hardship in communities where the individual's most valuable resources were collective: family, community, and a shared culture of resistance and mutual support. Affluence was viewed ambivalently by the writers of the New Left. It was dismissed as a myth, yet viewed with apprehension

(Westergaard, 1965). As families were moved out of the inner city slums into new housing estates which isolated them, the ties of community were, it was feared, being broken. Modern mass-produced (and shoddy) goods were offering new aspirations, new temptations. Hoggart's book crystallized these fears about the corrosion from within of working-class culture:

> In what ways may 'tolerance' help the activities of the newer entertainers? By what means may scepticism and nonconformity be made tarnished ghosts of themselves? Can the idea of ''avin a good time while y'can' because life is hard open the way to a soft mass-hedonism? Can the sense of the group be turned into an arrogant and slick conformity? Can a greater consciousness of these traditional values be developed into a destroying self-flattery? (Hoggart, 1957, p. 136)

The spate of writings set in the traditional Northern working-class community was a nostalgic affirmation of the values and strengths of a way of life whose imminent passing it lamented.

The shift of focus from work to leisure in delineations of the old and the new working class was certain to have gender implications, since the relationship of men and women to work and leisure, production and consumption, is a differentiated one. These implications have come more sharply into focus with the hindsight gained from twenty years of contemporary feminism. Today it is possible to 'look back in gender'.[1]

Looking back in gender

Because work was seen as the defining feature of working-*men*'s lives, characterizations of the traditional working-class community and its culture were masculine, work-related ones, even where the spotlight might happen to fall on the community at leisure. Humphrey Jennings's documentary *Spare Time* (1939), a powerful influence on film-makers of the New Wave, captured this ordering of leisure by work in its movement of imagery from high-angle long shots of the industrial landscape, with massive, ugly, smoke-belching plants, down into closer focus on the streets and houses huddled in their shadow, the setting of 'spare time'.

Where the community in question was dominated by a single heavy industry there might be little paid employment available for women, and this helped to naturalize the adult woman as wife and mother, rather than as worker. In spite of the way in which men's work ordered the terms within which such communities were identified, where the focus was on *community*, women figured prominently within the frame. Hoggart's community was the one experienced in childhood, and remembered with affection and, in spite of his best efforts, nostalgia, by the adult whose education had taken him away, literally and culturally. The memory of the working-class community as experienced by the boy who was marked from his 'eleven-plus' examination onwards for a different future, placed at its remembered centre not work, but that which would have had most salience in his own childhood experience, family and neighbourhood life.

The female heroine of *The Uses of Literacy* is the middle-aged, shapeless and a-sexual figure known as 'Our Mam'. Hoggart, and later Jeremy Seabrook, celebrated her from the perspective of the adult son. In these evocations of the working-class mother, the adult daughter is silent. When she speaks, argues Carolyn Steedman, our view of that landscape shifts, the figures in it change:

> The fixed townscapes of Northampton and Leeds that Hoggart and Seabrook have described show endless streets of houses, where mothers who don't go out to work order the domestic day, where men are masters, and children, when they grow older, express gratitude for the harsh discipline meted out to them. (Steedman, 1986, p. 16)

In telling the story of a very different working-class mother, Steedman produces a figure who 'is not to be found in Richard Hoggart's landscape. She ran a working-class household far away from the traditional communities of class, in exile and isolation, and in which a man was not a master, nor even there very much' (Steedman, 1986, p. 6).

The point of view of *The Uses of Literacy* is Hoggart's own – the son who became the scholarship boy. It is the position of an insider who has left. The book addresses a non-working class readership. It resembles an anthropological study written by an exiled native informant, returning to interpret the culture of his childhood to the inhabitants of the world of his exile.

Coronation Street, or 'Whatever happened to our Mam?'

The early episodes of *Coronation Street* give us a very conscious attempt to transpose the themes and concerns of this type of representation of the traditional working-class community into the form of the television long-running serial. The close resemblance between *Coronation Street* and Hoggart's working-class landscape has often been noted. Richard Dyer has traced out some of the parallels (Dyer, 1981). All the figures in Hoggart's landscape make an appearance in the very first episode. We are taken inside three of the terraced houses, where we find first the 'respectable' household of Hoggart's own childhood behind the front door of the Barlows at number 3. We recognize 'Our Mam' in Mrs Barlow, the 'mester' in Ken's dad. And here is Hoggart himself, the scholarship boy, 'our Ken', home from college, and looking with jaundiced eyes at the habits and practices of working-class life made strange by educational mobility.

The Barlows keep a 'good' living-room, defined by Hoggart in terms of gregariousness, warmth, and plenty of good – that is to say, 'tasty' – food. In number 11 there is no such comfort, for we are taken into the all-purpose kitchen of a 'rough' working-class household, the Tanners. The fire is unlit, the inhabitants come and go, and quarrel noisily. Elsie, long since abandoned by her husband because of her sexual misdemeanours, shouts ineffectually at her ne'er-do-well son Dennis, just out of prison and unemployed. Her daughter Linda has in her turn left her own husband. The differences between rough and respectable are signified with economy through the differences in the dress and physique of the two women. Mrs Barlow, in a shapeless apron, knits pullovers for Ken, the 'mother's boy', and places a 'proper' cooked meal of lamb chops, tea and bread and butter in front of the menfolk as they arrive home. Elsie exudes sexuality in her black sheath dress, and through her critical self-assessment in the mirror. She arrives home to a disordered household and a hand-to-mouth meal of cooked ham which has just been bought from the corner shop. There is a blazing row between Elsie and Dennis when she accuses him of stealing two shillings from her purse.

Next door to the Barlows at number 1 – a nice touch this – we find Uncle Albert, who identifies himself for us in terms of what, but for the grace of God, he might have been – one of the 'old ruins' in the reference library: 'those old men who fill the reading-rooms of the branch public libraries ... the solitaries' (Hoggart, 1957, p. 50). Every street, Hoggart tells us, has its corner shop which is the housewives' club that may have its notice, 'Please Do Not Ask for Credit as a Refusal Might Offend', and here we are inside Florrie Lindley's, who is taking over the corner shop from Elsie Lappin, who acts as Florrie's, and our, guide to Coronation Street and its inhabitants. The notice, she tells Florrie, has been taken down long since. Every street likewise has its pub, and Coronation Street has the now familiar 'Rover's Return'.

They quarrel less noisily in the respectable Barlow household, but it has tensions of its own, and as we might expect of a drama of this provenance, the main story-line of the first episode centres on the figure of the scholarship boy and his shamefaced critical consciousness of class habits very different from those that obtain in his new milieu. The chief antagonism is between father and son, and its immediate trigger is Ken's arrangement to meet his middle-class college girlfriend at the Imperial Hotel, where Ken's mother works as a cleaner. Ken's brother David, the 'father's boy', who works at a local factory, articulates the 'them/us' dichotomy which Hoggart finds to be so typical of working-class perceptions of class.

The credit sequence establishes a visual point-of-view 'outside and above' the Street and its inhabitants, positioning the viewer to move with the camera inside the houses and into their occupants' lives as unseen observers. To become a successful prime-time television serial, *Coronation Street* had to capture the interest of a broad spectrum of viewers. Although it has been argued that the conventions of realism in use in the series draw on the pleasures of recognition (Dyer *et al.*, 1981), it was essential in those early episodes to find ways of also drawing in the viewer who would not be able to see herself in this 'landscape' because it was *not* like her own. The gap between viewer/(class) outsider, and what was viewed had to be bridged *before* the characters became familiar to regular viewers so that the Street could begin to take on a life of its own.

Ken Barlow acts as one surrogate for the middle-class viewer, because of his status as insider/outsider: the man who moves back and forth across the class divide. The entry of his girlfriend Susan into the living-room brings a complete class outsider, whom Ken has attempted to keep away for shame of his home setting. The story is resolved by her good-natured willingness to 'muck in', as David and his father mend a bicycle puncture on the sitting-room floor. She shakes hands with David on a common dislike of David's boss (whom she knows because he lives in her own up-market locality), and is unconcerned when her hand is smeared by dirt from the bike.

With this narrative resolution, the unacceptable face of class is redefined away from relations of exploitation and on to questions of personal style and behaviour. David's boss is disliked not because he is one of 'them' but because he is personally unpleasant. The terms have shifted, and the divide between middle class and working class has become negotiable. It may be crossed by 'nice' middle-class individuals like Susan just as the Street will welcome viewers from more affluent sitting-rooms. We accepted the invitation and stayed for thirty years, in numbers that must have been beyond the wildest imaginings of the original programme planners.

Coronation Street has become one of the most successful long-running serials/soaps of British television history. Soap opera has attracted the attention of feminists because it is a 'woman-to-woman' form which usually centres on strong female characters. The strength is in part a function of age and experience. Soaps are among the few forms which offer key roles to middle-aged women, and in this respect they might seem particularly well-suited for the portrayal of households dominated by the formidable figure of 'Our Mam'. But while the interlocking stories that make up the narrative may feature older women, 'Our Mam' drops into the background, and is rarely at the centre of the plot. She entered as a stolid and immobile figure from Hoggart's memory-washed streets. There are not many stories to tell of her. Who now remembers Ken Barlow's mam? She fades into the background, like her ubiquitous apron. Our Mam's function is to be, not to do. Mrs Barlow died in an accident in 1961. At least she went out on a good story.

The feckless Tanners were another matter. Elsie not only became a major character in her own right, but has been used to identify a recognizable character type: 'There is an "Elsie Tanner type" – sexy, rather tartily dressed, hot-tempered, impulsive – who is also recognisable in other women ... Rita, Suzie, Bet' (Geraghty, 1981, p. 20). The new romances which follow the broken marriages and failed affairs, the new marriages which in their turn break up, provide the very stuff of soap, and starring roles for Elsie and her successors. The ordered community remembered and restructured by Hoggart gives place to a different order of imaginings structured more by the demands of this particular televisual narrative form than by any concern for 'truth to reality'. Family life on the Street was placed within a frame which dislodged it from Hoggart's immobile landscape. Today, thirty years on, the Street retains its physical look; the cat stretches sensuously in the sunshine which bathes the timeless terrace rooftops. But the human topography below bears little resemblance any more to Hoggart's Hunslet community. 'Our Ken' is the last survivor of that first episode. He leaves behind him a trail of corpses. Mother, father, brother David from the first episode are long since gone. His first wife was electrocuted by a faulty hair-dryer, his second committed suicide. A much married man, he recently embarked on an affair which caused an acrimonious break-up with his current wife, Deirdre. And if this sounds more like a furtive bluebeard than the rather timid scholarship boy from the respectable working-class home that we fondly remember, it is simply a measure of the problematic relationship between that image of the working-class community and the narrative demands of soap opera.

Domestic interiors of the British New Wave

The cycle of films classed together as the British New Wave date from the same period as *The Uses of Literacy* and the early episodes of *Coronation Street*, and they are deeply marked by the same 'structure of feeling', the same class and cultural concerns. The cycle began with *Room at the Top* (1959) and *Look Back in Anger* (1959), and ended with *This Sporting Life* (1963). All were adaptations of recent novels and plays: John Osborne's *Look Back in Anger*; Shelagh Delaney's *A Taste of Honey*; Kingsley Amis's *Lucky Jim* and *That Uncertain Feeling* (filmed under the title *Only Two Can Play*, 1962); John Braine's *Room at the Top*; Alan Sillitoe's *Saturday Night and Sunday Morning* and *The Loneliness of the Long-Distance Runner*; Stan Barstow's *A Kind of Loving*; David Storey's *This Sporting Life*.

The action of *Coronation Street* is largely contained by domestic interiors, plus the small-scale interiors of the pub, the corner shop, the little factory. In most of these spaces women are strongly present. Even that bastion of masculinity, the local, was for many years dominated by Annie Walker and her formidable barmaids, and although the factory in question is owned by a man, its employees are women; and when we are taken into this setting it is just as likely that the story-line will be about one or more of the middle-aged women who work the machines as that it will be about the owner, Mike Baldwin.

In *The Uses of Literacy* Hoggart sketches his domestic interiors with great care and, as we have seen, they provided models for the terraced homes of *Coronation Street*. This type of setting was well adapted to the needs and constraints of the low-budget television serial. Such working-class domestic interiors are also features of the New Wave films. But these films are more noted, visually, for their picturesque exteriors shot on location. We do not have the same convergence of economic, formal and narrative-mythologic constraints that Paterson identifies in the case of the cheap televisual serial and the realism of *Coronation Street* (Paterson, 1981, pp. 53-66).

Contrasting domestic interiors are not used, as they were in the first episode of *Coronation Street*, to mark the differences between rough and respectable households. In the films both rough and respectable carry the aura of 'authenticity' by comparison with those households that have adapted to the styles and values of mass consumerism, and it is this contrast that is drawn in the films. Household interiors, the space in the streets and the city outside, are organized along axes of old and new, middle-aged and young, masculine and feminine. Typically, the films take us early on into a traditional working-class terrace similar to those of *Coronation Street* and dominated by those Hoggartian figures, 'Our Mam' and 'the mester', where the young male hero lives, to move out with him again into the more actively masculine spaces of the street, the workplace, and the pub, where he negotiates potential sexual encounters. These in turn draw him back into the domestic interior, this time a new-style working-class home, often on a new housing estate.

Saturday Night and Sunday Morning (1960) and *A Kind of Loving* (1962) follow this pattern. Arthur Seaton, the hero of *Saturday Night and Sunday Morning*, is first located in and identified in relation to his workplace, and to the city streets as he cycles home. The camera follows him through the back entrance into the old terraced house where he lives with his parents. Caught in the frame with Arthur are icons which serve to signify an unreconstructed traditional working-class home: an old-style, free-standing, high kitchen cabinet, an elderly gas stove on legs, some battered pots and pans, and an antiquated round metal light switch with the electric cable on the outside of the wall. The men sit while 'Our Mam' stands and serves tea. The living-room is furnished with heavy wooden chairs and table. Arthur, like Ken Barlow, lends this scene a critical eye in a series of close-up and point-of-view shots. But it is not class habits that attract his censure and the camera's eye ('Why do we always have to have cups of tea with everything? Why do we always have bread and butter, and sauce?' Ken had asked). These things are present, but unremarked. Rather it is the television set which provokes Arthur's ire, and his parents' and their generation's passivity – 'dead from the neck up'. Arthur stops only long enough to down his tea and get changed, and we are out again with him on the street for his Friday evening's entertainment.

The second interior is another terraced house much like the first, where Arthur is an interloper as he spends the night with his work-mate's wife Brenda. In the morning we get a second series of point-of-view shots, this time around the bedroom, which returns to a close-up of a smiling Arthur well-pleased at his own temerity, from a pan which picks up the various markers that identify Robbo as the legitimate occupant. This, too, is an interior on which Arthur makes a temporary raid, careless of the risks he runs. As Robbo enters the back door, Arthur leaves by the front.

The third domestic interior we enter with Arthur is that of his new girlfriend Doreen's mother. This one is on a new working-class estate. As he did at Brenda's, so he again enters in pursuit of sexual conquest, and it is an interior from which he is twice ejected before making it with Doreen on the living-room floor. This interior bears all the marks of Hoggart's new working-class consumerism. The kitchen is a fitted one: the living-room furniture is 'fifties modern', with a glass fronted china cabinet. The walls are hung with 'contemporary' wallpaper, with wall-mounted lights and flush doors. Since Doreen's father has left fifteen years previously, the affluence we see flouts socio-economic logic. Arthur's household, with two adult male 'affluent workers' should, logically, be the more prosperous of the two. But this cycle of films persistently portrays the status-conscious woman as the vulnerable point of entry for seductions which might betray a class and its culture, and this moral imperative overrides, it seems, any commitment to sociological realism. The missing figure in the new status-conscious, high-spending household is the one which, paradoxically, is in reality a condition of its possibility, the relatively well-paid working man. Both

Saturday Night and Sunday Morning and *A Kind of Loving*'s 'new working-class' households are female-headed, father-absent, despite the anomaly that the working-class aspirations they represent could only be realized by women through access to a male wage. The young male protagonist has, then, a relationship to 'feminine' domestic space in these films which is problematic both personally and ideologically. Sexual encounters are typically initiated outside, in space which is conventionally regarded as masculine, but consummated inside, in stereotypically feminine space. He must therefore enter inside, but he risks either punishment (the beating of Arthur by the squaddies) or containment (marriage to Doreen) as a result.

Aesthetic strategies and urban landscapes

The basis on which the British New Wave staked its cinematic claims was a realism defined in terms of its working-class subject, and a more open treatment of sexuality, as well as its aesthetic form. Lindsay Anderson, one of the foremost New Wave directors and a leading figure in Free Cinema, had characterized the dominant British cinema of the 1950s in harsh terms. It was 'completely middle-class bound. Ealing Studios comedies – for example *Kind Hearts and Coronets*, and the like. Emotionally quite frozen' (Gelmis, 1970, p. 98). British cinema was disparaged for its class restraint, its snobbishness, its sexual repression, its general lack of cinematic flair. David Lean's *Brief Encounter* (1945) was the paradigm. Set in the North of England, so far as one can tell from road signs and railway announcements, its 'upstairs' characters spoke impeccable standard English while 'downstairs' (or rather, behind the counter in the station tea-room) they sported cockney – the multi-purpose accent which was made to serve for *all* working-class speech. But realism has suffered badly in the critical values created by developments within film theory in the past twenty years. And the repertoire of images, narrative concerns and characters of the New Wave quickly became over-familiar, and its style soon lost its initial freshness of effect. 'Poetic realism' began to seem to critics and film theorists less a break with the past than a confirmation of a limited cinematic imagination. 'Isn't there a certain incompatibility between the terms "cinema" and "British"?' Truffaut had asked Hitchcock in his famous interviews, an implicit judgement foreshadowed by Victor

Perkins writing about New Wave directors in 1962 (Truffaut, 1968, p. 100; Perkins, 1962, p. 5).

More recently, there has been a revival of critical interest in British cinema, but while this has produced some interesting studies of New Wave films, it has typically taken the form of deconstructing the ideological work of the films, dismantling the critical claims made under the banner of the new realism. Popular forms which had been dismissed within orthodox criticism, such as the Hammer horror, Gainsborough melodramas, or even the ubiquitous *Carry On* comedies, and the quirky idiosyncrasies of Powell and Pressburger, fared rather better in this critical reassessment of British cinema (see Curran and Porter, 1983).

The New Wave was the subject of a major study of British realist cinema by John Hill. In his chapters on the New Wave, Hill built on the work of Andrew Higson, who had subjected a number of the films to close analysis in the pages of *Screen* (Higson, 1984b and elsewhere in this collection: Hill, 1986, Chapters 6 and 7). The analysis developed by Higson centred on the representation of place in the New Wave, and on the films' use of exteriors rather than interiors. Although all the films of the cycle draw attention to their Northern industrial townscapes, the film which springs most readily to mind when its iconographical repertoire of place is recalled is *A Taste of Honey* (1961).

While frequently referred to in critical discussion of the New Wave, *A Taste of Honey* is rarely analysed. When it is, the analysis centres on the sequences shot on location. Shelagh Delaney's play was entirely set in 'a comfortless flat in Manchester'. While the film retains much of the original dialogue, it takes us out of this setting for the location sequences which give the film its most striking visual images. We are shown Jo in school, at work as a salesgirl in a local shoe-shop, walking the canals and streets of Manchester, at the fair, and on a trip to Blackpool. The director of photography was Walter Lassally, and his widely praised camerawork was responsible for imprinting the images that became shorthand for the Northern industrial working-class community. This repertoire of images soon staled into cliché. Each of the New Wave films has its shots of canals, street scenes, the pub, the fairground, the bus journey, the visit to the nearby countryside. *A Taste of Honey*, above all the other films, gives priority to place. 'It is place, rather than action, which assumes importance' (Hill, 1986, p. 131).

New Wave realism was characterized by many commentators at the

time as 'poetic realism' (Higson, 1984b, and elsewhere in this collection). The term was associated with the work of the documentary
film-maker Humphrey Jennings, who was a potent point of reference
for New Wave directors in general and Anderson in particular. The
concept of *poetic* realism allowed the New Wave directors to stress the
personal vision of the observer/film-maker as well as the authenticity of
what was observed. John Hill gives us a careful and convincing analysis
of the relationship between the aesthetic and narrative strategies of *A
Taste of Honey*. The film's photography draws attention to itself. It does
not create an unobtrusive backdrop to the narrative like the 'invisible'
style of realism favoured by French and British *auteur* critics, in which
camera movement is subordinated to the demands of the narratives; and
in which the mark of directorial 'art' is found in the *mise-en-scène*. Hill
observes that the shots of the urban landscape in *A Taste of Honey*, as in
other New Wave films, are redundant in terms of the narrative. They
serve to slow down the action and oblige the viewer to pay attention to
the film's pictorial beauty. For narrative drive we substitute the
pleasures of spectacle – townscapes made picturesque, squalor
aestheticized. Hill gives a number of examples: there are eight shots,
lasting twenty-seven seconds, of a Manchester street parade and its
crowd of onlookers before the scene is motivated by a cut to Jo; there is
a multiplication of shots in the sequence in which Jo returns from
school – seven shots lasting fifty seconds before the appearance of
Jimmie. Hill argues that this 'authentic' photography of recognizably
'real' landscapes has a double function. It signifies the 'real', but also
what would seem to be its opposite, creative art: 'It is precisely through
the production of a "realistic" surplus that the film marks the authorial
voice; the signification of reality becomes at the same time the site of
personal expression' (Hill, 1986, p. 132).

As modern linguistic theory has demonstrated, there is in all forms of
enunciation, even first-person speech about the self, a gap between the
point of enunciation and that which is spoken of: between the 'I' and
the 'me'. In New Wave realism, there is a good deal of conventional
point-of-view shooting, but this does not and cannot close the gap
between the camera's view and that of the protagonist. Even in those
early parts of *Saturday Night and Sunday Morning* where Arthur's
visual point of view is reinforced by his voice-over commentary, the gap
remains. The camera, by including Arthur within the frame, and by

showing more than Arthur sees, allows the film to establish some critical distance from him. But the highly stylized location sequences analysed by Hill, in particular the shot which Higson terms 'That Long Shot of Our Town from That Hill', a view, like that of the opening credit shot of *Coronation Street*, from 'outside and above', open up a broad chasm between the observing eye of the camera and that of the observer within the landscape. Higson argues that this shot, along with others which serve to place the character in the environment, inscribes a middle-class observer/outsider as viewer, and as the source of the film's enunciation. Hill concurs, arguing further that this outsider's point of view gives to the film's relatively open (for the period) treatment of sexuality a certain rather unpleasant voyeurism which he links to 'bourgeois obsession with cleanliness, fascination with working-class squalor and sexuality' (Hill, 1986, p. 136)

While acknowledging the existence of the gap identified in Hill's analysis between observer and observed, I would want to argue that it opens up space which the viewer may occupy in a number of ways, and that there is one category of viewer in particular who is best placed to enjoy the pleasures of these texts from that space, namely Hoggart's scholarship boy: the adult working-class male looking back with nostalgia at a remembered childhood landscape. It is not an outsider's perspective, but that of someone deeply implicated in and familiar with what is observed: someone who has left that life behind, yet with a considerable sense of loss in moving through the educational system, and who therefore brings to its observation the knowledge of the insider combined with the distance achieved by the move outside and beyond. It is this position which can align itself most readily and personally with the point of enunciation of many of the New Wave films. Within the familiar landscape, such a viewer is offered a potent figure of identification in the young, sexually active male worker, because he may identify in him a fantasy projection of the self he might have become had he remained.

And what of the female viewer? It is perfectly possible of course to identify across gender as well as class lines, and no doubt this frequently occurred in relation to these films. Hill recognizes the vividness of the New Wave's more direct acknowledgement of sexuality, but registers its gender bias. The sexuality that erupts in 'resistance to refinement and repression' is a masculine sexuality (Hill, 1986, p. 163). The women in the films are split between those who answer the sexual desire of the hero with an equal and equally raunchy desire of their own (Brenda in *Saturday Night and Sunday Morning*) and those who, while less confident of their own active sexuality, draw the hero into marriage and conformity through sexual attraction. Hill comments that the insufficiency of marriage is structured in relation to *male* desire, not, as in *film noir*, to female desire (Hill, 1986, p.166) and links the films' misogyny to the gendered perception of the transition from old to new working-class values of the New Left. It is characters like Doreen in *Saturday Night and Sunday Morning* and Ingrid and her mother in *A Kind of Loving* whose actions curtail the more radical emancipatory impulses of the hero. It is the scholarship boy, drawing on a Hoggartian analysis of the undermining of the traditional working class community by mass consumer culture, and perhaps himself married to a middle-class woman, who can most fully inhabit the point of enunciation identified by Higson and Hill.

In *A Taste of Honey* the positioning of the viewer is more mixed. Hill analyses those films which have a male hero in terms of the narrative choice he faces between the sexy but forbidden adulterous woman and the less experienced, more inhibited younger woman he eventually marries and who channels his sexuality into conforming domesticity in the new class style. The sexuality of the hero is contained by marriage in sexually conservative resolutions. Hill argues that films like *A Taste of Honey* which centre on a female protagonist present the heroine with a parallel choice between sexuality and domesticity. Jimmie is seen as the male equivalent of Brenda, Geoff of Doreen. For Jo the choice is only a little more starkly presented. With Jimmie she may have sexuality without domesticity; with Geoff domesticity without sexuality.

To make this reading of *A Taste of Honey*, we have to ignore much of the dialogue that passes between the characters as well as the associations which are created between Jo, Jimmie and Geoff on the one hand, and on the other, the children whose songs, skipping, and rhyming games are never long absent from screen or soundtrack. Jimmie is not a male equivalent of Brenda, and Jo's attraction to him is only ambivalently a sexual one, expressed in dialogue such as 'Don't do that' – 'Why not?' – 'I like it' – 'I hate love' and so on, all of which are taken from the play. It is Helen rather than Jo who is given an active, urgent sexuality. Jimmie, moreover, cannot be set against an a-sexual domesticated Geoff. They are alike in their possession of stereotypically feminine characteristics. In the play we are informed that Jimmie was a nurse before his national service took him into the navy. He is as much at home in Jo's kitchen as is Geoff. In the film, Jimmie is the ship's cook. He takes Jo on board to bathe and dress her grazed knee, lifting her onto the work-surface to do so as a mother might an injured child. The last time we see him he is sitting on deck, in his chef's cap, preparing vegetables as his ship moves slowly down the canal to the sea. His well-ordered galley produces substantial meals, whereas nothing except coffee comes out of Jo and Helen's squalid kitchen.

We have not only a generation role-reversal, then, between Jo and Helen, with Helen comprehensively refusing the maternal role, but two role-positionings between Jo and both Jimmie and Geoff which entail gender-reversals for the two males. Jimmie figures as mother-surrogate as much as lover; also as fellow child. Like Jo, he is associated with the children. He hopscotches his way along the pavement in a childish motion which repeats the games we have watched the children play. Jo and Jimmie play hide-and-seek around the ship, and play with a toy car ('what rubbish little boys have in their pocket'). Although the relationship with Jimmie is sexual, whereas that with Geoff is exclusively domestic, no sharp contrast can be drawn between the two men. Both are outsiders. Jimmie is doubly marginalized because he is a transient sailor and black; Geoff because he is gay and an art student (as Jo herself might have been). Both men nurture Jo. Geoff, like Jimmie, is skilled at domestic tasks. He cooks for Jo, cleans the flat, and sews baby clothes. He too offers the 'mothering' which Helen refuses and which Jimmie, because he must leave with his ship, can give only in passing.

Hill's and Higson's analyses work best on those parts of A Taste of Honey which were introduced in the film, and have no counterpart in Delaney's play – the location sequences in and around Manchester, and the visit to Blackpool. In these sequences we find the familiar concern with the quality of new working-class culture, expressed within the visual terms and references common to the New Wave. Richardson attempts to organize the contrast between old and new through his use of the children to represent the traditional community and its indigenous culture. Higson's claim that the children 'represent the future' is therefore misleading. They may be linked to the child which Jo, emotionally still a child herself, is carrying. But also in a stronger sense they represent the past: the childhood, as well as the childishness, of the young people of the story, and an earlier, more 'authentic' way of life which has been lost. This link, clearly drawn in the play, is obscured in the film. For its closing images of Jo and the children, watched in the shadows by Geoff as they light sparklers around the bonfire, their faces alive with childish wonder, belong in the play to *Helen's* childhood memories. In a speech towards the play's close, she says:

> You know when I was young we used to play all day long this time of the year; in the summer we had singing games and in the spring we played with tops and hoops, and then in the autumn there was the Fifth of November, then we used to have bonfires in the street, and gingerbread and all that. (Delaney, 1959, p. 85)

In transposing these associations from Helen's past to Jo, while retaining the punctuation of the action by the seasonal round of fairs and festive processions, the film actually succeeds in giving Jo a ten-and-a-half month pregnancy, in spite of its much proclaimed realism. Conceived after a Christmas-time visit to Blackpool, the baby is still awaited on Bonfire Night. In the film, then, adult memories of and longings for a lost childhood are replaced by real children who are used to forge a division between the adults and the young people. Instead of figuring Helen's lost past, they mock and plague her as she goes off with her 'fancy man' Peter. They are linked throughout with Jo and Geoff. They follow them to 'the arches', a local viaduct, and accompany them on the bus-ride to the country where we get the statutory Long Shot of Our Town from That Hill.

It is the adults who are made to represent the shoddy new consumerism. Helen's aspirations are epitomized by the bungalow which Peter buys on their marriage. Peter is a used car salesman, shifty, drunken and lecherous. The visit to Blackpool offers an opportunity for a sequence which could have come from any one of these films, and which is reminiscent, as Hill points out, of Anderson's Free Cinema documentary *O Dreamland* (1953) – no matter that these particular working-class pastimes cannot strictly be attributed to 'mass culture', belonging as they do to much older working-class cultural traditions. We are given close-up shots of Helen and Peter and their friends as they cavort around the funfair, with an angle of vision and closeness to the face that produce similar visual distortions to those of the hall of mirrors. A grotesquely dressed-up Jo, unwanted, bloody-minded, and trailing a few yards behind, offers a point from which the spectator can position him/herself in alienation from the scene while, just in case we haven't got the point, the whole montage sequence is accompanied by raucous pop music and the loud, empty laughter of a mechanical clown.

The mass culture/traditional culture paradigm is superimposed, then, on the narrative material of the play, and it is this original material as it is transposed into film which justifies Higson's perception that *A Taste of Honey* is a woman's picture (Higson, 1983). This leaves the film fractured, with a double vision, as it were. The mass culture themes cannot be effectively pursued through Delaney's narrative, because all her characters are, like Carolyn Steedman's mother, figures who have no place within the Hoggartian working-class landscape in which the dichotomies of these themes had their genesis. Helen and Jo exist on the margins of working-class culture and community. Both are single parents, Helen sexually promiscuous, Jo inexperienced yet pregnant at sixteen. Helen doesn't work, but has no visible means of support other than her 'fancy men'. Neither could be said by any stretch of the imagination to partake of Hoggart's 'full, rich life'. They flit from one bleak rooming house to another, living out of a couple of suitcases.

The economy of interior and exterior space in a film is organized in interesting ways when the protagonist is a woman rather than a man. The street and the public places of *Saturday Night and Sunday Morning* and *A Kind of Loving* are associated, as we have seen, with a dominant male sexuality that gains access to domestic interiors and sexual gratification, but ultimately is contained through marriage. Because private and public places are culturally gendered, they will be available for different sets of signification when the film centres on a young woman. Jo, like Arthur, moves between domestic interiors and the streets and countryside, but the two spaces are organized in this film less by gender than by generation. The streets are dominated not by sexually active young men but by children. Jo is poised between childhood and womanhood, precipitated into adult life by her affair with Jimmie and her pregnancy, and her moves outside may be related to her reluctance to abandon childhood rather than the masculine search for sex, while the interior of her flat is associated with her search for nurture rather than sex. The few actual and attempted sexual encounters take place not in the flat, but outside, from Jimmie and Jo's first kiss under a starlit sky on Jimmie's ship to Geoff's clumsy attempt to 'start something' on the hillside later. In the play, Jimmie and Jo make love in the flat when her mother is away in Blackpool. In the film they begin to make love on waste ground and there is no indication that they move indoors to take advantage of Helen's absence and the availability of an empty double bed. The effect of this open-air love-making is less to associate the outside with sex, than to associate the sex with the transition from childhood.

The temporalities of the film are rhythmic and cyclical, and it is not perhaps too fanciful to invoke here Julia Kristeva's concept of 'woman's time' (Kristeva, 1981). The action covers a little less than a year, a little more than the baby's nine month gestation. It is punctuated by the annual round of fairs and holidays. And Jo repeats Helen's story. When she kisses Jimmie on the ship, we cut to what we at first mistake for the starry sky overhead – to the ceiling of the ballroom, covered with crystal stars, where Helen and Peter dance the last waltz. What I want to suggest is that Delaney's play did not inhabit the structure of feeling articulated by *The Uses of Literacy* but was sutured onto it in the film adaptation. It is concerned in addition with a very different set of issues which we can begin to discern more clearly in the light of the women's movement which has since supervened.

In *Of Woman Born*, Adrienne Rich writes of the lack of stories of 'the passion and rapture' (Rich, 1977, p. 42) of mother–daughter relationships in a culture in which the father–child relationship is at the centre of one of the most powerful 'interpretive devices of our culture', Freud's 'family romance'. Freudianism theorizes what has been dramatized in high art from *Oedipus Rex* to *Hamlet*. It gives us a way of seeing the little boy as jealous of his father, the rival for his first love-object, his mother. It allows us to see the little girl, once she has shifted into her own Oedipal phase, as jealous of her mother, now rival for the attentions of her second love-object, her father. What is harder to see is the little girl jealous not of her mother, but of her mother's lover, raging against her own neglect.

The women's movement has radically altered the situation described by Rich. Its early years produced little of 'passion and rapture' in its presentation of mothers and mothering by the daughters who forged the movement. The tone of an earlier generation towards its mothers was distinctly hostile, while children featured as impediments at best in the struggle for liberation, to be cared for communally in twenty-four hour nurseries.

More recent developments within feminism have returned with a vengeance to the question of women's mothering, and mother–daughter/daughter–mother stories are now legion. In fiction we have a huge range of examples; Michèle Roberts's *A Piece of the Night*; to Jeanette Winterson's *Oranges are not the Only Fruit* (Roberts, 1978; Winterson, 1985); the poetry and essays of Adrienne Rich; the recovery and reworking of myths such as that of Persephone and Demeter; Nancy Chodorow's work, and that of the Woman's Therapy movement (Chodorow, 1978; Eichenbaum and Orbach, 1983); and there is no doubt that there are resources here to stimulate new readings of *A Taste of Honey*. But because of the masculine address of this whole group of New Wave films, the masculine identity of their visual enunciation, and because *A Taste of Honey* is visually and generically at one with them, it has attracted little attention from feminists.

I want to end where I began, with Carolyn Steedman's mother–daughter story. It would be as much of an error to map *A Taste of Honey* exclusively onto the terms in which mothering has been discussed recently within feminist thought as it would be to do the same with Steedman's tale. In Steedman we find no trace of yearning for a pre-Oedipal utopia, nor any echoing fragments of Kristeva's semiotic chora. The experiences of mother- and daughterhood are placed in historical and social time, not in Kristeva's non-linear 'woman's time'. They are mapped onto the lineaments of class as well as gender. We may look back in gender, drawing upon the (reworked) stories of Freud's family romance, but we would lose as much as we gained if, in the process, the context of mothering as a social institution with a history and a class and ethnic specificity were to be lost from sight.

Note

1. The title of a book by Michelene Wandor
   on post-war British drama (Wandor, 1987).

The British Avant-Garde and Art Cinema from the 1970s to the 1990s

Michael O'Pray

Derek Jarman's producer once remarked in a letter that 'the directors who should have made *Caravaggio* – Murnau, Pasolini, perhaps Cocteau – are dead.'[1] The association of Jarman's project with the work of classic directors of the so-called 'art cinema' is apposite. But Jarman, one of British cinema's leading figures over the past twenty years, also had close links with the apparently quite other traditions of avant-garde film-making. As his work shows, he was involved in two distinct film practices: a form of art cinema in his critically successful feature films and a form of avant-garde cinema in his Super 8mm films. In 1976, for instance, he completed the feature length *Sebastiane* but he also showed a multi-projection three-screen film work at London's Institute of Contemporary Arts (ICA) in their 'Festival of Expanded Cinema', an event in the very heartland of British avant-garde cinema, at that point arguably at it height. And in the 1980s he made films such as *The Last of England* (1987) and *The Garden* (1990) that shared elements of both avant-garde and art cinema in an eclectic, hybrid manner.

What I want to do in this essay is to begin to trace a history of British film culture in the post-1968 period which can take account of these twin projects, using as a key reference point Jarman's ability to straddle and eventually perhaps amalgamate the two. Existing accounts of art cinema and the avant-garde in this period rarely do justice to the full range of activities involved (see, e.g., Harvey, 1986; Wollen, 1993). While I cannot be exhaustive, I do want to try to indicate something of the richness and diversity of such film-making.

In the 1970s it makes sense to distinguish between avant-garde cinema, oppositional or independent cinema and art cinema – and even between a low-budget subsidized art cinema and a much more commercial and mainstream art cinema (Higson, 1994). By the late 1980s, the funding of film production and the general cultural context of cinema had changed to such an extent that it is much more difficult to make such clear-cut distinctions, with each of the strands absorbed into a broader front of film-making which yet has no shared project, whether cultural, political, or aesthetic. In the 1970s, however, the boundaries between such films as *Berlin Horse* (1970), *Performance* (1970), *Sebastiane* (1976) and *The Song of the Shirt* (1979) seemed much more obvious.

Malcolm Le Grice's avant-garde *Berlin Horse*, a few minutes in length, was made on 16mm for a few pounds, distributed by the London Film-makers' Co-op and shown there and at other such venues and on the art college circuit. In a way typical of the formalist experimentation of the 1970s avant-garde, it explored print processes, colour and repetition, using found footage. It also existed as a two-screen film, with the original black and white film before it was optically printed and colour-processed being projected on one of the screens. As such the film was also characteristic of the avant-garde movement's commitment to 'expanded cinema' in the early 1970s.

Derek Jarman's art movie *Sebastiane* was a feature-length colour film, made on a budget of tens of thousands of pounds from largely private sources, and premiered at London's Gate cinema, one of the major art-house venues of the period. Its casual narrative structure explored homosexual desire and the iconic status of St Sebastian, while its Latin dialogue and blatant homoeroticism singled it out in British film at the time, as did its obvious debts to the then influential art-house movies of Pasolini and Fellini.

Donald Cammell and Nicolas Roeg's *Performance* was a much more commercial and mainstream project which could, however, lay some claim to the tradition of art cinema; it was funded, distributed and exhibited through the Hollywood-based film industry with a budget of hundreds of thousands and used rock stars and major actors, but formally it shared many of the concerns of the European art film. Indeed, it was constructed in a way that can only be described as experimental, with its radical montage, complex time patterns, and desultory plotting. Similarly, its early focus on the mean streets of gangster London quickly shifts to the subjectivist distortions and existential angst of its characters locked away in a house in Notting Hill. In a slightly different vein, the rich colours and textures of the *mise-en-scène* for the drug scenes suggest the influence of the American underground film-maker Kenneth Anger, with whom Cammell worked in the 1970s. By comparison, Jarman's three features of the 1970s (the other two were *Jubilee*, 1978, and *The Tempest*, 1980), hardly exhibit the same sort of experimentalism. The quick, intuitive, almost documentarist style of *Jubilee*, for instance, seems closer to the British realist tradition, not something one normally associates with Jarman's work.

Jonathan Curling and Sue Clayton's *The Song of the Shirt* (1979) was a product of the oppositional independent cinema of the late 1970s, much influenced by the theoretical concerns of the film journal *Screen*. A feature-length film with self-consciously political and educational aims, it was financed by the British Film Institute (BFI), the Arts Council and Greater London Arts and shown at the ICA and at a handful of BFI-funded Regional Film Theatres in Britain's major cities. This kind of project, with its public arts funding, its political programme and its Brechtian aesthetic, was thus quite distinct from both Jarman's pleasure-based art cinema and Le Grice's formalist experimentation.

The 1970s films of Laura Mulvey and Peter Wollen (*Penthesilea: Queen of the Amazons*, 1974; *Riddles of the Sphinx*, 1977) also belong to this tradition of counter-cinema, with its strategies of dismantling and challenging mainstream Hollywood cinema and by implication much of traditional European art cinema. One of the key reference points for this oppositional independent cinema was the post-1968 work of Jean-Luc Godard and the modernism of Straub/Huillet, whom Wollen had identified as representatives of one wing of his two avant-gardes, over against the formalist experimentation of the other (Wollen, 1975).

By the early 1980s, the boundaries that apparently existed between these different strands of film-making were becoming increasingly blurred – as is more than evident in the films and writing of Mulvey and Wollen. In part, there was a general fragmentation of the avant-garde under the impact of the women's movement, the gay sensibility, and the rise of a younger generation of black film-makers. Film-makers like Jarman were increasingly bringing their avant-garde concerns to bear on the art cinema into which they seemed to be moving. To some extent, the possibility of such a move was created by the funding policies of the newly established Channel 4 and the BFI Production Board (Petrie, 1992a). For example, it was the latter body which allowed Peter Greenaway to move from the avant-garde experimentalism of his early work, based in fine art-cum-literary practices, to the far more self-consciously art house sensibility of *The Draughtsman's Contract* (1982). Similarly Sally Potter moved from avant-garde performance art, film and dance, via the short but art cinema inclined *Thriller* (1979), to the full-blown art cinema of *Golddiggers* (1983) and more recently *Orlando* (1992).

By the late 1980s, few of the distinctions made above any longer seemed meaningful, with the avant-garde itself barely recognizable. What I want to do in the rest of this essay is to begin to explore the relative distinctiveness of some of these traditions, and especially that of the avant-garde, but also some of the lines of convergence between the different traditions. As such, this essay is very much the first scratching at a history that needs much fuller research. In the meantime, I hope that it at least sets down some markers and provides an initial shape to the history of the avant-garde and its links with art cinema in Britain since the early 1970s.

One of the major institutions of the 1970s avant-garde was the London Film-makers' Co-op. Founded in 1966, it was an intensely democratic organization and a major production resource and cultural centre for avant-garde cinema. The openness of the Co-op was to some extent counteracted by the influence of two key figures of the period, Malcolm Le Grice and Peter Gidal. Both film-makers, their influence was felt through their writings (Le Grice, 1977, and Gidal, 1978) and through their teaching, the former at St Martin's School of Art and the latter at the Royal College of Art. The view we are left with of British avant-garde cinema in the 1970s tends to be dominated by what Gidal called 'structural-materialist' film-making. Structural-materialism as practised and defined by Gidal and others was an austerely minimalist and cerebral film form that sought to avoid what it saw as the illusionism of films which attempted in whatever way to represent or document something outside the filmic process itself. Thus films such as Gidal's own *Room Film 1973* (1973) and Le Grice's *Spot the Microdot* (1969) rejected narrative in favour of non-narrative means of structuring film form, and self-reflexively focused on the material qualities of the film itself: the flatness of the filmic image, grain, light, movement, and so on.

The merging of this aesthetic with the enormously influential concerns of *Screen* in the 1970s provided structural-materialism with a visibility that was never a full reflection of avant-garde film practice of the period, which was far more eclectic than this image suggests. There were many other aesthetic projects in the 1970s existing outside the confines of the structuralist aesthetic, associated with such film-makers as Chris Welsby, William Raban, Jeff Keen, Margaret Tait, David Larcher, and Steve Dwoskin.

Chris Welsby and William Raban developed a strongly Romantic school of landscape film-making in which systems and processes were used to film 'nature'. In Welsby's *Seven Days* (1974), for example, the placement of the camera was determined by the presence of sun and clouds. Formalism was thus translated into the connections made between the mechanism of the camera and the arbitrary aspects of nature such as sea tides and weather.

Jeff Keen, an older figure, born in 1923, had begun working in film in 1960. Unlike the younger generation of formalists, his influences were Dada, surrealism and popular culture ranging from Donald Duck, horror magazines of the 1950s and camp pornography to B movie film trailers. His techniques were collage-based and there was also a strong element of performance in films like *Mad Love* (1972–8). His work plugs into a tradition of English eccentricity bordering on bad taste found in the *Carry On* series, Michael Powell and Ken Russell. In many ways, Keen's work was a precursor of scratch video and the punk-anarchic non-sense films of Andrew Kotting (*Klipperty Klopp*, 1984, *Selfheal*, 1987, etc.) in the 1980s.

The Scottish film-maker Margaret Tait is another older figure, who studied film at the Centro Sperimentale di Cinematografia in Rome in the early 1950s. In many ways her poetic 'documentaries' owe something to Italian neo-realism, although her work has a strong diarist element, obsessed with the minutiae of her natural surroundings (Krikorian, 1983). In *On the Mountain* (1974), for example, she explores Rose Street in Edinburgh, contrasting its present-day state with its past by incorporating an earlier film, *Rose Street,* which she shot in 1956. She represents a vital connection with the documentary film movement of the 1930s, especially with the films of Humphrey Jennings, although her own films are more intensely personal.

David Larcher made only two films in the 1960s and 1970s – *Mare's Tail* (1969) and *Monkey's Birthday* (1973–5) – but they added up to eight and a half hours of viewing. Imagistic in the extreme, both films employ optical printer techniques to achieve a density of colour, texture and composition that was unmatched during this period. In many ways, the films represent the fusion of eclectic and exotic ideas and images associated with the hippy culture of the 1960s. To this extent, Larcher's work was culturally closer to the mystical undercurrents of *Performance* than to Le Gricean avant-garde formalism.

Steve Dwoskin began making films in 1961. He arrived in Britain from his birthplace, New York, in 1964, having already absorbed aspects of Warhol's minimal film-making at The Factory in the early 1960s. Dwoskin's *Moment* (1968), for instance, foregrounds the long take of Warholian cinema but also highlights aspects of human relationships and expression that were to be eschewed by, for example, Gidal's later version of Warholian film (Gidal, 1989, pp. 83–7).

By the late 1970s, Le Grice himself was moving away from a purely fine art based formalism towards a film-making that acknowledged the mainstream narrative as an ideological mechanism. In a film trilogy comprising *Blackbird Descending (Tense Alignment)* (1977); *Emily – Third Party Speculation* (1979) and *Finnegan's Chin – Temporal Economy* (1981), he experimented with the key elements of narrative – time, space and spectator identification. Le Grice's work and writings at the time seemed to be readily identified with *Screen*'s project (Le Grice, 1979–80), although they were criticized by his closest ally, Peter Gidal (Gidal, 1982).

Broader political, social and cultural transformations in British culture were also to have their effect on the avant-garde. One of these was feminism. In the late 1970s, there was a splintering of the London Film-makers' Co-op as women film-makers left to set up their own distribution and production units such as Circles and Four Corners under the impact of the women's movement. Circles, whose first distribution catalogue was published in 1980, refused the titles of feminist and avant-garde. Instead they saw themselves as representing and developing women's art work in the broadest sense so as to include video, slide tape and performance work (Oppe, 1981). In 1979, several women film-makers formed a breakaway group from the 'Film as Film' show on the history of avant-garde film practice at the Hayward Gallery in London. The women film-makers issued a statement attacking the show's patriarchal tendency (Nicolson et al., 1979) with Lis Rhodes citing distinctly non-formalist film-makers Alice Guy, Germaine Dulac and Maya Deren as precursors in women's struggle to make films (Rhodes, 1979). This represented immediately and quite dramatically a broadening of the so-called avant-garde film front and the beginning of the collapse of the formalist hegemony of the 1970s.

Lis Rhodes' own film *Light Reading* (1978) heralded a different kind of women's cinema which stressed the experiential and poetic above the formal, although without rejecting the latter. Its enigmatic 'narrative' centred on the repeated and vertiginous image of a bed, while a first-person voice-over explored time, memory and narrative event. The strong formal aspects of the film were successfully merged with its expressive concerns in relation to woman as experiencing being. Sally Potter's film *Thriller*, made around the same time, also explored the subjective female experience, although her reference points were art cinema rather than the formal film tradition of Rhodes. *Thriller* leans heavily towards narrative, using the opera *La Bohème* as a foil both for a critique of patriarchy and for a retrieval of subjectivity. The overwrought sense of anxiety, threat and death itself, plus the exploration of time and of the enigma of narrative event, are shared fascinatingly by both films.

Although, in many ways, the early 1980s was a period of consolidation for women's experimental film, there were film-makers who were pointing in new directions. Jayne Parker's films, for instance, were symbolist-inclined quasi-narratives which engaged with the thoroughly marginalized 'nude figure'. In *I Dish* (1982), for example, among other events a man washes his naked body in a kitchen sink and a woman uncovers a dead fish on the shoreline in a shifting tale of sexual and personal anxiety. Parker's influences also ranged across the American underground and European art cinema.

If by the end of the 1970s the old avant-garde was collapsing, then the art cinema proper in Britain barely existed at all. Derek Jarman, whose work in the 1970s could be aligned with neither the structural-materialism of Gidal, nor the related concerns of *Screen*, had in fact been one of the few British film-makers to produce art cinema-inclined work in his previously mentioned three feature films. It is important to consider Jarman's coming of age in the London of the 1960s when, like many others of his generation, he experienced the impact of the European art cinema of Antonioni, Godard, Visconti, Truffaut, Bergman, Pasolini and earlier figures such as Murnau. He shared with Le Grice and Gidal an antipathy towards American culture. He never embraced any aspect of Hollywood's mainstream, with the exception of *The Wizard of Oz* (1939), although he did favour and was influenced by the American underground, and especially the work of Andy Warhol and Kenneth Anger. But apart from these reference points Jarman's taste was predominantly European.

This preference for continental art cinema ran counter to the concerns of the *Screen*-dominated film theory movement of the 1970s with its commitment to Hollywood and political modernism. Within such circles, 'art cinema' became a derogatory term typifying the bourgeois high art position, at odds with the popular culturalists of the New Left. In this context, it was hardly surprising that the British art cinema of Jarman, Chris Petit (*Radio On*, 1979), Ron Peck (*Nighthawks*, 1978) and others should fall into a critical vacuum in which, for example, Petit's existential 'road movie' *Radio On* could be reviewed by *Screen* with barely a mention of the enormous debt it owed to the German art cinema director Wim Wenders (Nowell Smith, 1979–80). Instead, it was pointedly described by Nowell-Smith as 'a film without a cinema', a fitting comment on the lack of a British art cinema at the time.

Of course there were aspects of Jarman's work which made it difficult to appreciate within the conventional terms of art cinema criticism. One problem was the apparent lack of professional sheen in his films. *Radio On*, at least, seemed to look like a 'serious' art movie. On the other hand, *Jubilee*, an apocalyptic account of Britain in the near future with its punk inspired *mise-en-scène* and early Elizabethan fantasies, was edgy, raw and forthright. There was no existential angst at its core. It was a disconcerting mix of punk gig, pantomime, historical reconstruction, musical – a thoroughly postmodern hybridization.

Significantly, Jarman was unable to build on the relative success of his trio of feature films in the 1970s. Efforts to raise funds for his *Caravaggio* project repeatedly failed and the film was not made until 1986. Jarman turned once more to Super 8mm films, ironically in the context of the London Film-makers' Co-op, where he met his future producer James Mackay in 1979 (Jarman, 1984; Mackay, 1992). At this point Jarman's influence on a younger generation of experimental film-makers was beginning to coalesce around the young gay film-makers Cerith Wyn Evans and John Maybury (who, as a student, had been a design assistant on *Jubilee*). Jarman's work was an inspiration to Maybury and Wyn Evans, not only in its imagist style but also in its use of Super 8 with the latter's inbuilt 'anti-professionalism', its cheapness and not least, in the hands of Jarman, its celebration of gay eroticism.

Wyn Evans and Maybury's show of Super 8 films at the ICA in 1981 under the title 'A Certain Sensibility' proved to be a watershed in the British avant-garde. Maybury's statement in the programme, especially the final sentence of the quotation below, was provocative and addressed implicitly to his avant-garde film elders:

> Our criteria for visual response have been permanently altered – sophisticated advertising and slick promotional videos have picked up the line from where the Surrealists and German Expressionists left it. Experimentation was sidetracked up the blind alley of structuralism which effectively murdered under-ground film. (quoted in O'Pray, 1987, p. 8)

This was another rebuff to the 'Film as Film' selection committee which a few years earlier had omitted 'much of the mainstream of the American Underground film', including the work of Kenneth Anger, Jack Smith, Ron Rice, Gregory Markopoulos and Maya Deren, on the grounds that the 'underground', while rejecting the 'dominant mainstream institution', did 'not sufficiently [reject] its forms' (Le Grice, 1979, p. 114). It is perhaps not insignificant that this 'blacklist' involved three homosexual film-makers (Anger, Smith and Markopolous) and a woman (Deren). As has already been suggested, Deren became an icon of the women's avant-garde film movement. Similarly, Maybury *et al.* embraced Smith and Anger. Thus the two strongest tendencies in experimental film in the early 1980s – gay film and feminist film – became associated in this moment of exclusion. Interestingly, Maybury and Wyn Evans owed much to European art cinema too, and especially Godard, Fellini and Cocteau. Thus the break with formal film and the founding of another wave of experimental film-making was inspired in part by European art cinema.

Maybury and Wyn Evans were the leading members of a loose-knit group of film-makers in the early 1980s known as the New Romantics which included Michael Kostiff, Steve Chivers and the installation artist Holly Warburton. Their films shared an imagistic aesthetic sometimes involving a theatricality as in Chivers' Angeresque tableaux in *Catherine de Medici* (1984), sometimes a surrealist-like symbolism as in Wyn Evans' *Still Life with Phrenology Head* (1980), and sometimes the austere gaze of Warholian film as in Maybury's *Tortures that Laugh* (1983). All of them used music with their films – opera soundtracks were *de rigueur* for a time – played on manually synched cassettes. Different music would be used at different screenings of the same film. There were also strong connections with the London club scene, a new phenomenon at the time, with its mix of pop personalities, dancers, fashion designers and the clubland glitterati. Wyn Evans in his own statement for the ICA show speaks of 'the catwalk as a metaphor for existence' and the 'coffee-table as the ultimate mode of exhibition' (quoted in O'Pray, 1987, p. 8). The embracing of popular culture, of style as display and masquerade, of pastiche and ironic gestures and images, can be seen as an important postmodernist move. In other words, the New Romantics' aesthetic fully reflected the general art scene in the 1980s. It also represented a significant fragment of a steadily fragmenting film culture, one in which the notion of 'underground' cinema, with its connotations of social and sexual subversion, seemed more apt than that of an avant-garde.

Jarman's fate and that of some of the New Romantics during the 1980s reveals the steady involvement of the experimental cinema with the commercial world of advertising and pop music. For Jarman and others, music videos, for example, earned much-needed money and provided an opportunity for experimentation, sometimes with expensive video, and computer equipment. By the mid-1980s, Maybury had drifted into a successful career in music video culminating in three MTV awards in 1989 for his Sinead O'Connor video 'Nothing Compares 2 U'. Chivers moved into feature films. Wyn Evans jettisoned film for installation work after his BFI-funded, hi-tech video *Degrees of Blindness* was released in 1988. Jarman's music videos of the same period (most famously for The Smiths and the Pet Shop Boys) provided financial support, whilst he shot ambitious no-budget Super 8 films like *The Angelic Conversation* (1984) and later low-budget features (in commercial industry terms) like *Caravaggio* and *The Last of England* (1987). In television advertisements grainy Super 8 was fashionable as were the styles of Stan Brakhage, Zbigniew Rybczinski, Bruce Connor, Robert Breer, Jan Svankmajer and Jarman himself. This mixed economy of British cinema in the 1980s, comprising a variety of practices which included experimental film, video art, music video, television adverts and in Jarman's case feature-length art films, established a pluralism in which the values asserted by modernism and art cinema itself were thrown into serious disarray.

As an interesting backdrop to this scenario, the American independent cinema of the same period took on an art cinema-cum-underground style. *Eraserhead* (1976), *American Gigolo* (1980), *Rumble Fish* (1983) and *Blue Velvet* (1986) were all films that showed the strong influence of European art movies (Bresson, Godard, early French surrealism) and the American Underground (for example, Kenneth Anger's influence on *Blue Velvet*). Gus van Sant, in the late 1980s, admitted to the influence of Jarman's *The Last of England* (Fuller, 1994).

Perhaps the most profound impact on film practice, theory and criticism in the 1980s was that of the Black film movement (see Mercer, 1988a; and Malik elsewhere in this collection). This movement helped to circulate a set of theoretical concepts by which film could begin to be grasped in relation to cultural and national identity. What had in the past been ignored – the social and historical context of a film practice – was now an imperative (Mercer, 1994a). Two of the key Black film workshops were Sankofa, who produced such films as *Territories* (1984) and *The Passion of Remembrance* (1986), and Black Audio Film Collective, with their tape-slide piece *Signs of Empire* (1983) and the much discussed documentary *Handsworth Songs* (1986). In the work of collectives such as these, various formal and narrative strategies were adopted that crossed over many film practices and discourses. As Dick Hebdige remarks:

> In films like *Handsworth Songs* and *Territories* the film-makers use everything at their disposal: the words of Fanon, Foucault, C. L. R. James, TV news footage, didactic voice-over, interviews and found sound, the dislocated ghostly echoes of dub reggae, the scattergun of rap – in order to assert the fact of difference. (quoted in Mercer, 1994b, p. 89)

The Black film movement burgeoned as the New Romantics reached their highest visibility and impact on the experimental area. They shared a particular visual expressiveness and attitude (Isaac Julien of Sankofa is gay) and a post-modern bricolage method. Maybury's *Circus Logic* (1984), for example, used a 'found' sound track, a thick layering of found images with sensationalist newspaper headlines prominent, in a way that was not dissimilar to Black Audio's *Handsworth Songs* or Sankofa's *Territories*. Similarly, Jarman's *Imagining October* (1985), with its stylized tableaux, its historical recuperation, its imagist exploration of memory, both personal and historical, shared concerns and strategies with the new Black films. As Kobena Mercer observed, 'the 1980s have seen a reaction against the asceticism, demonstrated in the opulent excess of "new romantics" and more generally by the return to narrative.' (Mercer, 1988b, p. 19).

The debates around the influences on the British Black independent film movement tended to distance it from European avant-gardism (Mercer, 1994a) even though Isaac Julien, for instance, attended Le Grice's film unit at St Martin's School of Art. The desire and acute need to tackle the issues of cultural context and identity within the British Black film movement led to one of the few energetic debates about avant-gardism and modernism in the 1980s (Attille *et al.*, 1988). In this unresolved and often heated confrontation, Gidalian formalism was seen to remain a necessary theoretical and practical horizon in a 1980s context in which spectator pleasure, the need to reach non-sectarian audiences and the desire to explore narrative possibilities clashed headlong with formalism and to some extent European film modernism. Julien's move to a form of art cinema in such films as *Looking for Langston* (1988), and then to a genre-based film, *Young Soul Rebels* (1990), highlights the potential for adopting different film forms in Britain in the 1980s.

There is little doubt that Channel 4's imaginative funding strategy after its inception in 1982 created a space for a British art cinema of sorts to take shape in the 1980s. Films as diverse as *The Draughtsman's Contract*, *My Beautiful Laundrette* (1985), *Caravaggio* (1986) and *Distant Voices, Still Lives* (1988) had major financing from Channel 4 (Petrie, 1992a). In more recent years Patrick Keiller made *London* (1994), having worked for years on a series of brilliant short 'documentaries' like *The End* (1986) and *Valtos* (1987). A member of the London Film-makers' Co-op, his work is indicative of its more pluralist aesthetic in the 1980s, and in his move to a BFI-funded feature-length film like *London*, which develops his eccentric form of documentary, the distinction between avant-garde and art cinema seems not only opaque but perhaps meaningless. Similarly, the Quay Brothers' first feature film, *Institute Benjamenta* (1995), has the hallmark of art cinema in its auteurism and high art ambitions but seems to have little affinity with the psychologism and existential themes of much classic European art cinema. Equally, the so-called avant-garde cinema has consolidated the return to narrative and explicit social and political themes that began to appear in the late 1970s, as we have seen. Jarman's *The Garden* is the most extreme version of this hybrid film form. Its central theme of gay sexuality in relation to AIDS and to the Christian Passion is sieved through an avant-garde sensibility in which space and time are fractured, video and Super 8 home movie footage are juxtaposed and many other formal devices, like looped images and time-lapse photography, are used. Its hybridity and the fact that it has an audience marks it out as something exciting and new that enables it to escape across the boundaries of both avant-garde and art film forms.

In summary, the period between 1970 and the present has witnessed the rise and fall of the formal avant-garde film movement. Its eclipse by a more fragmented pluralist scene of different cinematic practices often with quite distinctive ends – as in the case of Black cinema and women's cinema – is quite obviously entwined in the broader social, political, technological and cultural forces at work in British society in the 1980s. What is plain is that the certainties of modernism encapsulated in the formal film movement, and of humanism, traditionally represented by the European art cinema, no longer exist as discrete areas. If an experimental film practice survives – which it undoubtedly does – it is as often as not in the form of something which looks like an art film. Jarman's *The Garden*, Patrick Keiller's *London* and the Quay Brothers' *Institute Benjamenta* are hybrid films that render many of the existing theoretical and critical frameworks cumbersome, if not useless.

Note

1. Letter from Nicolas Ward-Jackson to Mamoun Hassan of the National Film Finance Corporation, 29 April 1981, Derek Jarman Special Collection, British Film Institute.

12

A Post-National European Cinema: A Consideration of Derek Jarman's *The Tempest* and *Edward II*

Colin MacCabe

In some senses it is almost impossible to question the notion of European culture; the two terms seem necessarily to define each other. But this definition of culture is specifically European: it relates to the great national cultures of Europe and to their founding fathers, the Dantes, Shakespeares and Goethes. But you only have to sit, as I have sat, in conferences on Europe with Europeans whose forebears come from the Caribbean or from the South Asian continent to realize how pointless such a litany can sound, how far removed those national cultures are from the contemporary realities of multinational and multi-ethnic Europe. The real question is, how are we to understand the founding moments of those great national cultures in conjunction with a Europe whose other founding moment has come back to haunt it? If we think back to that period in the sixteenth century when Western Europe expanded to asset-strip the globe, what comes back in the twentieth century is the fundamental asset of labour which is now imported to service late capitalism.

The problem is that if we wish to grasp the reality of this moment it becomes difficult to know, or to understand, how we can define it as specifically European. In the movement from the sixteenth to the twentieth century we pass from a European to a global perspective, a perspective which demands that we analyse contemporary culture in terms of an imperialist imposition of authoritative norms which are then contested, negotiated, mimicked in the crucial emphases of our post-modernity. But that post-modernity would seem to have no more time for European than for national cultures as the crucial terms become the global and the local.

It might seem that we can short-circuit these theoretical difficulties by appealing to a practical political level at which European culture makes sense. Independently of the particular political rows about the single currency, or the powers of the European Commission, the European Union is becoming an ever-increasing political reality, and it is that political reality which is increasingly part of any European cultural agenda. It is such pragmatic realities which dominate many of the institutional concerns of bodies such as the British Film Institute, and have dominated the multitude of conferences on Europe and the cinema which have taken place in the last few years. These concerns and conferences are not without their successes. The MEDIA 95 programme for European film funding proliferates, growing new arms like a monster from a 1950s sci-fi movie. But it is when one reflects on an initiative like MEDIA 95 that one realizes that there is no real way to short-cut the theoretical problems by appeals to political reality. All the discussions around MEDIA 95 make two massive cultural assumptions: the first is that American cinema is a cultural threat, and the second, as a necessary corollary, is that there is some evident meaning to the notion of European cinema and European culture. Within such forums any attempts to raise genuine questions about European culture are treated as both impertinent and irrelevant. Impertinent because we all know what European culture is, irrelevant because we must eschew such intellectual levity for the realistic rigours of 'policy'. In fact, almost all appeals to 'policy', like its repellent semantic cousin 'management', are appeals away from a reality which is too various and too demanding. But it is the cultural reality of Europe which must be faced, and faced urgently, if we are not to bungle the enormous possibilities offered by the growing movement towards political unification.

To understand our current cultural situation, it is my own deep belief that one must step into the 'dark backward abysm of time'. These are the words that Prospero uses at the beginning of *The Tempest* as he reveals to his daughter the world beyond their island. The world that we need to understand is not the Milanese court and its intrigues, which Prospero addresses, but the cultural space of the Elizabethan and

Jacobean theatre which Prospero and Miranda inhabit. The film-maker who has been most preoccupied with this historical reality is Derek Jarman, ever since, in *Jubilee* (1978), the magus John Dee escorted Elizabeth I on a tour of her kingdom four hundred years on. For Jarman the investigation of what it is to be English is inseparable from a reworking of the controlling myths of the English Renaissance. Three years after *Jubilee*, Jarman made his own version of *The Tempest* (1980).

Let us start with Shakespeare's version. The play starts eponymously with a tempest and a consequent shipwreck. The ship carrying the King of Naples back from the wedding of his daughter to an African (itself an interesting fact in the light of the play's concerns) is separated from its flotilla and wrecked on an island. The wreck itself divides the passengers and crew: Ferdinand, the heir, finds himself alone; the nobles form one group and the crew, with the exception of Trinculo, are confined to the ship and kept there for the duration of the play. It is at this point that we learn from Prospero, the magician who rules the island, the history of the island, or rather the history of his arrival and conquest of the island. He disposes of the former ruler of the island, the witch Sycorax, frees her captive Ariel, the airy spirit, who is then bound to him for twelve years (a period which will coincide with the end of the play), and enslaves her son Caliban, this 'thing of earth'. The play then pursues two sub-plots in which the nobles plot against the king and Caliban conspires with Trinculo to overthrow Prospero, while the main theme follows the courtship of Ferdinand and Miranda, all these events obsessively supervised by Prospero with the help of his spy Ariel.

While the play may seem entirely European, set in the Mediterranean, its source is not (as for almost all of Shakespeare's other work) a European story but a contemporary event in the Caribbean. In 1609, while sailing off Bermuda, an expedition led by Sir Thomas Gates was caught in a tempest, his ship was separated from the rest, and he was presumed lost. A year later Gates arrived in Virginia, having spent the intervening year on a magical island, which furnished the survivors with all they needed to eat and drink. It is from this contemporary story that Shakespeare actually weaves his tale. In this context it becomes clear that the problematic of *The Tempest* is the problematic of the relationship between Europe and the New World which had only been discovered a century before and was in the process of colonial appropriation. Caliban is not simply this 'thing of earth', the savage man who has a long history in European thought, but also an anagram of his own name: the cannibal, the inhabitant of this new world. Prospero's relationship with him is evidently, among other things, an allegory of Europe's relation with the New World.

It is fashionable at the moment, in the current jargon of post-colonialism, to read *The Tempest* entirely in relation to Caliban, to stress the extent to which one must understand the play as Shakespeare's meditation on the particular way in which the colonial is constituted as what is not civilized but then, in a complicated and reciprocal moment, is considered to be that which defines civilisation (e.g. Greenblatt, 1990). In the contemporary critical climate this is defined as the political reading. From this point of view Jarman's *Tempest* is an embarrassment, for his Caliban is white and the concerns of colonialism are largely absent from his film. But these contemporary readings ignore another, and as important, political reading which concentrates on the formation of the new nation-states which will dominate global history for the next four centuries. Explicitly, these concerns are present in *The Tempest* in terms of the politics of the court of Milan. Jarman rigorously excludes all such concerns from his film.

In *The Tempest*, however, he makes clear how Prospero's reign is one of terror. It was, not that long ago, fashionable to imagine the Elizabethan age as one of social harmony. More recently, and in the wake of the new historicism, political divisions have been understood as contained by cultural power (Greenblatt, 1985; Mullaney, 1988). What both ignore are the twin foundations of the Elizabethan terror state, torture and espionage. If I want to think of London at that time, then I always think first of the gates, the walls of the city, outside which are the theatres along with the brothels and the new factories, but mounted on which are the bleeding quarters of those who have just been executed – noted by contemporary Protestant tourists to London as signs of England's civilization (Anon., n.d.).[1] The crucial element in this machinery of terror was Walsingham's secret service, and we can read Ariel in *The Tempest* as an allegory of that secret service, forced under pitiless conditions to spy on every corner of the island and to bring to his master Prospero that information which underpins his power. It is for this reason that Jarman's *Tempest* concentrates on the relationship between Prospero and Ariel, with its barely suppressed sexual undertones. Jarman's homosexuality is what leads him to concentrate on the repression at the heart of the English state from which all the other repressions follow. The complete containment of sexuality within sanctified heterosexual marriage, the rigorous policing of desire and excess, the focusing of male sexuality and the denial of female sexuality: these are the fundamental themes of *The Tempest*, the sexual politics which underpin the birth of capitalism as it appropriates its colonial surplus.

But Jarman clearly understands, even more clearly in his art than in his discourse, how this sexuality is linked to certain traditions of representation. For if the security apparatus is the skeleton of the state, then the new national culture is the flesh. At the heart of this culture is a rigorous divorce between representation and audience. The traditional, and much mocked, reading of *The Tempest* is that it is autobiographical, that Prospero is Shakespeare and that when Prospero at the end says that 'every third thought shall be my grave', it is Shakespeare's own voice that we should hear as he bids adieu to his audience 'Act V, Scene i, line 311'. (Shakespeare, Arden edn, 1990). In fact, if that traditional autobiographical account is placed within the wider context of theatrical history then it once again becomes very plausible. The theatre in which Shakespeare started to work at the beginning of the 1590s and in which Marlowe was already the transgressive star was a very different theatre from that to which he bid farewell in 1611. Not only was it more directly popular and addressed to a much wider social audience but it was also one which posed direct political and cultural threats to the state. By the time he wrote *The Tempest*, Shakespeare was writing for a representational space which was much more contained both aesthetically and socially. That is the crucial point of the masque that Prospero puts on for the lovers in Act IV, the masque that will celebrate their wedding. In his instructions to Ferdinand and Miranda, his attempts to control them as they sit, his order that 'No tongue! all eyes! be silent', Prospero reproduces the new relationship to the audience, a relationship where without tongues, reduced to vision, the audience is excluded from the representational space. It is this space, directly affiliated to an aristocratic culture, which disinherits the popular traditions on which Shakespeare had drawn so contradictorily. The biographical nature of the farewell comes in the recognition of what has been repressed and disinherited.

It is the fracturing of that representational space which makes *The Tempest* such a subversive film, for it sets itself not on an island but in a ruined aristocratic house, an imperial monument. If the viewer grasps that this is a house, there is no way in which he or she can organize the space that is presented. We cannot connect room to room or inside to outside. And, as if to make the point even more explicit, Caliban is played by Jack Birkett, the blind actor. It is this Caliban's blindness which places him categorically outside Prospero's cultural space. But if we can understand Jarman's undoing of the space of *The Tempest*, if we can see him using the cinema to undo the rigid distinctions of culture and sexuality which *The Tempest* so brilliantly performs, we must also admit that, in many ways, and whatever the borrowings from the popular culture of the twentieth century, it remains caught within that exclusive cultural space that it seeks to undermine. Brecht's 'fundamental reproach' to the cinema was that it could never escape that divorce between representation and audience which he termed 'Aristotelian' but which is more properly understood in terms of the Renaissance theatre (Brewster, 1977).

In the aftermath of *The Tempest*, one could be left wondering whether this filmic subversion of the relation between representation and audience could ever do more than endlessly interrogate itself. Jarman's disruption of cinematic space (in terms of costumes, sets, and articulation of shots and scenes) seems to invite (like so many leftist critiques) a nostalgic Utopia in which the ideal is a carnivalesque union of audience and representation, a return to a moment before any of the divisions of labour on which capitalism constructs itself. That carnival is, of course, realized for Jarman in the Super-8 films of the 1970s, but they remain irredeemably private, films which can only be truly enjoyed (as at their original screenings) by an audience entirely composed of their actors.

The counterpart of this personal privacy is the absence of any real public political sphere in *The Tempest*. Jarman excises the power politics of the kingdoms of Naples and Milan, but the film is then left in a curious vacuum in which the critique of representation and sexuality remains oddly unanchored. Jarman triumphantly solves this problem in *Edward II* (1991), when the political plot is made to turn (and turn even more emphatically in Jarman's version than Marlowe's) on direct sexual repression. *Edward II* would seem to mark a final settling of accounts with Jarman's chosen historical space: that interface between the Renaissance and the present which was first unveiled by John Dee in *Jubilee* and which has been investigated again and again, in *The Tempest*, in *The Angelic Conversation* (1985), in *Caravaggio* (1986). But all these films fade into prentice works beside the achievement of *Edward II*. Christopher Hobbs's sets and Sandy Powell's costumes triumphantly realize what one now sees was only hinted at in *Caravaggio* (and Italy may always have been a diversion): a world which is always both now and then (both twentieth and sixteenth century) but is always England. At its heart is the constitutive relation which founds the modern English state on a repressive security apparatus and a repressed homosexuality. Jarman makes all these arguments with the deftness and lightness of a painter's hand. From the moment that Mortimer appears with the dress and bearing of an SAS officer in Northern Ireland, the equations between past and present, between state and sexuality, are clearly visible on the screen.

Jarman's *Edward II* continues a debate about national and sexual identity which goes back four centuries to that moment at the beginning of the 1590s when the Elizabethan stage became the privileged symbolic space for a whole society. The exact date of Marlowe's play might seem of interest only to the most pedantic of scholars but, in fact, it is crucial to the play's significance that it comes right at the end of Marlowe's career, probably in 1592. Crucial both personally and culturally, for by 1592 Marlowe was a man deeply engaged not only with the Elizabethan theatre but also with that other alternative employment for a man of letters who did not want to join the church or to occupy the position of learned scholar in a great lord's house: he was deeply implicated in the modern foundations of the Elizabethan state – Walsingham's secret service.

Culturally the play can be seen as a direct response to Marlowe's new rival Shakespeare, whose trilogy *Henry VI* had attempted to produce a version of English history which would find ethical and political meaning in the bloody shambles which had produced the Tudor dynasty. Marlowe's response is that of the arrogant intellectual who has known the pleasures of both political and sexual transgression. There is no meaning to be deduced from these chronicles of blood and treachery, except Mortimer's wheel of fortune (a sixteenth-century version of Ford's dictum that 'History is bunk' but with none of that twentieth-century tycoon's optimism), and to emphasize the nihilism Marlowe places a perverse love at the centre of his story. But for Marlowe this perversity is very closely linked to the new learning from which he draws his own legitimacy. There is absolutely no warrant in the chronicles for turning Gaveston and Spenser into intellectual parvenus. Edward's minions they may have been, but they were as well born as Mortimer and the other barons. For Marlowe they represent the new class, of which he is a prominent member, who will sell their learning to the new state but will, in the end, be crushed by that very same state. It is Gaveston's and not Edward's death which uncannily foreshadows Marlowe's own end, that great reckoning in a small room when Ingram Frisar, almost certainly with the Privy Council's blessing, stabbed Marlowe days before he was to appear before that same Council to answer charges of blasphemy. Four hundred years on, Marlowe's death remains no less of a mystery, but it is not unreasonable to speculate (as has become wearingly and repetitively obvious in our own century) that political and sexual secrets make the most likely of bedfellows and that in an age when sodomy was a capital offence there may have been more than one member of the Council who was concerned that Marlowe's testimony might end with a lethal outing.

Jarman's film is not, however, Marlowe's play. Marlowe's identification with the new knowledge and learning of the Renaissance gets no response from the director ('such an intellectual queen', as Jarman remarks in a marginal note to the script [Jarman, 1991, p. 14]), and Jarman's Gaveston and Spenser are not overlearned smart young men working for MI5 but very rough trade indeed. What Jarman had always insisted on is that he be recognized for what he was, and *Edward II* is, in that sense, unquestionably his most autobiographical work in what has been a consistently autobiographical *oeuvre*. But it is the bovine, middle-class Edward that Jarman identifies with, not the street-smart Gaveston whom he loves but who is here presented without redeeming features except that 'he loves me more than all the world'. The film is also much more unambiguous in its misogyny than ever before. In that gay dialectic where identification with the position of the woman is set against rejection of the woman's body, *Edward II* is entirely, and without any textual foundation, on the side of rejection. For Marlowe, as for his age, the love of boys is merely the ultimate sexual transgression, not in any sense an alternative to heterosexual sex. It is here that Jarman does violence to his source, making Edward's passion for Gaveston a consequence of his inability to be roused by the queen's body, a truly chilling scene at the beginning of the film. This is itself horribly overtrumped at the end, however, by the murder of Kent when Tilda Swinton's magnificent Isabella literally tears the life out of him with her teeth; every fantasy of the castrating woman, the *vagina dentata*, rendered into all too palpable image.

But there is love in this film, and a love which redeems history. The film is punctuated by scenes from the end of the play as Edward and his murderer-to-be, Lightborn, discourse in the bowels of the castle where the king is imprisoned. We await throughout the film the fabled end, the vicious poker which will leave a king dead and humiliated and without a mark on him. It is this end that the film has prepared us for as we see the homophobia which courses as a vicious lifeblood through our history and our culture. No fault of Gaveston's can possibly excuse or justify the loathing which is spat out at him as he is forced through a gauntlet of hatred on his way to exile and a death unbearable in its explosion of destructive violence. As Mortimer comes to upbraid the king for his moral turpitude, the barons at his back suddenly reveal themselves as a moral majority stretching back and forth across the centuries, an endless, and endlessly unpleasant, Festival of Light.

But after the end that Marlowe and history has prepared us for, Jarman has contrived a happy end from the resources of his own fight against death (he was diagnosed HIV positive in 1986 and developed full-blown AIDs in the early 1990s; he died on 20 February 1994). As Lightborn approaches the king for a second time with the dreaded poker in his hand, it falls from his hands and in a moment of real tenderness he bends and kisses the king. With this kiss a whole history of homophobia and violence is annulled, a whole new history becomes possible.

It is at this point that *Edward II* becomes possible, drawing the audience into the most private of worlds, not merely as spectator but as participant (and in this respect the published screenplay is an integral part of the film). The Outrage slogans which punctuate the text, like the film itself, demand reaction. It is in the multiplication of the forms of address around the text that Jarman provides a solution to Brecht's 'fundamental reproach'. For Brecht, the theatrical setting is still a unity, the alienation devices simply fragment that unity from within. Jarman, here working with the grain of advanced capitalism, breaks the unity of the cinema experience from without. The celebrity interview, that crucial tool of marketing, is here turned into a method of disrupting any separation of public and private, and thus deprives the moment of viewing of any simple aesthetic unity.

It is this multiplication of address, and its refusal of the divorce between public and private, which enables Jarman to solve the problems of *The Tempest* in *Edward II*. The private is made public and, as a result, the public sphere can be incorporated into the film. The state, which disappears from his *Tempest*, is now centre-stage but that stage can also be the most public proponent of the abolition of privacy, the militants of Outrage. It is not, I think, unreasonable to suggest that it is the pressure of death, that unique meeting of the public and private, that has been the catalyst for the extraordinary experiments that marked the last five years of Jarman's work. This is signalled within the film itself when, as the screen dims, the final lines, which are Jarman's rather than Edward's or Marlowe's, are: 'Come death, and with thy fingers close my eyes, Or if I live let me forget myself.'

It is striking at this point, and in the context of the politics of any future European film, to compare Jarman's film with Kenneth Branagh's *Henry V* (1989). *Henry V* is a crucial play for Shakespeare – both the final answer to the problems that Marlowe had posed him seven years earlier in *Edward II* and the first play in the new Globe theatre. The power politics with which the bishops open the play is transcended by the national divinity which Henry represents. And the final farewell to an older cultural space is witnessed in the death of Falstaff, standing in for the refusal of Will Kemp (the great clown who had embodied Falstaff) to join the new company. It can come as a surprise only to those who refuse to understand the links between sexuality and representation that it is in this play that the formal mastering of the female body is accomplished by the naming of Katherine's body in English and her marriage to the English king. It says a lot about the sheer bad taste of Branagh's film that his idea of taking licence with the text is to have Falstaff appear in flashback and to rehearse the famous Chimes at Midnight speech (which only makes sense as a conversation between two old men) as a dialogue between Hal and Falstaff. But this is all of a piece with the cultural nostalgia of Branagh's project (which is exactly captured in the name of his company, 'The Renaissance Film

Company'). The Renaissance theatre will now use the cinema to reproduce the Elizabethan stage shorn of all its contradictions. What in Olivier's magnificent version of *Henry V* (1944) is the cultural corollary of the last tragic moment of the English state (extinguishing its own empire in the fight against Fascist Germany) becomes in Branagh's tepid offering the farcical analogue of Thatcher's hideous mimicry of Churchill. Jarman's use of his Renaissance model has absolutely nothing to do with Branagh's. *Edward II* (as in Olivier's *Henry V*) is placed at the service of pressing contemporary concerns. Unlike Olivier, however, Jarman's film responds to both public and private need and calls the very distinction into question.

I think that these reflections should enable us to understand something of the specificity of European film. What is specific to Europe, within a global context which emphasizes the local and the international, is the question of the nation-state. It is no accident that Jarman never hesitates to stress his cultural conservatism, for what he returns to, again and again, are the founding myths of Englishness. Jarman, it could be argued, is trying to rescue, from underneath the monument of the nation, the last ethnic minority – the English. It is exactly the release of these buried ethnicities which constitutes the reality and risks of European culture and politics today. This is not to say that there is no question of cultural prescriptivism, that all European film-makers should now address the question of the nation. What it does say is that in so far as European film-makers make films that are specifically European, those films will focus on the reality of national identities and the possibilities that are contained in their transgression.

Note
1. My attention was drawn to this pamphlet by my colleague Curtis Breight; see Breight, 1996.

13

Beyond 'The Cinema of Duty'?
The Pleasures of Hybridity: Black British
Film of the 1980s and 1990s

Sarita Malik

During the 1980s, Black British cinema emerged as one of the most diverse and innovative areas of British film-making. Since then, it has continued to draw on and document the rich but often complex experiences of the Asian, African and Caribbean diaspora. Films as diverse as *Handsworth Songs* (John Akomfrah, Black Audio Film Collective, 1986), *Bhaji on the Beach* (Gurinder Chadha, 1993) and *Young Soul Rebels* (Isaac Julien, 1991) have raised vital questions about ethnicity, identity and the cultural politics of difference, while also re-examining notions of 'Britishness' and national cinema. The form, content and production contexts of such work have varied greatly, from the politically and aesthetically challenging workshop films of the mid and late 1980s produced by collectives such as Sankofa (*The Passion of Remembrance*, Isaac Julien and Maureen Blackwood, 1986) and Ceddo (*The People's Account*, Milton Bryan, 1988) to the more recent populist narrative features by Gurinder Chadha (*Bhaji on the Beach*) and Isaac Julien (*Young Soul Rebels*). There have also been social realist dramas such as Retake's *Majdhar* (Ahmed A. Jamal, 1985), experimental shorts from artists such as Ruhul Amin (*Rhythms*, 1994) and Shakila Maan (*Ferdous*, 1990), and generically hybrid features such as *My Beautiful Laundrette* (Stephen Frears, 1985).

Despite the diversity of practices identified, it makes sense to group these films together as Black British films, a term I shall use to refer to all such films which draw on the manifold experiences of, and which, for the most part are made by film-makers drawn from the Asian, African and Caribbean diaspora (many production teams include practitioners from more than one ethnic group). I shall also use the working definition British-Asian film to refer to those films which deal specifically with the British-Asian experience or are made by those who descend from the Indian sub-continent. I shall trace the development of Black British film by examining the struggles which led to the emergence of a distinct Black film movement in Britain in the mid-1980s and the economic, political and cultural shifts which have occurred within it since.

Black British films of the 1980s and 1990s have developed the traditions and extended the frameworks established by Black cinema activists and cultural practitioners in the 1960s and 1970s. One of the major turning points for Black artists in general was the publication of an influential report by Naseem Khan in 1976, 'The Arts Britain Ignores'. The report was instrumental in opening up a debate about funding for Black artists. Khan called for a reassessment of the overall distribution of financial and other resources invested in the Black community, and her intervention led to the establishment of the Minority Arts Advisory Service. Prior to developments such as these, Black experiences rarely found an outlet in media representation. The politics of multiculturalism began to redress the balance and, by the early 1980s, an increasing number of 'minority artists' received funding from public arts institutions such as the British Film Institute (BFI), the Arts Council and regional bodies such as the Greater London Council. However, most Black film-makers found it virtually impossible to organize independently, given the comparatively expensive nature of the medium.

During the 1960s and 1970s, there was consequently only a handful of 'practising' Black film-makers who, with little public funding, made films such as *Jemima and Johnny* (Lionel Ngakane, 1963), *Ten Bob in Winter* (Lloyd Reckord, 1963), *Baldwin's Nigger* (Horace Ové, 1969) and *Reggae* (Horace Ové, 1970). Many of these productions fall into the category of what Cameron Bailey has described as 'cinema of duty' films:

> Social issue in content, documentary-realist in style, firmly *responsible* in intention – [the cinema of duty] positions its

subjects in direct relation to social crisis, and attempts to articulate 'problems' and 'solutions to problems' within a framework of centre and margin, white and non-white communities. The goal is often to tell buried or forgotten stories, to write unwritten histories, to 'correct' the misrepresentations of the mainstream. (Bailey, 1992, p. 38)

Most of the Black British films made in the 1970s, productions such as *Pressure* (Horace Ové, 1975), the first Black British feature-length film to be funded by the BFI, *A Private Enterprise* (Peter Smith, 1975), the first BFI-funded feature to examine British-Asian identities and experiences, and *Step Forward Youth* (Menelik Shabazz, 1977), were exemplary of the documentary realist, social issue genre even if they were categorized as 'dramatic features'. Such films are important for the way in which they 'answered back' to what Jim Pines has called the 'official race relations narrative' (Pines,1988, p. 29), by offering an alternative view of the diasporic experience.

By the mid-1980s, national identity was increasingly contested as a central political and social issue. This was due, in part, to three key factors. First, the Conservative Government under the leadership of Margaret Thatcher since 1979 had shifted increasingly to the Right. In this context, the uprisings in 1980 in St Paul's, Bristol and in 1981 in Toxteth and Brixton were followed by strategies of police containment and the contentious Scarman Report (1982). Secondly, a number of anti-fascist movements such as Rock Against Racism and the Anti-Nazi League emerged alongside, and partly in response to, a resurgence in fascist politics. And finally, many Asian, African and Caribbean people in Britain chose to adopt the term 'Black' as an umbrella political term. This collective category came into usage not only to trample on a history of negation, but also to find a cohesive voice in order to fight collectively for greater political rights and better representation. It was the shared experiences of both colonialism and British racism which united Black British citizens and allowed them to construct an identity for themselves. Blackness, in Kobena Mercer's terms, was 'de-biologized' (Mercer, 1992, p. 430). This rearticulation of Black British identity in the 1980s 'showed that identities are not found but *made*; that they are not just there, waiting to be discovered in a vocabulary of Nature, but that they have to be culturally and politically *constructed* through political antagonism and cultural struggle' (Mercer, 1992, p. 427).

In the politically turbulent atmosphere of the mid-1980s, the audiovisual space for Britain's independent cinematic practitioners was being redefined, which had a profound effect on the formations of Black and Asian film production. The lobbying and debate about training and access for Britain's Black film-makers helped prepare the ground for the formation of Channel 4, which began broadcasting in November 1982 and was soon to become a vital source of finance for British film production. Channel 4's remit to 'say new things in new ways', its minority-based rationale (with Sue Woodford and subsequently Farrukh Dhondy as Commissioning Editor for Multicultural Programming), along with its commitment to independent film-making, meant that it could offer a new form of cultural support to Black British film-makers.

By the mid-1980s, different modes of Black British film production were emerging. There were independent production companies such as Kuumba Productions, Anancy Films, Penumbra Productions and Social Film and Video, which were commissioned by the mainstream television industry to make individual films. There was also the grant-aided or subsidized workshop sector, a space in which collectives such as Sankofa, Retake, Ceddo and Black Audio Film Collective could produce relatively small-scale, innovative and experimental films. The support of public bodies such as the BFI and Channel 4, and general agreements about pay negotiated with the Association of Cinematograph, Television and Allied Technicians, meant that such groups could avoid the constraints of commercialism and the logic of the market-place.

Although the workshops of the mid-1980s were crucially shaped by the cultural politics of arts subsidy in this period, the founding members of these workshops were also motivated by their personal histories. As the first generation of sons and daughters of those who had come to Britain in the post-war years, and the first wave of arts graduates from British universities and film schools, these film activists approached film in a unique way. As Isaac Julien, then of Sankofa, put it:

> A different perspective has emerged, a perspective that has been
> more critical because we've been allowed the space to think – and
> that is a luxury for a lot of Black people, to be allowed a space to
> think about what we are doing, to have the time to discuss, the

time to look at films and be critical about what we are looking at, etc. (quoted in Pines, 1985, p. 7)

The dynamics of the personal and the political equipped the film and video workshops of the 1980s with the creativity and commitment to tell the types of stories which the mainstream British media had, to date, largely ignored. There was, too, a commitment to new *forms* of representation, new ways of seeing Black people in the context of wider society and the newly developing cultural politics.

If such developments involved a strong sense of 'independence', film-makers also needed funding to survive and to feed their craft. A degree of dependency was therefore inevitable, since money needed to come from external sources and often in fact from local or central government. In practice, this meant that Black film-makers were often expected to produce what funding bodies considered to be 'a *black* film' (Pines, 1988). For example, it was easier to get the money to make a 16mm documentary about race than for a 35mm fictional feature. Many workshop practitioners were pigeon-holed as 'experimental film-makers' and 'avant-gardists', rejecting Hollywood's story-telling conventions, even though this often had as much to do with the funders' cultural expectations than with any conscious decision by the film-makers themselves to refuse commercial fictional treatments. At the same time, many black film-makers in the 1980s clearly regarded the creative space they had struggled for as a critical terrain for artistic experimentation where an entire approach to film could be reconstituted.

There were other pressures too. In a culture in which cinematic images of Blackness are so rare, many Black film-makers have found themselves weighed down by what Kobena Mercer has called the 'burden of representation', the sense that any film made by a Black film-maker has to solve all the problems of Black representation at once (Mercer, 1994b, p. 81). As Martine Attille of Sankofa explains:

> There is a sense of urgency to say it all, or at least to signal as much as we could in one film. Sometimes we can't afford to hold anything back for another time, another conversation or another film. That is the reality of our experience – sometimes we only get the *one* chance to make ourselves heard. (quoted in Pines, 1986, p. 101)

This 'sense of urgency' produced some very powerful filmic explorations of notions of race and identity, many of them as much concerned with history and memory as with the contemporary realities of Black experience. *Handsworth Songs*, for instance, perhaps the most significant documentary of the 1980s, complicates the traditional race relations documentary form by interweaving news footage from the 1985 Handsworth riots with archival newsreels of Black historiography. In 'the struggle ... to find a new language' (Hall, 1987), *Handsworth Songs* focuses on the problem of representation rather than on the problem of race. In developing several non-linear narratives, alternative viewpoints to those we are familiar with from the traditional riot documentaries, and an overall 'cut 'n' mix' style, the film offers an unsettling yet pleasurable viewing experience. The power of decades of reductionist images of Blackness taken as 'truth' is such that a transgressive text like this is inevitably noticed, and seen by some as extreme (for a range of responses, see Mercer, 1988a). What Black Audio Film Collective make us remember is that 'the truth' we once believed in (or at least settled for) was in fact based on little more than an easily palatable myth.

With *Handsworth Songs* and other films of the period such as *Territories* (Isaac Julien, 1984) and *The People's Account*, Black Audio, Sankofa and Ceddo were trying to bring pleasure to the documentary form and to problematize the audience's relation to the images on the screen. In terms of format and medium, they were typical of the type of Black British films being made in the 1980s. In compiling a list of Black and Asian films in distribution in Britain, June Givanni found that the majority of films had running times of less than sixty minutes, while two-thirds of them were documentaries (Givanni, 1987). Of course, there were exceptions. Several of the films produced by Sankofa, for instance, were dramatic narratives, including *The Passion of Remembrance*, which was a full-length feature film, *Dreaming Rivers* (Martine Attille, 1988) and *Looking for Langston* (Isaac Julien, 1989).

Meanwhile, many British-Asian film-makers continued with the drama-documentary mode of address in an attempt to recode the 'official' master discourses on race. The first British-Asian feature film to materialize from the workshop sector was *Majdhar* by the Retake Film and Video Collective, a group of Asians 'who felt that there was an urgent need to challenge the stereotyped images of black people in the media'(*Majdhar* publicity leaflet).

Majdhar, like earlier British-Asian films such as *Mirror Mirror* (Yugesh Walia, Birmingham Film and Video Workshop, 1980), is organized around a female protagonist who undergoes a gradual change of consciousness. In such films, progression tends to be measured in terms of how 'Westernized' or British the Asian subject becomes. In *Majdhar*, once Fauzia, the decentred subject, is 'freed' by her Pakistani husband, she is able to embark on a journey from dependence to independence. The Fauzia we first meet, wearing traditional Indian dress, connotes powerlessness, silence and lack whereas the 'new' Fauzia is free to wear 'Western' clothes, work, and date English men. Fauzia opts for British middle-class culture and adapts her identity accordingly. As well as reiterating racist ideologies which align the East with oppression and the West with freedom, this 'between two cultures' film also reveals how social realism as a mode of enunciation can be limiting when dealing with the complexities of identity for the diasporic subject. As such, *Majdhar* has an explicit assimilationist project.

Where films such as *Handsworth Songs*, *My Beautiful Laundrette* and *The Passion of Remembrance* refused to be confined by the (imaginary) parameters of form and subject matter, films such as *Majdhar* and *Mirror Mirror* were limited by their insistence on positioning a troubled subject within a social realist framework. Where the first set of films open up the form to 'let the image speak', the latter are stifled both aesthetically and technically by reducing the diasporic experience to a confused 'in-betweenness'.

The tenacious investment in the notion of identity, the use of the realist mode and the dependence on the visual image with minimal use of dialogue in films such as *A Kind of English* (Ruhul Amin, 1986) were all important aesthetic and political trademarks of 1980s British-Asian films. Although the production contexts and types of stories told in these films were diverse, the critical debate about British-Asian film was standardized and repetitive. This was perfectly embodied in the critical response to *My Beautiful Laundrette*, one of the few British-Asian films to have entered the realm of Black arts criticism. Many found the film problematic because of the apparent incompatibility of creative thinking with 'political correctness'. The unremitting politicization of discourse when reading a Black film produced a focus on 'positive' and 'negative' images. *My Beautiful Laundrette* was praised by many precisely for script writer Hanif Kureishi's refusal to create 'one dimensional, positive images'. But there could be no uniform agreement about what constituted a 'positive image'. Keith Vaz, for instance, argued that the images of Asians in *My Beautiful Laundrette* were 'too positive' – 'there were no poor Asians in the film, Asians living on the margins of poverty, which is what we have in this country' (*Saturday Review*, BBC2, 16 November 1985). Mahmood Jamal, on the other hand, perceived those same images as too negative, with the emphasis on 'money grabbing, scheming, sex-crazed people' (Jamal, 1985). The 'British-Asianness' of *My Beautiful Laundrette* overdetermined most approaches to it. The most publicized responses to the film refused to see it as anything but realist, or the characters as determined by anything other than their ethnic identity. Clearly, quite different readings of this markedly hybrid film are perfectly legitimate.

The 'Black Film, British Cinema' Conference at the Institute of Contemporary Arts in London in 1988 highlighted the diverse and often contradictory responses provoked by recently exhibited Black films such as *The Passion of Remembrance*, *Playing Away* (Horace Ové, 1986) and *Handsworth Songs*. The varied critical reception revealed three key things. First, that Black audiences are heterogeneous and active. Secondly, that we have transcended the 'siege mentality which says that anything we do must be good' (Henriques, 1988, p.18). And finally, that the cinema has become, in Kobena Mercer's words, 'a crucial arena of cultural contestation' (Mercer, 1994b, p.73).

By the late 1980s, a number of public arts institutions had begun to feel financial strain, largely as a result of the Conservative Government's abolition of the Greater London Council and other metropolitan authorities in 1986, its increasing stranglehold on public expenditure and dwindling allocations to the Local Authorities Support Grant. The Government's hostility towards the public sector led Channel 4, the BFI and other public institutions to reassess their commitment to the independent film and video sector. By 1990, the revenue funding of film and video workshops had virtually ceased. Some workshops subsequently closed and others began to operate a mixed economy, relying partly on public grants, partly on earned income.

Changes in the television infrastructure also inevitably affected independent film and video production. The development of cable and satellite, combined with the Government's deregulatory, market-led approach to broadcasting, saw the prioritizing of commercialism over access, artistic concerns and a basic commitment to public service broadcasting. Many feel that Channel 4 has 'sold out' and relinquished its commitment to the independents in the quest to attract a larger audience share and advertising revenue. Despite the recent trend to commodify Black culture, and particularly Black youth culture, the perception still remains that 'minority art' does not make money. The emphasis today is more on the marketable end product than on cultural diversity or equal opportunities issues such as training. This undermines the 'non-commercial' premise on which most of the film and video workshops had been based, and their commitment to integrating training into their activities.

At the same time it cannot be overlooked that television has provided a space in which Black British films can be seen. Several of the films cited above have been aired on (and often funded by) Channel 4. More recently, there have been a number of funding and scheduling slots such as 'Funky Black Shorts' and 'Synchro', which have been reserved for Black short films; other short film slots like 'Short and Curlies' and 'S/He-Play' have found space for Black work such as *Roots* (Taghi Amirani, 1992) and *A Nice Arrangement* (Gurinder Chadha, 1989). BBC2 has also brought 'one-offs' such as *My Sister Wife* (Lesley Manning, 1992) and *Two Oranges and a Mango* (Lindsay Posner, 1994) and series such as *The Buddha of Suburbia* (Roger Michell, 1993) to our screens. Television, largely thanks to short film slots, is now the main entry-point for emerging Black film-makers. There are also narrative screenplay programmes for Black writers such as Screenwrite, a partnership between the London Film and Video Development Agency, the BFI and British Screen Finance.

Alongside the television developments (and setbacks) of the 1990s, a number of relatively populist Black British feature films have been made. *Young Soul Rebels*, *Wild West* (David Attwood, 1992) and *Bhaji on the Beach* are the first Black British features since *My Beautiful Laundrette* to have 'crossed over' from relatively selective, small-scale art-house audiences to larger, more varied, commercial ones. Each film makes an explicit break from the aesthetic and ideological principles of the earlier 'cinema of duty' films. They refuse a simple focus on racial politics and acknowledge other facets of identity. They are multilayered and complex films, not only in terms of narrative, but also in terms of genre, style and film form. As such, they render redundant those critical discourses which depend on the rigid dichotomies of Black versus White, negative versus positive, representative versus unrepresentative, realism versus fantasy and so on.

Each of these films – and we can add to the list the BBC's four-part serialization of Hanif Kureishi's book *The Buddha of Suburbia* – deals with the evolution of a myriad of fluid, complex and sometimes conflicting identities. In so doing, these films realize and profile 'the end of the innocent notion of the essential Black subject' (Hall, 1988, p. 28). Chris and Caz's version of growing up Black and British in 1970s Britain in *Young Soul Rebels* is thus very different from Karim's experience of the same period in *The Buddha of Suburbia*.

Productions such as these shift the focus from the political arena to the cultural arena, where the 'politics of race' are interwoven with the 'politics of the dance-floor', the former inextricably linked to the latter. Such films use popular culture and music to bridge the gap between academic critiques of essentialism and the lived reality of displacement. In dealing with and reaching the popular, they encourage a more applicable and accessible reading of 'otherness'. This is not to suggest that film practice and critical practice are exchangeable entities, but that new Black film practices, in dealing with community, identity and social action, can help us make sense of notions of ethnicity, Third Cinema and the diasporic experience which have been so central to critical discourse in recent years, particularly in the theoretical writings of leading Black cultural critics such as Stuart Hall, Paul Gilroy, Homi Bhabha and Kobena Mercer.

Wild West, for instance, profiles Zaf Ayub, a young British Asian growing up in Southall. Music provides him and his Country and Western band, the Honky Tonk Cowboys, with a voice. They dream of success and Nashville but others demand that they 'bring back the Bhangra'. The narrative is cemented as fantasy largely through the depiction of Southall as a lawless Western frontier town. The film repudiates an essential racial identity, instead offering fluctuating points of identification, emphasizing questions of performance and pastiche. Zaf's mother represents an extreme condition of alienated and isolated individualism. Blinded by her nostalgic desire for her 'imagined homeland' of Pakistan, she does not consider that an authentic return to an unproblematized homeland is impossible. *Wild West* deconstructs the suggestion made by the 'between two cultures' films which see only three possible paths for the British-Asian subject to follow (a journey to the heartland of Britain, return to the Indian subcontinent or a confused in-between path). *Wild West* provides a fourth option, represented by Nashville, which points to the indeterminacy and impossibility of clearly categorizing Black British identity.

Like *Wild West*, *Bhaji on the Beach* is a British-Asian film which really can be taken on its own terms as a more or less successful fiction. British-Asian identity is not dwelt on in the film, it just is. At the same time, the fact of Asianness is not naturalized and assimilation is not simply urged. Gurinder Chadha, the film's director, makes it clear that the 'British-Asianness' of the text informs the creative process:

> In *Bhaji* what I found emerging ... is the pull between a very British film on the one hand and being quite Indian on the other and that pull is present in every single scene, every single character, every single frame of the film. ... We as Black people live with this duality – this pull – every day of our lives but it's also the force that feeds me as a film-maker. (Chadha in Givanni, 1993, p. 10)

This 'pull' between British and Asian identities and between British and Indian cinema aesthetics generates the pleasures of hybridization in the cinematic form. This form of duality is different to the 'in-betweenness' of the 'cinema of duty' films in that it does not locate its protagonists solely within a problem-oriented discourse and diasporic experiences are not limited to victimhood and struggle. Furthermore, Chadha does not treat her own 'hybrid' identity as a hurdle and does not see it as limiting the range of issues or characters she can explore.

Both *Wild West* and *Bhaji on the Beach* incorporate comic elements in the narrative, a mode of address not generally associated with cinematic representations of race. *Bhaji on the Beach*, the first feature film to be directed by an Asian woman in Britain, combines slapstick *Carry On*-style humour with high drama. Indeed, the film constantly moves across generic boundaries. Just as *Young Soul Rebels* can be seen as part thriller, part disaffected youth drama, part love story, *Bhaji on the Beach*'s generic positioning is equally ambiguous. It is part soap opera, part road movie, part romantic comedy, while also borrowing from the British realist tradition and Bombay popular cinema (particularly *Bajju Bawara* [Vijay Bhatt, 1952] and *Purab Aur Pachhim/East or West* [Manoj Kumar, 1970]).

In exploring the generational, class, political and personal differences and tensions within a group of Asian women on a day trip to the seaside, *Bhaji on the Beach* depicts the reality of Asian women's heterogeneous and often complex lives. In the melodrama of other British-Asian films such as *A Nice Arrangement, Majdhar, Mirror Mirror* and *My Sister Wife*, Asian women have been confined to the 'private' space of the home. In *Bhaji on the Beach*, we see an ensemble of Asian women temporarily inhabiting a public sphere (Blackpool beach) which is predominantly associated with 'Englishness' and 'Whiteness'. The quintessential 'Englishness' of Blackpool is juxtaposed with the 'Indianness' of the female protagonists, both culturally and visually. At the same time, we do not get the sense that any one culture has 'crossed over' or been assimilated, but that a new form of cultural identity is emerging. This hybrid identity is 'British-Asianness', a fluid evolving entity, which cannot be reduced to any one thing.

While the workshops were losing their support in the late 1980s, Gurinder Chadha and Ngozi Onwurah, the director of the controversial *Welcome II The Terrordome* (1994), were setting up their own production companies and exploring how to reach multiple audiences. Although some have argued that Black British Cinema can never be Commercial British Cinema, the increasingly populist stance and box-office success of new Black film appears to suggest otherwise.

The 1980s ethos of collective and integrated practice seems to have given way to a far more individualistic approach to film production. We have almost come full circle – without public funds, many of today's Black British film-makers are being forced to subsidize their own productions, just as the Black British film-makers of the 1960s and 1970s had to. It may well be the case that those who cultivated the Black British film movement in the 1980s will be left behind since they lack the funds to survive in today's increasingly competitive broadcasting and film environment. Although creative power has emerged from diasporic difference, Black film-makers are still limited by cultural expectations and production finance. Black film-makers are still predominantly considered as 'minority artists', not an easy position from which to negotiate when trying to survive in the free market, while for those reliant on public arts funding the future seems even bleaker. There is less room for experimentation and the 'sense of urgency' and obligation to make a 'Black film' still remain.

In foregrounding notions of identity and community, Black British films have diversified and enriched not only the concept of British cinema, but also the entire notion of Britishness. There has been an increasing desire, by Black British film-makers, to re-examine notions of British national identity without being nationalist. The emergence of a wide range of Black British films in the 1980s and 1990s has broadened the somewhat narrow repertoire of British national cinema by interrogating otherwise taken-for-granted notions of British culture and British film. As Thomas Elsaesser points out,

> British films ... have been rather successful in marketing and packaging the national literary heritage, the war years, the countryside, the upper classes and elite education, and in doing so have also succeeded in constructing and circulating quite limiting and restricting images of 'Britishness'. (Elsaesser 1984, p. 208)

In recent Black British films, that limited and restricted agenda has been discarded. Now, we have the image of Johnny licking Omar's neck in front of his fascist thug-like gang (*My Beautiful Laundrette*), we have an old Indian woman on Blackpool beach gleefully sprinkling chilli powder on her fish and chips (*Bhaji on the Beach*), and we have two Black men dancing over a superimposed image of a burning Union Jack (*Territories*). We have been offered a version of Britishness that does not necessarily belong to the English.

In redefining what is assumed to be unchangeable, Black film activists have challenged the concept of identity as a fixed core. They have shown us that identity, as Stuart Hall has reminded us, 'is never complete, always in process, and always constituted within, not outside, representation' (Hall, 1990, p. 222). Recent Black film-makers have refused to be bound by a rigid national boundary or a singular (cultural, ethnic or national) identity.

There is, however, an urgent need to debate the aesthetics of these diverse productions. In particular, much needs to be done to reverse the situation whereby the specific role and contribution of British-Asian film has been culturally marginalized (both critically and institutionally) within an already culturally marginalized Black British film sector. There are important similarities, but there are also significant differences between the experiences of Asian and African-Caribbean film practitioners and the films which they have produced. In the same way, it is important that we record the contribution of Black women to cultural production.

Several of the more recent films to have emerged from the Black British diaspora have revealed that we do not all necessarily share the same political ground and are not all motivated by the same experiences. It is not enough to say that the same critical framework applies to all films to have emerged from the Black British diaspora. There has not been a simple progress model in the history of Black British film, from the 'cinema of duty' to a 'cinema of freedom'. There are aesthetic and political concerns which overlap the two, and there is nothing to suggest that, with institutional support, both types of films will not continue to be made.

14

Crossing Thresholds:
The Contemporary British Woman's Film

Justine King

The recent success of Sally Potter's *Orlando* (1992) and Gurinder Chadha's *Bhaji on the Beach* (1993) suggests that the feminist cultural politics of the woman's film have finally found a place in mainstream British cinema in the 1990s. Certainly, the so-called 'renaissance' of British cinema during the 1980s yielded scant opportunities for women film-makers to break into mainstream feature film production. Yet despite the continuing marginalization of 'women's cinema' (that is, films made *by* women) in this country, it was, perhaps somewhat paradoxically, a period marked by the emergence of a series of memorable and innovative British woman's films (that is, films made *for* women; for a discussion of the distinction between women's cinema and the woman's film, see Mayne, 1990, pp. 2–6). Although these films were, with only one exception, the products of all-male scriptwriting and directing collaborations, they nonetheless occupied much of the terrain traditionally held by 'women's cinema'. Thus they tackled headlong the conflicts and vicissitudes of contemporary gender relations; they foregrounded charismatic and transgressive female protagonists; and they offered what were, within the context of mainstream cinema at least, refreshingly radical resolutions to the conflicts they portrayed.

The series of movies I have in mind comprises David Goldschmidt's *She'll be Wearing Pink Pyjamas* (1985) from a script by Eva Hardy, Chris Bernard's *Letter to Brezhnev* (1985), David Leland's *Wish You Were Here* (1989) and Lewis Gilbert's two screen adaptations of Willy

Russell's stage plays, *Educating Rita* (1983) and *Shirley Valentine* (1989). These are by no means the only British woman's films of the 1980s. Indeed, if the principal defining features of the genre are the privileging of female point of view structures (both diegetic and spectatorial) and a preoccupation with thematic concerns designated as 'feminine' within a patriarchal culture, then the category might well be opened up to include such films as *Dance with a Stranger* (1985), *The Dressmaker* (1988), *Wetherby* (1985), *A Room with a View* (1985) and *Scandal* (1989), to name but a few (for more extensive definitions of the woman's film genre, see for example, Brunsdon, 1986; Gledhill, 1987; Doane, 1987; Basinger, 1994).

However, with the benefit of hindsight at least, it does seem to me that the level of intertextuality and the continuity of certain staple themes and narrative patterns across the five films I will focus upon suggests that they form a coherent cycle. In what follows, I will use this cycle to map out the characteristic features of the burgeoning new British woman's film as it emerged and developed during the 1980s and to assess its position within British film production and the culture at large. This will be very much a text-based analysis; attention to the marketing and reception of these films – clearly important areas of enquiry – will have to await another occasion. Finally, I will return to the question of the 1990s British woman's film, and explore the extent to which this 1980s cycle established useful paradigms for women film-makers currently breaking into mainstream British film production.

While the five films in question are as a group innovative and distinctive in various ways, they are also patchworked together out of a variety of well established filmic, theatrical and televisual styles. This is hardly surprising, given that *Shirley Valentine* and *Educating Rita* were adapted with many elements of their original hugely successful theatrical staging intact, and that *Wish You Were Here, Letter to Brezhnev,* and *Pink Pyjamas* were Channel 4 films, conceived and developed with an eye to their suitability for television broadcast. But they also all quite knowingly mobilize and rework the familiar stock-in-trade of the conventional woman's film: the portrayal of the competing demands of women's prescribed social and sexual roles, the valorization of female friendship and camaraderie, and the concomitant inter-rogation of the dynamics of heterosexual relationships.

As woman's films, they follow convention in portraying their heroines as railing against the constraints of their roles as wives, mothers, daughters and lovers within a rigidly confining patriarchal order. But their status as British films often signals this confinement as specifically symptomatic of a still hopelessly class-bound and politically polarized British culture (which, as with these films, so often in practice becomes reductively subsumed within the terms of what is considered representative of *English* culture).

In *Wish You Were Here*, it is not only Lynda's (Emily Lloyd) hostile Oedipal relationship with her dogmatic widowed father which drives her to transgress at every turn (hence, on one level, the title of the film, which refers to the dead mother); it is also the suffocating, petit-bourgeois morality of a 'Little England' scandalized by a bike on a bowling green (the film is set in an English seaside town in the early 1950s). Similarly, in *Educating Rita*, it is not only the persistent demands of her husband and father that Rita (Julie Walters) should fulfil her class and gender *raison d'être* and have a baby (considered well overdue at the age of twenty-six) which prompts Rita to turn to education; it is also her belief that education will empower her to defy the petty moral and social strictures of her working-class positioning. Thus, there is undoubtedly an intersection of discourses in these films which attempts to codify conflicts of class and gender as corollary to one another in English culture. However, it seems to me that these discourses may not always be so conveniently or seamlessly elided, either politically or aesthetically, and that the critique of gender conflict in these films may be superseded or compromised by an overarching project to interrogate wider issues of class and national identity.

There is, though, another more insidious problem attendant upon any discussion of the British woman's film. As Richard Dyer has perceptively pointed out, the 'official' characterization of British cinema almost precludes the recognition of its propensity for melodramatic emotionality (Dyer, 1994). The conceptualization of the 'typically English film' consistently seems to attract the ideologically loaded epithet 'restrained' (which reflects not only a middle-class bias but, I would argue, a masculinist bias too) whereby demonstrative displays of 'excessive' emotionality – worst of all, tears – are regarded as inappropriate, both on and off screen. It is, then, an easy enough matter to see why the woman's film might be regarded as something of an unwelcome cuckoo-in-the-nest here. For, despite twenty years or more of sustained critical attention which has repeatedly demonstrated the aesthetic and ideological complexities of the genre, the woman's film still carries the taint of triviality, emotional excessiveness and brash Hollywood populism. In short, it might well be considered as rather 'un-British'.

One could speculate at length as to the various motivations underpinning such a conceptualization, but, whatever the case, it is, as Dyer also notes, a peculiarly skewed and selective characterization which fails to take account of British cinema's sustained investment in melodramatic emotionality. It is of course possible to trace a legacy of films such as *Millions Like Us* (1943) and *Two Thousand Women* (1944), *A Taste of Honey* (1961) and *The L-Shaped Room* (1962), *Jane Eyre* (1970) and *A Room with a View* (1985), which adhere to the fundamental tenets of the woman's film, but which are swept under the umbrella of other film movements or genres (the wartime morale film, the New Wave film, the 'quality' literary adaptation) in order to fit them, however reductively, into a dominant scheme of national cinema. The same generic eclipse seems to have overtaken *Shirley Valentine*, *Educating Rita*, *Wish You Were Here*, *Letter to Brezhnev* and *Pink Pyjamas* (all of which were predominantly promoted and apparently received as comedies), for it certainly strikes me as curious – not to say negligent – that these films have been explicitly discussed neither within their generic context as woman's films nor in juxtaposition to one another as a cycle of real significance to 1980s British cinema.

What, then, at a thematic level, constitutes this group of films as a distinctive cycle? As I have already suggested, these films concern themselves with the representation of transgressive women who circumvent the prescribed norms of their cultural and sexual positioning, but this hardly distinguishes them from their numerous British and American generic counterparts. What unifies and distinguishes these films as a coherent cycle is, above all else, the all-pervasive and recurring motif of escape. This escape takes a variety of narrative forms: a foreign holiday in *Shirley Valentine*, a ticket to the USSR in *Letter to Brezhnev*, an all-women adventure holiday in *Pink Pyjamas*, the removal from the patriarchal home in *Wish You Were Here*, an Open University course in *Educating Rita*. But the function of escape is consistent: all five films allow their respective female protagonist to resist the generically conventional drive toward a reinscriptive or punitive ideological and narrative closure.

Whenever one speaks of escape in connection with the woman's film genre, however, it is all but inevitable that alarm bells should begin to sound. For alongside the promising possibilities afforded by this motif of escape, there must also be the less positive suggestion of escap*ism*, with all its attendant insinuations of triviality, 'reality' avoidance and, perhaps most problematically, spectatorial passivity (all of which again echo the same entrenched prejudices implicit in the woman's film's virtual proscription from critical discussions of British national cinema). There is, though, a crucial distinction which needs to be drawn here. On the one hand, escape offers the radical prospect of a *permanent* removal of the constraints and imperatives imposed upon the female protagonist within patriarchal culture (and, by extension, the constraints imposed upon the female spectator by the patriarchal film). Conversely, escapism must be seen as only a *temporary* withdrawal, a spatially and temporally limited retreat which ultimately may well serve as a cathartic process reconciling the protagonist (and spectator) to the apparent inevitability of her prescribed position.

The motif of escape is thus perhaps best understood here in terms of a movement through a *liminal* space, a realm of possibility (Van Gennep, 1960; Turner, 1969 and 1977; Ashley, 1990). Once this threshold is crossed, once she enters this realm of possibility, the female protagonist is able to remove herself from her initial narrative (and cultural) situation, distance herself from the demands and entrapment of everyday life, and undergo a redefining and re-empowering transformation of identity or rite of passage. In *Shirley Valentine*, *Pink Pyjamas* and *Letter to Brezhnev*, this liminality is explicitly located as a topographical space (Greece, the Lake District, the USSR) which the female protagonist journeys to or through. In *Educating Rita* and *Wish You Were Here*, liminality is not a concrete, physical space, but a symbolic trajectory. For both Rita and Lynda, the liminal threshold is located within the rites of passage through which they pass (the educational process for Rita, sexual initiation and motherhood for Lynda) in order to redefine their initial narrative positioning.

In *Pink Pyjamas*, the liminal space subsumes the entire diegesis. The film opens at the beginning of the holiday, the first all-female Outward Bound course of its kind (the success or failure of which is explicitly signalled as a feminist 'test case' around which all the other feminist issues that the film explores are to be oriented). The dynamics of the first scene prefigure many of the subsequent formal and discursive elements of the narrative. Eight women are seated around a table nervously introducing themselves and explaining why they have chosen this 'unusual holiday'. It is a scene reminiscent of the opening session of a group therapy meeting, which of course is precisely how the holiday does function. As the women reveal their identities, some fairly standard female stereotypes seem to emerge: the cynical, sexually disillusioned woman; the radical feminist who, true to type, has read about the course on the Woman's Page of the *Guardian*; the timid young wife and mother and her own formidable, domineering mother; the childless, uptight career woman; the ageing spinster; the 'mumsy', down-to-earth middle-aged woman; the quietly discontented middle-class wife.

It is difficult to escape the initial impression that these characterizations trade upon clumsy, misogynistic stereotypes of femininity, but as the diegesis is entirely located within a liminal space set apart from the culture that constructs and deploys them, the codification of these stereotypes breaks down; detached as they are from their cultural frame of reference, the women in this film gradually become defined solely in terms of their relationship to one another.

Cut into this opening scene are various shots of the women taking their first tentative steps into the Great Outdoors (canoeing, swimming, running through the woods). The intersection of contrasting images here demonstrates the way in which the film's deployment of liminality straddles the codes of implicitly gendered genres. On the one hand, the outdoor liminal space is a realm of adventure, action and potential danger more generally associated with 'male' genres such as the action movie or the Western. On the other hand, the film demonstrates a reliance upon dialogue reminiscent of the soap opera (for a wider discussion of the valorization of dialogue and oral culture in soap opera, see Brown, 1994). By far the greatest proportion of screen-time is devoted to the various discussions which take place between the women as they open up to one another and forge bonds of camaraderie and mutual sympathy. It is essentially this recourse to therapeutic talk that affords the women the capacity for introspection and transformation, but it is important to recognize that it is only when the women cross the liminal threshold and remove themselves from their everyday, familiar surroundings (the world of work, familial responsibilities and men) that inhibitions are dissolved, confidences established and self-transformations effected.

The liminality of *Wish You Were Here* is far less prominent or protracted. Indeed, for much of the narrative, it is entrapment rather than escape that seems likely to prevail. Lynda is regarded as something of a problem teenager by her exasperated father. She has an abiding fascination for blue language, embraces promiscuity long before the 1960s made it acceptable, and spends her life flitting from one menial job to another (the range of which provides a politically pointed demonstration of the painfully limited career opportunities open to women after the war).

For much of the narrative, the film oscillates between the possibilities of escape and entrapment, as Lynda's exuberant, rebellious outbursts (the bike on the bowling green, mooning at the neighbours, the striptease in the bus depot) are juxtaposed with the recurring image of Lynda seated at her bedroom window staring out to the space beyond the patriarchal home. Towards the end of the film, the narrative seems to move inexorably towards a closure that will mete out a predictable come-uppance. There is what appears to be Lynda's final outrageous outburst of carnivalesque rebellion, as she jumps on a table and proclaims to the assembled company of the sedate seaside tearoom where she works that she is pregnant. This is followed by an anti-climactic scene in which Lynda's aunt admonishes her for causing her father so much grief and humiliation and she is given money to go off quietly and have an abortion (which Lynda appears to do, as the following scene shows her poised to enter the house of a backstreet abortionist). Thus Lynda's final entrapment by a culture whose rules can only be broken at great expense seems unavoidable at the close of the film.

But this is not quite the end of the film. As if by magic, we next see Lynda disembarking from a bus in the depot where she once worked, dressed in vibrant, conspicuous, unapologetic yellow, defiantly meeting the half-lecherous, half-censorious gazes of the men with whom she once worked. She walks along the same bowling green where once she rode her bike to the consternation of the club members, only this time she proudly promenades with the pram bearing her illegitimate child. Here, the liminality which provides the female protagonist's escape route is not so much a trajectory as an ellipsis which magically rescues her from what seemed the inevitability of a reinscriptive and punitive closure. The final shot of the film shows Lynda standing outside the patriarchal home smiling delightedly at the baby she proudly holds aloft, waiting for her father to open the door. We are left to speculate as to whether her reception will be hostile or reconciliatory, for, as with *Pink Pyjamas*, the film positively refuses to gesture beyond this final moment of apparent wish fulfilment. However, this final image which ostensibly suggests that Lynda has escaped the imposition of the prescribed norms of femininity is perhaps rather more ambivalent. After all, what she escapes *to* is arguably the most forcibly prescribed feminine role of them all: motherhood. True, by keeping the baby, Lynda has defied the petty moral constraints of her milieu which, at the very least, demand that she should be bowed by shame. But the final image of mother and child draws upon a pantheon of sentimentalized iconography which represent motherhood as the ideal of femininity. Thus it seems to me that it would be difficult to assert that Lynda's characterization at the end of the film is quite so thoroughly transgressive as it is at the outset.

In *Educating Rita*, liminality is not so much a space as a process. At the beginning of the film, Rita is characterized as brash, disarmingly outspoken and apparently assertive. She is the kind of stereotype of working-class femininity (vulgar, sexy, funny) that would not look amiss in *Coronation Street*. But, at the age of twenty-six, Rita's life is closing in around her. Having left school without qualifications and married young, Rita is desperate to broaden her horizons. She undertakes an Open University course and changes her name from Susan to Rita to emphasize the change of identity she intends to affect. Her weekly tutorials with Frank (Michael Caine) increasingly become the central focus of her life; they represent a kind of liminal space where she can shape and assert her new identity. Her husband burns her books, demands a baby and delivers an ultimatum that Rita must give up the course or end the marriage. But his power to impose his expectations upon her simply dissolves. As in all the films of this cycle, what appeared, at the beginning of the narrative, to be the very real and immediate threat cast by patriarchy is gradually exposed to be little more than a rather comic impotence.

Rita's escape route is thus secured. She moves out of the marital home, shares a flat with a neurotic bohemian, goes to summer school and begins to socialize with the 'proper students' she once found so intimidating. By the end of the movie, Rita has been empowered to resist the pattern of stifling domesticity and motherhood that, at the outset, seemed to beckon inexorably. However, it is difficult to ignore the ironic undertones of her apparent triumph. Whilst Rita aspires to join the ranks of the 'educated classes' because she believes them to be free from the petty constraints of her own class, the text continually belies such a prospect, most obviously by juxtaposing Rita's wide-eyed enthusiasm and unrestrained honesty with Frank's cynicism, apathy and worsening alcoholism. As such, the positive aspects of Rita's escape must be tempered by the fact that the world she escapes into is one of repression and pretension.

As in *Wish You Were Here*, it becomes difficult to avoid the conclusion that Rita's rite of passage renders her a rather less transgressive female figure than when the film began (she gives up smoking, stops dyeing her hair, wears muted casual clothes and is generally a good deal more restrained). But I would argue nonetheless that, in some important ways, Rita's transformation is still a predominantly positive one. Perhaps this is where the rift between the text's concurrent discourses of class and gender begins to make its presence felt. Whilst Rita's entrance into the educated middle classes is portrayed as merely trading one form of entrapment for another, reading the film as a woman's film (and therefore privileging the significance of its gender discourse over that of class), it is clear that Rita's escape from her socially and sexually prescribed roles remains quite a radical one. The closure resists reinscribing Rita within the all too convenient heterosexual coupling that has been threatening to take place throughout the narrative (a disgraced Frank goes off to Australia to find his own liminality alone), and instead leaves us with the positive image of a single woman who has some real choices available to her.

The distinction between escape and escapism is central to the construction of liminality in *Letter to Brezhnev*. The first half of the narrative, which recounts Elaine (Alexandra Pigg) and Teresa's (Margi Clarke) night on the town, maps out a narrative liminality which seems to be confined to the prospect of an escapist adventure. Elaine's yearning to escape the monotony and hardship of her life as an unemployed Kirkby girl for more romantic climes is explicitly signalled at the very beginning of the movie when she tells her friend Tracy, 'I'm sick of the men up here, they've got no romance in them. ... I wish I was in Casablanca or somewhere.' The comment clearly locates Elaine's narrative goal within the terrain of the woman's film with its reference to one of the most memorable romantic weepies of them all.

Casablanca being out of the question, Elaine limits her sights on the prospect of 'getting away for a few hours'. Having stolen a bulging wallet from two lecherous Greek Cypriots who have tried to buy a dance (demonstrating that not all foreign men fit the bill of the romantic hero), Elaine and Teresa embark upon a no-holds-barred night to remember. As Teresa quite literally lets her hair down, transforming herself in the toilets from factory worker to vamp, Elaine surveys the scene of a down town nightclub. It is during her wait that Elaine first spies Peter (Peter Firth), a Russian sailor on shore leave for one night only (a necessary narrative device to heighten the sense that their encounter must be an intense one-night stand). The moment of their instant mutual attraction is dealt with in a highly ironic, self-conscious set of shots which continually cut between Elaine and Peter's transfixed gazes, the spectacle of the contemporary street fashions of the dancers and Teresa's resourceful improvised vamping up in the toilet cubicle. The music of the nightclub (the gay song, 'Beat Boy' by Bronski Beat, which is surely intended to provide a further level of irony to this highly clichéd moment of heterosexual romance) fades into an extra-diegetic Russian score which emphasizes (if further emphasis were needed) that this exaggeratedly romantic moment of love at first sight is out of time and out of context within this unromantic contemporary scene of modern courtship.

When Peter sets off for home the following day, the narrative moves on to another stage in which Elaine attempts to transform the temporary escapism of their one-night stand into a more permanent form of escape. Here, *Letter to Brezhnev*'s ironic mobilization of the romance formula (with its anticipation of the heterosexual union as closure) and its commitment to delivering a stinging critique of a recession-hit 1980s English culture no longer seem to fit together so easily. Elaine's rite of passage becomes dependent upon the outcome of her relationship with Peter. Her journey to the USSR is one which takes her *towards* her sexually allotted roles (as she tells the pompous Home Office official who attempts to deter her from her politically embarrassing plans, she *wants* to be a wife and mother).

The positive aspects of her escape must therefore be limited to the fact that she has secured her removal from her social positioning as a working-class (though out of work) girl in a down-on-its-luck Northern city, rather than opening up any prospects beyond the traditional expectations of her gender. In this way, it seems to me that *Letter to Brezhnev* ultimately utilizes the motif of escape in order to privilege a social critique over that of gender; its primary polemical drive is to deliver an indictment of a class-bound Northern English culture polarized and demoralized by Thatcherism.

It is impossible to deal with the motif of escape in *Letter to Brezhnev* without paying some attention to the secondary narrative that revolves around Teresa. Of the two women, she is by far the more subversive (her characterization again trading upon the codes of transgressive femininity set out in *Educating Rita* and *Wish You Were Here*). But for Teresa there is little prospect of any permanent escape; her life is a vicious circle whereby she continues to do a job she loathes in order to earn enough money to enjoy herself, and spends her nights desperately chasing a good time to make the prospect of another day in the chicken factory tolerable. Like Elaine, she fantasizes about the possibility of foreign travel. She boasts to an uncomprehending Sergei (Alfred Molina) of a fantasy jet-set job in which she 'gets to travel everywhere: Paris, New York, Amsterdam, the moon'.

At the end of the movie, as Elaine prepares to board her flight to Moscow, Teresa tells her that she is lucky. It is a moment which seems to imply that the liminal trajectory that has been afforded at the end of the narrative is extraordinary and 'unrealistic', that Elaine's escape is a fairy-tale ending in a world where there are far more Teresas than Elaines. I would therefore agree (though perhaps for different reasons) with Paul Giles's reading that '*Letter to Brezhnev* deals more convincingly with containment than escape' (Giles, 1993, p. 7), a point which is borne out by the way in which the narrative closes. Despite its adherence to the romance formula, the expected closure – that of Peter and Elaine's (re)union – is never realized on screen. Instead, the film closes as the two women say their goodbyes (surely confirming that their strong, mutually supportive friendship is the privileged pairing of the text). The final image, then, is one of passive entrapment as Teresa watches her friend walk towards the boarding gate (perhaps another ironic reference to *Casablanca*?) and we learn, way too late, that Teresa has entertained the same romantic fantasies of escaping to join Sergei, but has reconciled herself to the fact that their encounter can only ever be another short-lived moment of escapist fun.

If the liminal trajectory in *Letter to Brezhnev* can be aligned to that of a rite of passage which takes its female protagonist towards a life as a wife and mother, then precisely the reverse process is in operation in *Shirley Valentine*. Shirley's escape to an idyllic Greek island enables her to cross back over the threshold of her passage into adult femininity and the attendant constraints and disappointments that it has imposed. As the opening song clearly informs us, Shirley's narrative goal is to rediscover the freedom and courage she once took for granted, to become once again 'the girl who used to be me, she could fly, she was free'. For, at the age of 42, Shirley (Pauline Collins) is consigned to a life of shopping, cooking and talking to the wall, which has long since proved to be a more animated listener than her husband Joe (Bernard Hill). She dreams of escape, of foreign travel, of 'drinking wine in the country where the grape is grown', and keeps a poster of her intended place of escape on the back of the larder door. The motif of liminality, then, is constructed here in terms of two polar realms of containment and freedom: the dull, regulated and claustrophobic monotony of Shirley's drab suburban home and fading marriage, and the bright, expansive, adventurous world she discovers on her Greek island where inhibitions dissolve and anything seems possible.

As with *Letter to Brezhnev*, *Shirley Valentine* ironically inflects the codes of the classical woman's film. Perhaps the most noticeable way in which these codes are inflected is through the device of direct address which, according to conventional wisdom, is a defamiliarizing device which disrupts the process of identification between protagonist and spectator by continually emphasizing the act of spectatorship and the fictionality of the world laid out before us. But it seems to me that this device has far more radical potential when deployed, as it is here, within the context of the woman's film. It completely precludes the possibility of passive spectatorship or spectatorial voyeurism and in fact functions to heighten our complicity with the female protagonist with whom we share a private joke (of being aware of the intermediary presence of the camera) of which the other characters are apparently oblivious.

Another productive subversion of the codes of classical cinema takes place around the deployment of the holiday romance motif. When Shirley meets Costas (Tom Conti), who invites her for a trip on his brother's boat, the audience's expectations are undoubtedly manipulated to anticipate a formulaic resolution to Shirley's quest for escapist adventure. Thankfully, however, *Shirley Valentine* does not settle for such clichés. The scene in which Shirley and Costas consummate their relationship upon the boat (moored in a deserted bay where the water, like Shirley's liminality, might well go on forever) is a moment of supreme pastiche where the hackneyed clichés of the romance formula are foregrounded to ironic effect. As the passion mounts, the camera cuts to ebbing waves and the increasingly rapid rocking of the boat (a reference, no doubt, to the days when a full-blown sexual encounter was beyond the pale of representation). At the moment of orgasm, the music reaches a crescendo and the camera cuts to Shirley's flushed face, anticipating her cry of pleasure. What comes instead is Shirley's deflating question, 'Where did that orchestra come from?', which acknowledges the incongruous presence of the extra-diegetic mood music.

Shirley Valentine's parodic treatment of the conventions of the romantic woman's film does not necessarily imply an attempt to undermine the viability of the genre. On the contrary, it seems to me that, of all the films of this 1980s cycle, *Shirley Valentine* makes the fewest compromises and concessions as a mainstream British woman's film. Coming, as it does, at the end of the cycle, its closure is perhaps the most positive and radical of all.

As in *Letter to Brezhnev*, its liminal trajectory is codified as a journey to a foreign country. But unlike in *Letter to Brezhnev*, the valorization of this foreign space seems less bound to a specific critique of English culture and more concerned with providing a space where the imperatives of Shirley's life as a middle-aged mother and wife may be suspended and a new identity asserted. Moreover, this new identity is one which explicitly rejects the prescribed roles of femininity. Whereas both *Letter to Brezhnev* and *Wish You Were Here* affect a rite of passage which simply trades one familial role (as daughters) with those of adult femininity (as wives and/or mothers), Shirley's transformation resists such reinscription. At the end of the movie, as a repentant Joe, who has come to Greece to 'reclaim' his absent wife, fails to recognize the new (or rather the 'old') Shirley, it is explicitly stated that her redefinition renders her identity independent of such conventional roles. As she finally tells Joe, 'I used to be the mother, I used to be the wife. But now I'm Shirley Valentine again.'

The film closes on the conventional image of the heterosexual couple who share a drink as the sun sets. But behind this image there is none of the capitulation of the female protagonist's independence with which such a closure is generally inscribed. Joe has entered Shirley's liminal space and has done so on her terms, and there is little or no suggestion that Shirley's final escape is about to be undermined.

By way of conclusion, I want to speculate upon the possible legacy that this cycle of films has left for the 1990s. Whether or not these films appropriated a discursive space that could or would have been better exploited by women film-makers is no longer an issue that can be productively explored. What should concern us now is the extent to which these films established a commercially, aesthetically and politically viable paradigm which might usefully be continued and extended in the current climate. Given the thematic continuity that exists within this cycle of films spanning the greater part of the 1980s, it seems safe to argue that their directors and scriptwriters knew that they had hit upon a winning formula. Whilst there can never be any solid guarantees of success – least of all within the capricious climate of the British film industry – current film-makers (whether female or male) can ill afford to ignore the viability of such a paradigm.

It is high time that movies like *Letter to Brezhnev* and *Wish You Were Here* were regarded less as fortuitous, quirky aberrations and more as exemplary instances of what British cinema does best. The fact that what must be the most successful woman's film of the 1990s to date, Ridley Scott's *Thelma and Louise* (1991), portrays precisely the same need of its female protagonists for escape and liminality (though arguably with rather less radical or positive consequences than its British forerunners), must surely stand as testament to the continuing political and aesthetic currency of this narrative paradigm.

On home ground, Mike Newell's *Enchanted April* (1991), in which four women escape the monotony of their drab English lives for a halcyon month in the idyllic Tuscan countryside, also undoubtedly retraces the steps mapped out by *Shirley Valentine*, *Pink Pyjamas* and company. It is worth noting, though, that Newell's critically acclaimed film was, predictably enough, promoted and received as a 'quality' costume drama rather than a woman's film. Of course, *Enchanted April*, like James Ivory's equally successful *Howards End* (1993), is a costume drama, and I do not advocate that the recognition of their status as woman's films should come at the expense of obscuring other useful categorizations. But the success of Jane Campion's *The Piano* (1993) should demonstrate once and for all the close generic relationship that often exists between the woman's film and the costume drama. One need only remember the plethora of Gainsborough costume melodramas of the 1940s (discussed by Pam Cook elsewhere in this volume) to see how a mythologized construction of the past has the capacity to function as a liminal space in the woman's film.

Perhaps most encouragingly, however, as noted at the beginning of this chapter, two British women film-makers have also extended the paradigm of the 1980s cycle. Potter's *Orlando* and Chadha's *Bhaji on the Beach* both mobilize the concept of narrative liminality, though in quite diverse ways. *Orlando*'s picaresque romp through history (which must surely stand as the most tongue-in-check deployment of the codes of the costume drama by a woman's film to date) constructs the past as a liminal trajectory through which the hero/heroine journeys. Whenever the social realities of patriarchy threaten to overtake Orlando (for example, when, during the Victorian period, Orlando is disinherited because she is now a woman), the narrative simply propels its protagonist forward into a new era and a new set of circumstances until she/he finally accesses the present day where (in a somewhat utopian closure) Orlando is at last able to assert something approaching an androgynous identity.

In *Bhaji on the Beach*, the racial, gender and generational conflicts which look set to overwhelm the women at the outset of the narrative are worked through and resolved on an all-women day trip to Blackpool. As in *Pink Pyjamas* and *Enchanted April*, Chadha's film mobilizes a liminal space to bring together a heterogeneous group of women in a space marked off from the everyday world of men, work and family commitments (see Malik in this volume for a further discussion of *Bhaji*).

All these British films mark an important shift in the generic idiom of the woman's film. Like their British and American forerunners, these films afford a space where the conflicts arising from women's positioning within patriarchy may be explored, dissent articulated, fantasies rehearsed and transgressions sanctioned. The point at which these films significantly depart is in their ability to sustain this space until the very end of the movie. Gone are the final five minutes of the narrative when, suddenly but inevitably, the female protagonist would be forced to concede to the pressures she has railed against for the previous eighty-five minutes or so: the final five minutes of self-sacrifice, renunciation or heterosexual coupling so characteristic of the classical woman's film genre. Instead, the female protagonist of the contemporary British woman's film does not have to pay the final price of her transgressions. She is allowed the opportunity to transform her initial narrative situation in a quite radical way, to remove herself *permanently* from the site of conflict. All this may well indicate substantial progress, both within the woman's film genre (which, after all, is still largely the product of male directors, scriptwriters and producers) and within the wider culture whose imposition of gender difference generates the contingency of such a genre in the first place. And by and large I would argue that there is room for real optimism here, though perhaps a final note of caution should be sounded.

In narrative terms, it is clear that the motif of escape and the movement through a liminal space has enabled the genre of the woman's film to extend its boundaries beyond the once virtually mandatory ideological and narrative closure. But the very fact that these films increasingly represent the demands and conflicts of patriarchal culture as far from overwhelming or insurmountable arguably suggests a somewhat premature optimism. It seems to me that in the endeavour to realize the radical potential that the new British woman's film undoubtedly affords, we must guard against the possibility of succumbing to a utopianism which might veer towards a form of escapism in itself.

My thanks to Andrew Higson for his many valuable suggestions which helped to clarify the issues I have raised in this chapter. Thanks too to Laura Mulvey, whose MA course, 'Contemporary Film Theory and Narrative Space', at the University of East Anglia in 1993 introduced to me the theory of liminality.

15

The Heritage Film and British Cinema

Andrew Higson

Heritage cinema, as a more or less pejorative term, has gained a certain currency as a means of describing a strand of contemporary cinema, and especially British cinema. Indeed, it seems to have become part of the common sense of film culture. In 'Re-presenting the national past', my own contribution to the debate about heritage discourses and contemporary British cinema, I identified a narrow range of quality costume dramas of the 1980s and early 1990s as heritage films (Higson, 1993b). The list of films stretched from *Chariots of Fire* (1981), via *A Room With a View* (1986) to *Where Angels Fear to Tread* (1991). To that list we can now add Merchant-Ivory's *Howards End* (1992), yet another adaptation of an E. M. Forster novel, and, in a slightly more problematic way, Sally Potter's *Orlando* (1992). But what exactly are we talking about when we refer to the heritage film? Is it a *genre* of films, in the same way that we define a Western or a science fiction film? And if so, does it have a history, or does the genre emerge only in the 1980s? In trying to answer these and related questions, I will be going back to and reflecting upon the argument I developed in 'Re-presenting the national past' – and in due course I will also look at some of the criticisms of my argument made by other writers.

First, however, there is this question of the generic status of the so-called heritage film. The term genre, of course, implies a shared group style and set of shared thematic concerns, but also some sort of institutional substance. In 'Re-presenting the national past', I defined what I saw as the key formal, thematic, iconographic and industrial characteristics of the heritage films of the 1980s and 1990s. I suggested that such films operate primarily as middle-class quality products, somewhere between the art house and the mainstream 🙰 one of the better kinds of British film', as the *Daily Mail* remarked of *Howards End* (1 May 1992, p. 34). Such films tend to be relatively low-budget independent productions, at least by comparison with mainstream Hollywood star vehicles, with the emphasis on authorship, craft, and artistic value. That is to say, these films tend to be valued for their cultural significance rather than their box-office takings, though profitability clearly cannot be removed from the equation altogether. Distribution tends to be specialized, with films carefully geared to target audiences, with exclusive runs in the right sorts of cinemas rather than saturation release, especially in the crucial North American market.

As I argued in 'Re-presenting the national past', one of the central pleasures of the heritage film is the artful and spectacular projection of an elite, conservative vision of the national past. These films are intimate epics of national identity played out in a historical context. They are melodramas of everyday bourgeois life in a period setting, projecting, like the National Trust, a country house version of Englishness (Samuel, 1994, p. 160). Several of them are set in the early decades of this century, when the culture of the country house was already in disarray – hence the almost pervasive sense of loss, of nostalgia, which infuses these films.

Many of these so-called heritage films are adaptations of culturally prestigious and canonic literary and theatrical properties. Such literary heritage properties are, however, only a small sample of the properties on display in such films, which also include the large and small country houses, and the more select landscapes, interior designs and furnishings conserved by such bodies as English Heritage and the National Trust. To this list we need to add costumes, and the social types we expect to inhabit these properties. This is, as others have noted, a museum aesthetic: the particular visual style of the films is designed to showcase these various heritage attractions, to display them in all their supposed authenticity (Dyer, 1994). The acting honours tend to be carried by almost a repertory company of key players, many of them drawing on the heritage of the English theatrical tradition.

The narratives of these films are typically slow moving and episodic, avoiding the efficient and economic causal development of the classical film. The concern for character, place, atmosphere and milieu tends to be more pronounced than dramatic, goal-directed action. Camerawork generally is fluid, artful and pictorialist, editing slow and undramatic. The use of long takes and deep focus, and long and medium shots rather than close-ups, produces a restrained aesthetic of display. Indeed, although I do not have the space to develop the argument here, it seems to me that these heritage films owe as much to the cinema of attractions of very early film-making as they do to the classical cinema of narrative integration (Higson, 1993b; 1995a, pp. 90–7).

Questions of genre

One of the issues raised by the sort of generic definition of the heritage film just offered is of course the relation of the so-called heritage film to other genres. Is the heritage film distinct from other costume drama or period drama or historical films, or is it a cycle within those genres? And what about its relation to the woman's picture, the quality literary adaptation, the television classic serial, soap opera, and the art-house film?

There are two general problems of genre to confront here. First, we should recognize that all genres and cycles are hybrid categories, drawing on a variety of representational practices, filmic and otherwise, each film the product of its particular historical conditions of existence, each cycle or genre emerging as it evolves, constructing its own terms of reference, its own intertexts.

Secondly, genres are both critical and industrial categories; that is to say, genre definitions are both means of organizing production and marketing, and ways of grouping films analytically, at the level of critical reception. As far as the heritage film is concerned, we should recognize that the term is a critical invention of recent years, loosely applied to a group of contemporaneous British films which appear to share the characteristics identified earlier, and which are all the product of a culture and an economy in which the heritage industry – the commodification of heritage, the commodification of the past – has become highly visible.

There is plenty of evidence that these shared characteristics are in part the product of decisions made at the level of production and marketing. The success of one film facilitates and perhaps even to some extent determines the production and marketing of subsequent films, and gradually a cycle emerges. But I don't think there is any evidence that the term 'heritage film' has itself figured in production and marketing decisions; indeed, it seems very unlikely that this would be the case since the term is to some extent – if not entirely – pejorative.

Even so, it does seem to me useful to use the term heritage cinema, perhaps, if possible, in a non-pejorative way, to describe a certain strand of contemporary film-making in Britain, in continental Europe, and to some extent in America. In any event, America must figure large in such discussions, both as export market and as producer of the cinema against which the various European national heritage films are defined, but also as producer of its own variants of the cycle, such as *The Age of Innocence* (1993) and *Little Women* (1995).

As critics, we should not try to regulate the genre or cycle too closely or too loosely, however – not all of the films I would see as part of the heritage cycle in Britain are literary adaptations, for instance (*Chariots of Fire* is a good example). The definition of the heritage film is only as good as the critic makes it, and there is no point in defining the term 'heritage film' too tightly – no point, for instance, in saying that the heritage film never deals with the great events of national history; the most we can really do is to say that, as critics, we have identified a cycle of films which *tend* to operate in this way rather than that. But there are no hard and fast rules to be adhered to or broken. After all, it is we critics who make up the rules as we write.

There is in fact something rather tautological about most definitions of the heritage film. I have, for instance, argued that the typical heritage film projects a particular image of the national past, but there are other images of the national past circulating in other recent British films. They are not generally graced with the name 'heritage film', however, precisely because they don't offer this same vision of the national past. But as Raphael Samuel has argued so persuasively, 'heritage' is a very diverse term, applied to a whole range of cultural, political and economic practices involving people from all walks of life; the national heritage is a rich, and richly hybrid, set of experiences and should not be reduced to the apparently singular experiences of elite, conservative patriotism (Samuel, 1994).

Just as Samuel shows how ideas of heritage and the national past have been expanded, modernized and democratized, so we might want to take on board other recent British costume dramas as diverse as *Comrades* (1987), *The Fool* (1990), *Hope and Glory* (1988), *A Private*

Function (1984), *Dance with a Stranger* (1985), *Wish You Were Here* (1987), *Distant Voices, Still Lives* (1988), *Scandal* (1989), and *Backbeat* (1993). Many of these films are set in the quite recent past, all of them deal with 'ordinary people', often working-class people, and they all engage with the idea of the national past in a national context. That is, they all offer a version of heritage. Having said this, I do want to continue to focus on what we might call the bourgeois heritage films.

Historical antecedents

What are the historical antecedents of these bourgeois heritage films? Are we dealing with an entirely new genre here? Or a specific contemporary cycle of costume dramas, a specific variant of a well-established genre? Or is the heritage film a unique genre with its own long history?

In Britain at least, the heritage cycle of the last decade and a half does have its historical antecedents. The heritage industry may have become increasingly visible in the last few years, but it is not new. Indeed, 1995 may be the centenary of the first public film screenings, but it is also the centenary of the founding in Britain of the National Trust, which has always been a major player in the heritage market. The National Trust was by no means unique in its projection of ideas of national heritage in the 1890s and the heritage project has been constantly reinvented over the last hundred years. Cinema has always played a part in this heritage project, and heritage cinema has since the 1910s been a vital plank in efforts to construct, maintain and reproduce a national cinema in this country.

When I use the term heritage cinema in this historical context, I am probably using it more loosely than when identifying the fairly tight and self-contained cycle of recent years. My own starting point for the idea of the heritage film was a passage in Charles Barr's introduction to his book *All Our Yesterdays: 90 Years of British Cinema*: '*Henry V* [1945],' he writes, 'is the culmination of a wartime series, almost a genre in itself, of "heritage" films'; Barr goes on to list several other films, and to suggest that 'none of these was simply recreating a bit of heritage in an inert, Trooping-the-Colour manner', but was an important part of the wartime bid to create a quality national cinema (Barr, 1986, p. 12).

In my own work, I have tried to follow Barr's lead and to map out a much longer trajectory of British films which invoke the idea of national heritage as part of the bid to construct a distinctive national cinema drawing on indigenous cultural traditions. I have considered these issues at length in *Waving the Flag: Constructing a National Cinema in Britain*. One of the case studies in the book focuses on Cecil Hepworth's much admired quality English film-making of the late 1910s and early 1920s, and in particular his film *Comin' Thro' the Rye* (1924), a charming and tasteful period adaptation of a now-forgotten but once enormously popular Victorian novel (Higson, 1995a, pp. 26–97). Elsewhere, I have applied the same sorts of arguments to Maurice Elvey's patriotic bio-pic, *Nelson* (1918), which appeared just after the end of the First World War (Higson, 1995b).

Indeed, we can find numerous films even from the turn of the century which in various ways mobilize heritage discourses, including 'topicals' depicting the Royal family, interest films about old England, adaptations of canonic novels and plays, or scenes from them, and films which drew on the nineteenth-century cult of the national hero.

My point here is to suggest that while there clearly is an identifiable cycle of heritage films with a strong group style and institutional coherence in the 1980s and 1990s, this type of film-making has a much longer history which can be traced right back to the beginnings of cinema. It is a history which is vital to the question of national cinema, for the heritage film is in part a nationally specific form of product differentiation based on indigenous cultural traditions, a historical effort to carve out a space for British, or English, films in a market dominated from the mid-1910s by the American film industry.

However, I am not at all sure that it is helpful to suggest that the heritage film is a long-standing *genre*. It would be more useful to suggest that heritage discourses have always informed particular currents within the national film culture, surfacing more visibly at some times than at others. Thus not all costume dramas are heritage films – which is to say that not all costume dramas have the same prestige cultural status, or the same engagement with conservative and elite heritage discourses. Think of *The Wicked Lady* (1945), for instance, and the other Gainsborough costume dramas of the 1940s (discussed elsewhere in this collection by Pam Cook): such films are less concerned to play out overtly nationalistic concerns and display authentic heritage attractions; they are, as Cook suggests, far more promiscuous in their relation to the past; they are more concerned with tight economic narrative action than with character and setting; identity tends to be much less stable, much more fluid.

Ambivalence

My argument in 'Re-presenting the national past' was heavily marked by a very ambivalent response to the films I was discussing. I embarked on the research for that paper with the intention of performing an ideological critique of what I started to call the heritage film, linking it to what I saw as the conservatism of the heritage industry and of middle-class quality cinema. But I had to take on board the fact that I also rather enjoyed these films, although I'm not sure I felt that I could admit as much, since this would reveal my own class formation, my own cultural inheritance, my attachment to the wrong sort of cinema for a Film Studies lecturer. For Film Studies, it seemed to me, had established itself as a distinct discipline precisely by breaking away from respectable middle-class English literary culture, by celebrating the central texts of political modernism, by exploring what was seen as the specifically filmic, and by embracing popular culture. Despite the fact that heritage cinema did not really seem to fit any of these categories, the more I worked on these films, the more I realized I enjoyed them, and the more I wanted to acknowledge that enjoyment in the paper I was writing, while at the same time wanting to hang on to my ideological critique.

More importantly, it does seem to me that the films of the recent heritage cycle are very ambivalent, and can be read in a variety of ways. Most of them seem to me to deal in nostalgia for an old England, but nostalgia is itself a profoundly ambivalent phenomenon. Nostalgia is always in effect a critique of the present, which is seen as lacking something desirable situated out of reach in the past. Nostalgia always implies that there is something wrong with the present, but it does not necessarily speak from the point of view of right-wing conservatism. It can of course be used to flee from the troubled present into the imaginary stability and grandeur of the past. But it can also be used to comment on the inadequacies of the present from a more radical perspective. As I tried to show in 'Re-presenting the national past', several of the bourgeois heritage films of the 1980s and 1990s can be read as liberal-humanist critiques of the Thatcherite and post-

Thatcherite present. Not flights from the present, but a return to a version of the past in order to comment on the present, to contrast the individualist and materialistic values of Thatcherism with the values of the liberal consensus, making connections across social boundaries of class, gender, sexuality, nationality, etc.

If we take the example of *Howards End*, we can see that this is precisely about combining the values of the prosaic, business-minded Wilcoxes with those of the more open-minded, intellectual, artistic and philanthropic Schlegels, but also the educated middle-class aspirations of Leonard Bast. Howards End, the house, is the key heritage property of this narrative, and inheritance is what is at stake. Who is to inherit Howards End – or, to put it more symbolically, who is to inherit England? Is it to be the new money of the Wilcoxes, a capitalist class whose power depends upon their colonial exploitation and their patriarchal swagger? Or is to be the caring, sharing, feminine line of the Anglo-German Schlegels? In the end, of course, the house is to be inherited by the offspring of the union between Sam West's out of work clerk, Leonard Bast, and Helena Bonham-Carter's wayward Schlegel sister. England is to belong to the middle classes – the target audience for the film version.

This question 'who shall inherit England?' is central to the heritage film. *Chariots of Fire, Another Country* (1984), *A Handful of Dust* (1987), *Orlando* – they all deal with this question of inheritance. But it is not a simple question, for it also raises questions about Englishness, and about the nature, shape and depth of England itself, its traditions and its topography.

Narratives of instability, images of stability

What I argued in 'Re-presenting the national past' is that, at the level of narrative, these questions are posed quite provocatively. The films constantly scratch away at the idea of an essential England, noting the instability, the flux in identity, the hybrid quality of Englishness. The films also dramatize the dissolution of a particular version of England and Englishness, the decay and the decadence of aristocratic life and its hold on the reins of power, the loss of inheritance.

But in that paper, I also argued that at the level of the image, narrative instability was overwhelmed by the alluring spectacle of iconographic stability, providing an impression of an unchanging, traditional, and always delightful and desirable England, the England of 'English Heritage', where social difference but also the possibility of making connections across social boundaries, are replaced by social deference, each person in their allotted place and transgression forbidden. At the level of the image, I argued, we are presented with an upper-class version of the national past, secured in images of exclusive and private heritage property which no longer seem to speak of social union, and which depict England as once more great.

This raises the whole question of how we read films, and particularly how we read images. There is always a problem of reading images in the heritage films of the 1980s and 1990s. How, for instance, are we to read the hospital scene in *Howards End* which marks the death of Mrs Wilcox? After a scene of Mrs Wilcox scribbling her last will, we move to a wide long shot from a high camera position of the exterior of the hospital, a splendid period facade. The camera pulls back and pans slightly, to reveal Charles Wilcox and his wife looking out of a window, but in the opposite direction to the view we have just been presented with. And gradually the scene picks up from here.

Now, this brief fragment from a scene, with its unmotivated view of the hospital building, and its unmotivated camera movement, could be read in a variety of ways. The shot could be read as a slightly unconventional establishing shot; the unconventionality of the shot (the lack of narrative motivation, the fluid camera movement) could be read as a mark of art-house style; it could be read as expressive of the mourning of the characters, an indication of their emotions; or it could be read as a shot designed to display heritage properties (the hospital building). I will return later to this question of how we read images.

What I want to do now is to look at some of the implicit and explicit criticisms that can and have been made of my argument about British heritage films of the 1980s and 1990s as put forward in 'Re-presenting the national past'. Several of these criticisms come back to this same question of how we read images.

The question of emotionality

In 'Re-presenting the national past', I suggested that the heritage films of the 1980s and 1990s were superficial in a typically post-modern way, and that as such they were emotionally empty, marked by what Fredric Jameson called a loss of affect (Jameson, 1984). Richard Dyer, among others, has argued on the contrary that such films do not lack passion, they are not skin-deep, they do have emotional depth, and the power to move audiences emotionally (Dyer, 1994).

As Dyer and others have suggested, British films will often deal very effectively with emotional repression, the representation of which in itself can be a very moving experience. But I would still maintain that these films are ambivalent enough to be read in different ways, even by the same viewer at a single viewing. For while story situations and character psychologies do cue emotional engagement, the richly detailed and spectacular period *mise-en-scène* also cues the distanced gaze of admiring spectatorship, as we can see in the hospital scene from *Howards End*.

Melodrama and *mise-en-scène*

This question of the emotional engagement of the so-called heritage film can be taken further. Claire Monk, among others, has argued that the *mise-en-scène* of these films should not be read in terms of heritage display but as expressive of what E. M. Forster would call 'the inner life' (Monk, 1994). Heritage films, from this point of view, are akin to the classical melodrama or the woman's picture; the *mise-en-scène* should not be read as a separate discourse of scenic display, in conflict with the narrative, but should be read as expressing the emotional intensity of the scene, props acting not as spokespersons for the heritage industry but as symbolic indications of the inner life of the characters. Again, this seems to me persuasive, but again, we are confronted with the problem of reception.

It seems to me perfectly feasible to argue once again that the films are ambivalent enough to be read in both ways, possibly even at the same time. Take another scene from *Howards End*, the scene when Henry Wilcox is showing Margaret Schlegel round his London house and proposes to her on the stairs. It is a wonderful scene, perfectly capturing the emotional turmoil of the characters, their propriety and their repressiveness. And it also has some magnificent decor, furnishings and interior designs on display. The space and the props are clearly used expressively, with the emotional distance between the characters conveyed by the distance between them on the stairs, with the staircase and the props literally overwhelming them. But there can be no denying that the scene also makes the most of the opportunity to display some fine authentic period properties, which are of course the properties of a very privileged class. It is interesting to compare the scene in the film to the equivalent passage in the novel, where Margaret's ironic view of the *mise-en-scène* suggests a much sharper criticism of the overdecoration and the masculinity of the space, and its source in colonial exploitation ('Such a room admitted loot') (Forster, 1989, pp. 166–7).

The problem here is how to take reception into account, how to attend to a range of different readings. A comparison with readings of Douglas Sirk's melodramas of the 1950s may be salutary. Barbara Klinger has recently argued that we need to try to recover something of the context in which Sirk's films circulated and were received. She suggests that we need to make sense of his films in terms of contemporary discourses of consumerism, which might lead to a quite different set of readings of the *mise-en-scène* of such films from those produced by the a-historical readings of the 1970s which stressed the melodramatic excess of the image (Klinger, 1994).

In the same way, we need to make sense of the heritage films of the 1980s and 1990s in the light of prevailing heritage discourses which dominated in public discussion of these films. This is not to say that the *mise-en-scène* of *Howards End* should never be read as expressive of the inner life, symbolizing the emotions of the characters. But we do need to recognize the extent to which critical debate around *Howards End* and related films has foregrounded notions of heritage, either in the pejorative sense of a problematic museum aesthetic, or in the more celebratory sense of *This England* patriotism, nostalgic consumerism and historical tourism. The work of Merchant-Ivory and images from their films are not infrequently used in more general promotion of such ideas, as the following fairly random examples show.

A recent *Sunday Times* review (12 February 1995) of Raphael Samuel's book *Theatres of Memory* (1994), a lengthy discussion of heritage and related ideas and practices, was illustrated with a large still of Helena Bonham Carter in *Howards End*, with the caption 'Sentimentalizing the past? Helena Bonham Carter as Helen Schlegel in *Howards End*'; neither the review, nor the book, it should be noted, mentions the film.

When *The Remains of the Day* (1993) came out, there was a full-page advertisement in the *Guardian* (22 January 1994) for a competition linked to the film, which was described as having 'a very English setting'. The main prizes were 'two luxurious weekend breaks to the elite, and very English, five star Hanbury Manor ... a restored Jacobean-style mansion built in 1890 and set in two hundred acres of Hertfordshire countryside, similar to the manor featured in *The Remains of the Day*'. The second prizes were 'ten hampers by Crabtree and Evelyn, including fine English biscuits, teas, preserves and other delicacies ...'

The release of *Shadowlands* (1994) was the excuse for a long article, also in the *Guardian* (2 March 1994), about American attitudes towards Englishness, illustrated with a large still of Anthony Hopkins in *Howards End*. The release of *Howards End* prompted *The Times* to devote a long article to a discussion of the archival research that went into planning the 'authentic Edwardian interiors' of the film, the techniques the set designer had used for ageing and distressing fabrics and materials, and the exhibition of designs for the film that was held at Sanderson's in London, source of most of the wallpaper designs (30 March 1992).

At about the same time, the *Independent on Sunday* ran a half-page article about Forster, the novel, cinema, and Englishness (3 May 1992). Another long article in the sister paper, the *Independent*, mused over the life and times of the original house on which Howards End was based, and the Poston family who occupied it for some years. The article opens: 'Thanks to Merchant-Ivory's justly acclaimed film adaptation of *Howards End*, Rooks Nest House near Stevenage can expect a busy summer' (30 May 1992). A year or so later, the *Daily Telegraph* (26 May 1994) and *The Times* (25 April 1994) ran articles about the sale of the house which stood in for Howards End in the film, with details of the heritage of the house.

Almost all the reviews of *Howards End* that I have read – some twenty or thirty – acknowledge the proximity of the film to the so-called heritage industry. Either they criticize the film because they see it precisely as a heritage film in the pejorative sense; or they specifically dismiss 'heritage' readings of the film, usually by some reference to Alan Parker's disparaging remark that this is 'the Laura Ashley school of film-making'; or they celebrate the film precisely because it offers the preferred version of the national past; or – and this is quite frequent – they hover somewhere in between each of these positions, ironically referencing the heritage problem as perceived by others, but praising the film at the same time.

In other words, images from the heritage films circulate widely in middle-class culture, and elite heritage discourses are frequently mobilized in discussions of the films themselves. They have a cultural resonance much wider than the films themselves. And this suggests to me that there is a powerful cultural overdetermination to read the heritage film precisely as heritage film rather than as melodrama (or at least 1970s film theory's version of melodrama), and to read individual images for their display of authentic period detail rather than for narrative symbolism. At the same time, the types of properties on display in heritage films are themselves part of a much longer tradition of imagining England, the heritage tradition of English Heritage, the National Trust, *This England* – images from their publications already circulate widely and are invested with a particular set of what might loosely be called official heritage meanings. This is not to imply some governmental conspiracy but to indicate something of the way in which images circulate in public culture. Nor is it to deny that audiences can resist such overdetermined readings.

Marginal voices

Another criticism of my earlier work is that I do not make enough of the closeness of the heritage film to the classical woman's picture or to romance fiction (the criticism is implicit in Dyer, 1994). Clearly, while heritage films often present grand national narratives, public histories, they do also present personal stories, private romances. And as with the classical woman's picture, heritage films, it is argued, are often sites where otherwise marginalized voices can be heard, where concerns so often rendered peripheral in other cinemas are here given space – feminist concerns, gay concerns, concerns about identity generally, especially national identity. While on the one hand heritage films seem to present a very conventional version of the national past, a view from above, conservative, upper-class, patriarchal, on the other hand they very often seem to move marginalized social groups from the footnotes of history to the narrative centre.

Again, this seems to me a very valid and persuasive argument, and one that I do try to develop in 'Re-presenting the national past', although perhaps not as forthrightly as some critics would like. But once again, we need to remember the extent to which films like *Howards End* are promoted and circulated within the culture precisely as heritage films, and not as woman's pictures or queer dramas.

Trivial histories

Elsewhere in this collection, Pam Cook argues that my dismissal of the quality middle-class cinema of the heritage film is akin to the dismissal by quality critics of the 1940s of the popular Gainsborough costume dramas of that period. In both cases, it is argued that the critic has a problem with historical inauthenticity, that we dismiss the film versions of novels or of historical periods because they are not true to the original, that we cannot cope with populist rather than academic versions of history, that we are anxious about the way in which history is transformed into commodified spectacle. As Cook notes, costume drama has traditionally been dismissed by mainstream male critics of the left and right as lightweight; feminine; obsessed with mere decor-ation and display; lacking the seriousness of real history; dealing in images, which rarely have the authority of written scholarship; and so forth.

We can situate this debate in a wider context by looking at Raphael Samuel's argument in *Theatres of Memory* (1994). Samuel takes to task those writers like Robert Hewison and Patrick Wright who have advanced the most trenchant critiques of the so-called heritage industry, and whom I have drawn on heavily for my own argument (Hewison, 1987; Wright, 1985). Samuel argues that aesthetes of the right and the left simply reveal their own difficulties with popular culture when they dismiss those versions of heritage which seem to package the past in Disneyland style. The widespread use as terms of revulsion, of such words as 'superficial', 'vulgar', 'trivializing', and 'commercial' speaks of a fear of the popular, Samuel suggests, and of popular versions of the past, and of a preference for the real thing, the authentic.

While I will readily admit that there is an anxiety about the popular running through my work, I don't think my critique of the heritage films of the 1980s amounts to the same as the dismissal of Gainsborough costume dramas of the 1940s by mainstream British film critics. My argument is not that heritage films offer a trivial view of the history. If I concentrate on the surface images of decoration and display, the visual attractions of heritage, it is because they are writ so large in the films, but also in the culture in which those films circulate. Obviously, spectators can read these images differently, but there seems to me to be a massive encouragement in the culture at large to read the images as heritage images.

My argument is not that these films are unworthy or trivial; on the contrary, it is that we must try to understand the particular version of the national past, the particular view of history, which these films construct, and the function that it may have. Now of course, the function of a film is dependent as much on its reception as on textual formation, and this takes me on to the final critique of the argument presented in 'Re-presenting the national past'.

The question of reception

The problem that *I* have with with my argument in that chapter is that I don't deal with questions of reception (and I know that I am not alone in this view). In fact, as will already have become clear, it seems to me that reception is one way of dealing with all the previous criticisms. They all suggest different ways of reading the films from the ones I advance in 'Re-presenting the national past' – but they are all in the end no more than readings. How do we decide to validate one reading over another?

Richard Dyer and Ginette Vincendeau, for instance, have suggested in a leaflet about their 'European Heritage Cinema Project' that certain readings of heritage films are only available to those who possess the subtle reading skills of a female spectator, or, by implication a gay man (Dyer and Vincendeau, 1995). While this is undoubtedly an interesting argument, it also implies that there is an essential truth hidden at the heart of the heritage film which is only available to the most subtle of readers. Surely that 'truth' is in fact just another reading?

But those other readings are important, and 'Re-presenting the national past' does tend to advance my reading of the films as the *correct* reading. Although I made some attempt there to relate the films of the 1980s to developments in the heritage industry more generally, I did not attempt to ground my reading in a thorough analysis of reception – though I think it could have been done. For, as I have tried to show above, both positive and negative critics of the films have treated them as paeans to a particular vision of England: this is the dominant view of them that has been circulated in print and on television. In other words, my reading of the films does have a certain cultural status, even a quasi-official status, and it is important to take that cultural status seriously.

Of course it is always possible to resist 'official' readings of texts, to use them in different ways and for different purposes. Hence the importance of reading these films not as celebrations of a particular version of the national past, but as woman's pictures, etc. I'm not sure that in 'Re-presenting the national past' I really allowed for this diversity of uses to which a text can be put. I think I envisaged a sort of critical historical discourse which apparently requires an active engagement with and exploration of the ways in which ideas of national heritage are produced and circulated. And I used this ideal discourse to challenge the superficial historical discourse which I associated with the heritage film, and which I assumed required a somewhat passive spectating position.

In a sense, it was *Orlando* versus *Howards End*. *Orlando* with its residue of political modernism, its anti-realist narrative developments, its outspoken commentary on representation itself, and the assumption that all this requires an active spectator; and *Howards End* with its conventional story-telling style, its avoidance of ironic verbal commentary, its self-contained narrative space, and the assumption that all this needs no more than a passive spectator. But of course *Orlando* can be read as a heritage film, and *Howards End* as a critique of capitalism, or as a feminist text, or as a celebration of multi-culturalism. The key here lies precisely in how the spectator reads the text, what uses she or he puts it to.

The same is true of those diverse practices that I have here reduced somewhat monolithically to the heritage industry. As Raphael Samuel has pointed out, people from all walks of life engage with the past in a variety of projects, both formal and informal (Samuel, 1994). Heritage is not simply an elite version of the national past purveyed by bodies such as English Heritage; the past can be and has been appropriated in all sorts of ways, many of which are central facets of popular culture.

And of course, films like *A Room with A View* and *Howards End* were very popular at the box office. But I still think there is a sort of official version of heritage which enables the way in which such films are read and the ways in which they circulate in the public culture.

I want to finish this discussion with a typically ambivalent review of *Howards End*, a review which seems to acknowledge the difficulties of the heritage project, but which also celebrates the film for its 'quintessential Englishness', a review which seems to be both ironic and patriotic, a review which seems to see the film as both carefully historical, speaking poignantly to present-day audiences, and as superficially nostalgic – a review which, like the film, offers itself up for a variety of competing readings:

> This is an instant national treasure [*sic!*]. ... [This] is because historic insights into British character – social snobberies, self-sacrifice – still ring as true as village church bells. The past speaks to the present as The Laura Ashley School of Nostalgic Film-making finally gets a masterpiece with an E. M. Forster story about Edwardian morality. ... The film ... is one to lift the spirits with the magnificence of its teeming set pieces and the eloquence of its intimate moments. In retreating into the past, the Ivory-Merchant-Jhabvala team has finally returned with something relevant and contemporary – the timelessness of a great movie. That it should be a country-house classic makes it the ultimate confirmation of their style. But that it should be an epic about class makes it an immediate part of the British heritage. (*Mail on Sunday*, 3 May 1992, p. 39)

It is worth recalling that this 'instant national treasure' was produced by an Indian, scripted by a Pole, directed by an American, and funded with British, American and Japanese money. And of course its narrative can be read as a gentle exploration of the peculiarly hybrid ethnicities that we reductively call Englishness.

This is a revised version of a paper presented at 'The European Heritage Film: A Workshop Conference' at the University of Warwick, June 1995.

Bibliography

Agate, J. (1946) *Around Cinemas* (2nd series). London: Home and Van Thal.

Allen, C. (1958) *Homosexuality: Its Nature, Causation and Treatment*. London: Staples Press.

Anderson, L. (1949) 'Alfred Hitchcock', *Sequence*, 9, pp. 113–23.

Anderson, L. (April–June, 1954) 'Only Connect: Some Aspects of the Work of Humphrey Jennings', *Sight and Sound*. Reprinted in Jennings, M-L. (1982) *Humphrey Jennings: Film-maker, Painter, Poet*. London: BFI Publishing, pp. 53–9.

Anderson, L. (1981) *About John Ford*. London: Plexus.

Anon. (n.d.) 'A short admonition or warning upon the detestable treason wherewith Sir William Stanley and Roland York have betraied and delivered for monie unto the Spaniards, the town of Deventer, and the sconce Zutphen.' Sig A iiii recto.

Ashley, K. (ed.) (1990) *Victor Turner and the Construction of Cultural Criticism*. Bloomington: Indiana University Press.

Aspinall, S. and Merck, M. (September–October, 1982) 'So That You Can Live II', *Screen*, 23, (3–4), pp. 157–60.

Aspinall, S. and Murphy, R. (eds) (1983) *BFI Dossier 18: Gainsborough Melodrama*. London: BFI Publishing.

Aspinall, S. (1983) 'Women, Realism and Reality in British Films, 1943–53', in J. Curran and V. Porter (eds) (1983) *British Cinema History*. London: Weidenfeld & Nicolson, pp. 272–93.

Attille, M., Auguiste, R., Gidal, P., Julien, I. and Merck, M. (Spring 1988) *Undercut*, 17, pp. 32–9.

Bailey, C. (1992) 'What the Story Is: An Interview With Srinivas Krishna', *Cineaction*, 28, pp. 38–47.

Balcon, M. (1969) *Michael Balcon Presents. ...* London: Hutchinson.

Barr, C. (1977) *Ealing Studios*. London: Cameron and Tayleur/David and Charles.

Barr, C. (1983) '*Blackmail*: Silent and Sound', *Sight and Sound*, 52 (2), pp. 122–6.

Barr, C. (ed.) (1986) *All Our Yesterdays: 90 Years of British Cinema*. London: BFI Publishing.

Barthes, R. (February 1978) 'The Realistic Effect', *Film Reader*, 3, pp. 131–5.

Basinger, J. (1994) *A Woman's View: How Hollywood Spoke to Women, 1930–1960*. London: Chatto and Windus.

Bazin, A. (1967) *What is Cinema?, Vol. 1*. Berkeley, Los Angeles and London: University of California Press.

Bazin, A. (1971) *What is Cinema?, Vol. 2*. Berkeley, Los Angeles and London: University of California Press.

Behn, M. (ed.) (1994) *Schwarzer Traum und weisse Sklavin. Deutsch-dänische Filmbeziehungen 1910–1930*. Munich: Edition Text und Kritik.

Behr, S., Fanning, D. and Jarman, D. (eds) (1993) *Expressionism Reassessed*. Manchester and New York: Manchester University Press.

Bellour, R. (1979) *Analyse du Film*. Paris: Editions Albatros.

Berlin, S. (1949) *Alfred Wallis: Primitive*. London: Nicolson and Watson.

Bordwell, D. and Thompson, K. (Summer 1976) 'Space and Narrative in the Films of Ozu', *Screen*, **17** (2), pp. 41–73.

Bordwell, D., Staiger, J. and Thompson, K. (1985) *The Classical Hollywood Cinema*. London: Routledge.

Breight, C. (1996) *Surveillance, Militarism and Drama in the Elizabethan Era*. London: Macmillan.

Brewster, B. (Summer 1977) 'The fundamental reproach (Brecht)', *Cine-tracts*, **1** (2), pp. 44–53.

Brown, M. E. (1994) *Soap Opera and Women's Talk: The Pleasure of Resistance*. London: Sage.

Bruno, E. (ed.) (1981) *Per Alfred Hitchcock*. Montepulciano, Italy: Editori del Grifi.

Brunsdon, C. (ed.) (1986) *Films for Women*. London: BFI Publishing.

Campbell, B. (1984) *Wigan Pier Revisited: Poverty and Politics in the Eighties*. London: Virago.

Carrick, E. (1948) *Art and Design in the British Film*. London: Dobson.

Chandler, R. (1950) *Pearls Are a Nuisance*. London: Hamish Hamilton.

Chodorow, N. (1978) *The Reproduction of Mothering*. Berkeley: University of California Press.

Christie, A. (1935) *Death in the Clouds*. London: Collins.

Christie, A. (1936) *The ABC Murders*. London: Collins.

Christie, I. (1978a) 'The Scandal of *Peeping Tom*', in I. Christie (ed.) (1978) *Powell, Pressburger and Others*. London: British Film Institute, pp. 53–8.

Christie, I. (1978b) *Powell, Pressburger and Others*. London: British Film Institute.

Christie, I. (1994, first pub. 1985) *Arrows of Desire: The Films of Michael Powell and Emeric Pressburger*. London: Waterstone.

Clarke, J. (September–October 1982) 'So That You Can Live I', *Screen*, **23** (3–4), pp. 153–6.

Collini, S. (1979) *Liberalism and Sociology*. Cambridge: Cambridge University Press.

Cook, P. (1996) *Fashioning the Nation*. London: BFI Publishing.

Corner, J. and Harvey, S. (eds) (1991) *Enterprise and Heritage: Crosscurrents of National Culture*. London: Routledge.

Curran, J. and Porter, V. (eds) (1983) *British Cinema History*. London: Weidenfeld & Nicolson.

Delaney, S. (1959) *A Taste of Honey*. London: Eyre Methuen.

Dennis, N., Henriques, F. and Slaughter, C. (1956) *Coal is Our Life*. London: Tavistock.

Doane, M. A. (1987) *The Desire to Desire: The Woman's Film of the 1940s*. Bloomington: Indiana University Press.

Dodd, K. (1990) 'Cultural Politics and Women's Historical Writing. The Case of Ray Strachey's *The Cause*', *Women's International Forum*, **13** (1–2), pp. 127–37.

Dodd, K. and Dodd, P., (1992) 'From the East End to *EastEnders*: Representations of the Working Class, 1890–1990', in Strinati, D. and Wagg, S. (eds) *Come on Down? Popular Media Culture in Post-War Britain*. London: Routledge, pp. 116–32.

Dodd, P. (1986) 'Englishness and the National Culture', in R. Colls and P. Dodd (eds) *Englishness: Politics and Culture, 1880–1920*. Beckenham: Croom Helm, pp. 1–28.

Donald, J. (1992) 'How English Is It? Popular Literature and National Culture', in *Sentimental Education: Schooling, Popular Culture and the Regulation of Liberty*. London: Verso, pp. 48–70.

Dyer, R. (1979) *Stars*. London: BFI Publishing.

Dyer, R. (1981) 'Introduction', in R. Dyer, C. Geraghty, M. Jordan, T. Lovell, R. Paterson and J. Stewart (1981) *Coronation Street*. London: BFI Publishing, pp. 1–8.

Dyer, R. (1993) 'Victim: Hegemonic Project', in The Matter of Images: Essays on Representation. London/New York: Routledge, pp. 93–110.

Dyer, R. March (1994) 'Feeling English', Sight and Sound 4 (3), pp. 17–19.

Dyer, R. and Vincendeau, G. (eds) (1992) Popular European Cinema. London: Routledge.

Dyer, R. and Vincendeau, G. (1995) 'The European heritage cinema', leaflet circulated by the Warwick European Heritage Cinema Project, University of Warwick.

Eichenbaum, L. and Orbach, S. (1983) What Do Women Want? London: Fontana/Collins.

Ellis, J. (1978) 'Art, Culture, Quality: Terms for a British Cinema in the Forties and the Seventies', Screen, 19 (3), pp. 9–49.

Ellis, J. (1982) Visible Fictions. London: Routledge and Kegan Paul.

Elsaesser, T. (1972) 'Between Style and Ideology', Monograph, 3, pp. 2–10.

Elsaesser, T. (September 1984) 'Images for England (and Scotland, Ireland, Wales...)', Monthly Film Bulletin, 268, pp. 267–9.

Elsaesser, T. (1993) 'Heavy Traffic: Perspektive Hollywood: Emigranten oder Vagabunden?', in J. Schöning (ed.) (1993) London Calling. Deutsche im britischen Film der dreissiger Jahre. Munich: Edition Text und Kritik, pp. 21–41.

Fielding, S., Thompson, P. and Tiratsoo, N. (1995) England Arise!: The Labour Party and Popular Politics. Manchester: Manchester University Press.

Forster, E. M. (1989, first pub. 1910) Howards End. Harmondsworth: Penguin.

Freud, S. (1977, first pub. 1909) 'Family Romances', in On Sexuality, Vol. 7. Harmondsworth: Penguin, pp. 217–26.

Fuller, G. (1994) 'Gus van Sant: swimming against the current', in G. van Sant (1994) Even Cowgirls Get the Blues and My Own Private Idaho. London: Faber and Faber, pp. vii–liii.

Gaines, J. and Herzog, C. (eds) (1990) Fabrications: Costume and the Female Body. New York and London: Routledge.

Garland, R. (1961, first pub. 1953) The Heart in Exile. London: Four Square.

Gelmis, J. (1970) The Film Director as Superstar. New York: Doubleday & Co.

Geraghty, C. (1981) 'The Continuous Serial – a Definition', in R. Dyer, C. Geraghty, M. Jordan, T. Lovell, R. Paterson and J. Stewart (1981) Coronation Street. London: BFI Publishing, pp. 9–26.

Gibbons, L. (1983) '"Lies that Tell the Truth"; Maeve, History and Irish Cinema', Crane Bag, 7 (2), pp. 148–55.

Gidal, P. (1978) Structural Film Anthology. London: BFI Publishing.

Gidal, P. (July 1982) 'On Finnegans Chin', Undercut, 5, pp. 21–2.

Gidal, P. (1989) Materialist Film. London: Methuen.

Giles, P. (1993) 'History with Holes: Channel Four Television Films of the 1980s', in L. Friedman (ed.) (1993) British Cinema and Thatcherism. London: University College of London Press, pp. 70–91.

Givanni, J. (compiled by) (1987) Black Film and Video List. London: BFI Publishing.

Givanni, J. (1993) 'Blackpool's Bhaji', Black Film Bulletin, 1 (1), p. 10.

Gledhill, C. (ed.) (1987) Home is Where the Heart Is: Studies in Melodrama and The Woman's Film. London: BFI Publishing.

Gough-Yates, K. (1971) Michael Powell in Collaboration with Emeric Pressburger. London: British Film Institute.

Gough-Yates, K. (1989) 'The British Feature Film as a European Concern: Britain and the émigré film-maker 1933–1945', in G. Berghaus (ed.)(1989) Theatre and Film in

Exile. Oxford: Oswald Wolff and Berg, pp. 135–66.

Gough-Yates, K. (1992) 'Jews and Exiles in British Cinema', in (1992) *Leo Baeck Yearbook, No. 37*. London: Secker and Warburg, pp. 517–43.

Graham, P. (1963) *The Abortive Renaissance: Why Are Good British Films So Bad?* London: Axle Publications.

Greenblatt, S. (1985) 'Invisible Bullets: Renaissance authority and its subversion – *Henry IV* and *Henry V*', in J. Dollimore and A. Sinfield (1985) *Political Shakespeare: New Essays in Cultural Materialism*. Manchester: Manchester University Press, pp. 18–47.

Greenblatt, S. (1990) *Learning to Curse – Essays in Early Modern Culture*. New York and London: Routledge.

Greenleaf, W. H. (1983) *The Rise of Collectivism*. London: Methuen.

Gunning, T. (1990) 'The Cinema of Attractions', in T. Elsaesser with A. Barker (eds) (1990) *Early Cinema: Space, Frame, Narrative*. London: BFI Publishing, pp. 56–62.

Hall. S. (1981) 'Notes on 'Deconstructing "the popular"', in R. Samuel (ed.) (1981) *People's History and Socialist Theory*. London: Routledge and Kegan Paul, pp. 227–40.

Hall, S. (15 January 1987) 'Song of Handsworth Praise', *Guardian*. Reprinted in K. Mercer (ed.) (1988) *Black Film, British Cinema*, ICA Document 7. London: Institute of Contemporary Arts, p. 17.

Hall, S. (1988) 'New Ethnicities', *Black Film, British Cinema*, ICA Document 7. London: Institute of Contemporary Arts, pp. 27–30.

Hall, S. (1990) 'Culture, Identity and Diaspora', in J. Rutherford (1990) *Identity: Community, Culture and Difference*. London: Lawrence and Wishart, pp. 222–37.

Hardy, F. (ed.) (1946) *Grierson on Documentary*. London: Collins.

Harper, S. (1983) 'Art Direction and Costume Design', in S. Aspinall and R. Murphy (eds) (1983) *BFI Dossier 18: Gainsborough Melodrama*. London: BFI Publishing, pp. 40–52.

Harper, S. (1988) 'The Representation of Women in British Feature Films, 1939–1945', in P. Taylor (ed.) (1988) *Britain and the Cinema in the Second World War*. London and Basingstoke: Macmillan, pp. 168–202.

Harper, S. (1994) *Picturing the Past: The Rise and Fall of the British Costume Film*. London: BFI Publishing.

Harvey, S. (1986) 'The "Other Cinema" in Britain: Unfinished business in oppositional and independent film, 1929–1984', in C. Barr (ed.) (1986) *All Our Yesterdays: 90 Years of British Cinema*. London: BFI Publishing, pp. 225–51.

Hauser, R. (1962) *The Homosexual Society*. London: Bodley Head.

Heath, S. (Spring 1975) 'Film and System: Terms of Analysis: Part I', *Screen*, 16 (1), pp. 7–77.

Heath, S. (1981) 'Narrative Space', in *Questions of Cinema*. London: Macmillan, pp. 19–75.

Henriques, J. (1988) 'Realism and The New Language', *Black Film, British Cinema*, ICA Document 7. London: Institute of Contemporary Art, pp. 18–20.

Hewison, R. (1987) *The Heritage Industry*. London: Methuen.

Higson, A. (July–October, 1983) 'Critical Theory and "British Cinema"', *Screen*, 24 (4–5), pp. 80–95.

Higson, A. (1984a) 'Five Films', in G. Hurd (ed.) (1984) *National Fictions: World War Two in British Films and Television*. London: BFI Publishing, pp. 22–6.

Higson, A. (1984b) 'Space, Place, Spectacle: Landscape and Townscape in the "Kitchen Sink" Film', *Screen*, 25 (4–5), pp. 2–21.

Higson, A, (1986) 'Britain's Outstanding Contribution to the Film: the Documentary-Realist Tradition', in

C. Barr (ed.)(1986) *All Our Yesterdays: 90 Years of British Cinema*. London: BFI Publishing, pp. 72–97.

Higson, A. (1992) 'Film-Europa: Dupont und die Britische Filmindustrie', in J. Bretschneider (ed.) (1992) *Ewald Andre Dupont, Autor und Regisseur*. Munich: Edition Text und Kritik, pp. 89–100.

Higson, A. (1993a) 'Way West: Deutsche Emigranten und die britische Filmindustrie', in J. Schöning (ed.) (1993) *London Calling. Deutsche im britischen Film der dreisiger Jahre*. Berlin: Edition Text und Kritik, pp. 42–54.

Higson, A. (1993b) 'Re-presenting the National Past: Nostalgia and Pastiche in the Heritage Film', in L. Friedman (ed.) (1993) *British Cinema and Thatcherism: Fires Were Started*. London: UCL Press, pp. 109–29.

Higson, A. (1994) 'A diversity of film practices: renewing British cinema in the 1970s', in B. Moore-Gilbert (ed.) (1994) *The Arts in the 1970s: Cultural Closure?* London: Routledge, pp. 216–39.

Higson, A. (1995a) *Waving the Flag: Constructing a National Cinema in Britain*. Oxford: Oxford University Press.

Higson, A. (1995b) 'The Victorious Re-cycling of National History: *Nelson*', in K. Dibbets and B. Hogenkamp (eds) (1995) *Film and the First World War*. Amsterdam: Amsterdam University Press, pp. 108–15.

Hill, J. (1986) *Sex, Class and Realism*. London: BFI Publishing.

Hoggart, R. (1957) *The Uses of Literacy*. Harmondsworth: Penguin.

Hood, S. (1983) 'The Documentary Film Movement', in J. Curran and V. Porter (eds) (1983) *British Cinema History*. London: Weidenfeld & Nicolson, pp. 99–112.

Hurd, G. (ed.) (1984) *National Fictions: World War Two in British Films and Television*. London: BFI Publishing.

Jacobsen, W. (1989) *Erich Pommer. Ein Produzent macht Filmgeschichte*. Berlin: Argon.

Jamal, M. (Autumn 1985) 'Dirty Linen', *Artrage*, **17**. Reprinted in K. Mercer (ed.) (1988) *Black Film, British Cinema*, ICA Document 7. London: Institute of Contemporary Art, pp. 21–2.

Jameson, F. (1984) 'Post-modernism, or the Cultural Logic of Late Capitalism', *New Left Review*, 146, pp. 53–92.

Jarman, D. (1984) *Dancing Ledge*. London: Quartet.

Jarman, D. (1991) *Queer Edward II*. London: BFI Publishing.

Kapsis, R. (1992) *Hitchcock: the Making of a Reputation*. Chicago and London: University of Chicago Press.

Keating, P. (ed.) (1976) *Into Unknown England: Selections from the Social Explorers*. London: Fontana.

Keiller, P. (March 1982) 'The Poetic Experience of Townscape and Landscape, and Some Ways of Depicting It', *Undercut*, 3–4, pp. 42–8.

Khan, N. (1986) 'The Arts Britain Ignores', in Kwesi Owusu (ed.) (1986) *The Struggle for Black Arts in Britain*. London: Comedia, pp. 47–66.

Klinger, B. (January–February 1984) 'Cinema/Ideology/Criticism Revisited: The Progressive Text', *Screen*, 25 (1), pp. 30–44.

Krikorian, T. (Spring 1983) '*On the Mountain* and *Land Makar*: Landscape and Townscape in Margaret Tait's Work', *Undercut*, 7–8, pp. 17–19

Krish, J. (Spring 1963) *Society of Film and Television Arts Journal*, issue on 'The New Realism and British Films'.

Kristeva, J. (1981) 'Women's Time', *Signs*, 7 (1). Reprinted in Moi, T. (ed.) (1986) *The Kristeva Reader*. Oxford: Blackwell, pp. 187–213.

Kuhn, A. (Summer 1978) 'The Camera–I: Observations on

Documentary', *Screen*, **19** (2), pp. 71–83.

Landy, M. (1991) *British Genres: Cinema and Society 1930–1960*. Princeton, NJ: Princeton University Press.

Lant, A. (1991) *Blackout: Reinventing Women for Wartime British Cinema*. Princeton, NJ: Princeton University Press.

LaValley, A. (ed.) (1972) *Focus on Alfred Hitchcock*. New Jersey: Prentice-Hall.

Le Grice, M. (1977) *Abstract Film and Beyond*. London: Studio Vista.

Le Grice, M. (1979) 'The History We Need', in Arts Council of Great Britain (1979) *Film as Film: Formal Experiment in Film 1910–1975*. London: Hayward Gallery, pp. 113–17.

Le Grice, M. (Winter 1979–80) 'Towards Temporal Economy', *Screen*, **20** (3–4), pp. 58–79.

Lejeune, A. (ed.) (1991) *The C. A. Lejeune Film Reader*. Manchester: Carcanet.

Lejeune, C. A. (1947) *Chestnuts in Her Lap*. London: Phoenix House.

Light, A. (1991) *Forever England: Femininity, Literature and Conservatism Between the Wars*. London: Routledge.

Lovell, A. (1972) 'Free Cinema', in A. Lovell and J. Hillier, (1972) *Studies in Documentary*. London: Secker and Warburg, BFI, pp. 133–59.

Low, R. (1971) *The History of the British Film, 1918–1929*. London: George Allen and Unwin.

Low, R. (1985) *Film-Making in 1930s Britain*. London: Allen and Unwin.

MacCabe, C. (Summer 1974) 'Realism and the Cinema: Notes on Some Brechtian Theses', *Screen*, **15** (2), pp. 7–27.

Mackay, J. (1992) 'Low-budget British Production: A Producer's Account', in D. Petrie (ed.) (1992) *New Questions of British Cinema*. London: BFI Publishing, pp. 52–64.

Macnab, G. (1993) *J. Arthur Rank and the British Film Industry*. London: Routledge.

Maeder, E. (ed.) (1987) *Hollywood and History: Costume Design in Film*. Los Angeles and London: Los Angeles County Museum of Art/Thames and Hudson.

Mangan, J. (1981) *Athleticism in the Victorian and Edwardian Public School: The Emergence and Consolidation of an Educational Ideology*. Cambridge: Cambridge University Press.

Mayne, Judith (1990) *The Woman at the Keyhole: Feminism and Women's Cinema*. Bloomington: Indiana University Press.

Medhurst, A. and Tuck, L. (1982) 'The Gender Game', in J. Cook (ed.) (1982) *Television Sitcom*. London: BFI Publishing, pp. 43–55.

Mercer, K. (ed.) (1988a) *Black Film, British Cinema*, ICA Document 7. London: Institute of Contemporary Arts.

Mercer, K. (1988b) 'Sexual Identities: Questions of Difference: Introduction', *Undercut*, **17**, pp. 19–21.

Mercer, K. (1992) '"1968": Periodizing Politics and Identity', in L. Grossberg *et al.* (eds) (1992) *Cultural Studies*. London: Routledge, pp. 424–37.

Mercer, K. (1994a) 'Diaspora Culture and the Dialogic Imagination: The Aesthetics of Black Independent Film in Britain', in *Welcome to the Jungle: New Positions in Black Cultural Studies*. London: Routledge, pp. 53–66.

Mercer, K. (1994b) *Welcome to the Jungle: New Positions in Black Cultural Studies*. London: Routledge.

Millett, K. (1972) *Sexual Politics*. London: Abacus.

Modleski, T. (1988) *The Women Who Knew Too Much: Hitchcock and Feminist Theory*. New York and London: Methuen.

Monk, C. (1994) *Sex, Politics and the Past: Merchant-Ivory, the Heritage*

Film and its Critics in the 1980s and 1990s Britain. MA Dissertation, BFI/Birkbeck College.

Montgomery Hyde, H. (1970) *The Other Love*. London.

Morley, D. (1980) 'Texts, Readers, Subjects', in S. Hall, D. Hobson, A. Lowe and P. Willis (eds) *Culture, Media, Language*. London: Hutchinson, pp. 163–73.

Mullaney, S. (1988) *The Place of the Stage: License, Play and Power in Renaissance England*. Chicago and London: University of Chicago Press.

Mulvey, L. (1975) 'Visual Pleasure and Narrative Cinema', *Screen*, **16** (3). Reprinted in L. Mulvey (1989) *Visual and Other Pleasures*. London: Macmillan, pp. 14–29.

Neale, S. (Spring 1979) 'Triumph of the Will – Notes on Documentary and Spectacle', *Screen*, **20** (1), pp. 63–86.

Nicolson, A., Sparrow, F., Clarke, J. Iljohn, J., Rhodes, L., Leece, M. P., Murphy, P. and Stein, S. (1979) 'Woman and the Formal Film', in Arts Council of Great Britain (1979) *Film as Film: Formal Experiment in Film 1910–1975*. London: Hayward Gallery, pp. 118–129.

Nowell-Smith, G. (Winter 1979–80) 'Radio On', *Screen*, **20** (3–4), pp. 29–39.

Oakley, C. (1964) *Where We Came In*. London: Allen and Unwin.

Oppe, F. (1981) 'Distribution and Exhibition: The Practices of the Women's Movement', in R. Stoneman and H. Thompson (eds) (1981) *The New Social Function of Cinema: Catalogue BFI Productions '79–80*. London: BFI, pp. 136–9.

O'Pray, M. (1987) 'The Elusive Sign: From Asceticism to Aestheticism', in D. Curtis (1987) *The Elusive Sign: British Avant-Garde Film and Video 1977–1987*. London: Arts Council/British Council, pp. 7–10.

Orwell, G. (1962, first pub. 1937) *The Road to Wigan Pier*. Harmondsworth: Penguin.

Parkinson, D. (ed.) (1993) *Mornings in the Dark: A Graham Greene Film Reader*. Manchester: Carcanet.

Paterson, R. (1981) 'The Production Context of Coronation Street', in R. Dyer, C. Geraghty, M. Jordan, T. Lovell, R. Paterson and J. Stewart (1981) *Coronation Street*. London: BFI Publishing, pp. 53–66.

Penguin Film Review (1977, first pub. 1946–49). London: Scholar Press.

Perkins, V. F. (1962) 'The British Cinema', *Movie*, **1**, pp. 2–7.

Petrie, D. (ed.) (1992a) *New Questions of British Cinema*. London: BFI Publishing.

Petrie, D. (ed.) (1992b) *Screening Europe. Image and Identity in Contemporary European Cinema*. London: BFI Publishing.

Pevsner, N. (1956) *The Englishness of English Art*. Harmondsworth: Penguin.

Phillips, P. (1963) 'The New Look', in M. Sissons and P. French (eds) (1963) *Age of Austerity*. London: Hodder and Stoughton, pp. 127–48.

Pines, J. (1985) 'Territories: Interview with Isaac Julien', *Framework*, **26–7**, pp. 2–9.

Pines, J. (1986) 'Interview With Sankofa Film Collective', *Framework*, **32–3**, pp. 92–9.

Pines, J. (1988) 'The Cultural Context of Black British Cinema', in Mbye B. Cham and Andrade-Watkins (1988) *Blackframes: Critical Perspectives on Black Independent Cinema*. Massachusetts: Massachusetts Institute of Technology Press, pp. 26–36.

Priestley, J. B. (1967, first pub. 1934) *English Journey*. Harmondsworth: Penguin.

Reisz, K. (1953) *The Technique of Film Editing*. London: Focal Press.

Rhodes, L. (1979) 'Whose History?', in Arts Council of Great Britain (1979) *Film as Film: Formal Experiment in Film 1910–1975*. London: Hayward Gallery, pp. 119–20.

Rich, A. (1977) *Of Woman Born*. London: Virago.

Richards, J. (1988) 'National Identity in British Wartime Films', in P. Taylor (ed.) (1988) *Britain and the Cinema in the Second World War*. London and Basingstoke: Macmillan, pp. 42–61.

Roberts, M. (1978) *A Piece of the Night*. London: The Women's Press.

Ross, A. (1983) *Colours of War: War Art 1939–45*. London: Jonathan Cape.

Rotha, P. (1936) *Documentary Film*. London: Faber and Faber.

Rotha, P. (ed.) (1975, first pub. 1947) *Richard Winnington, Film: Criticism and Caricature 1943–53*. London: Elek.

Rothman, W. (1982) *Hitchcock: the Murderous Gaze*. Cambridge, MA and London: Harvard University Press.

Ryall, T. (1986) *Alfred Hitchcock and the British Cinema*. London and Sydney: Croom Helm.

Ryall, T. (1993) *Blackmail* (BFI Classics series). London: BFI Publishing.

Salt, B. (1983) *Film Style and Technology: History and Analysis*. London: Starword.

Samuel, R. (1994) *Theatres of Memory*. London and New York: Verso.

Scannell, P. and Cardiff, D. (1991) *A Social History of British Broadcasting. Volume One: 1922–1939*. Oxford: Basil Blackwell.

Schöning, J. (ed.) (1993) *London Calling. Deutsche im britischen Film der dreissiger Jahre*. Munich: Edition Text und Kritik.

Schöning, J. (ed.) (1995) *Deutsch-russische Filmbeziehungen*. Munich: Edition Text und Kritik.

Schwarzbach, F. (1982) '"*Terra Incognita*" – an Image of the City in English Literature', in P. Dodd (ed.) *The Art of Travel: Essays on Travel Writing*. London: Frank Cass, pp. 64–8.

Shakespeare, W. (1990 edn) *The Tempest*, Arden Shakespeare. London: Routledge.

Sight and Sound (Winter 1938–39) 7 (28), p181.

Sinfield, A. (1983) 'Four Ways with a Reactionary Text', *LTP: Journal of Literature Teaching Politics*, 2, pp. 81–96.

Sorlin, P. (1980) *The Film in History: Restaging the Past*. Oxford: Blackwell.

Spoto, D. (1983) *The Dark Side of Genius: The Life of Alfred Hitchcock*. New York: Ballantine. Published in Britain as (1983) *The Life of Alfred Hitchcock: The Dark Side of Genius*. London: Collins.

Stedman-Jones, G. (1983) *Languages of Class: Studies in English Working-Class History 1832–1982*. Cambridge: Cambridge University Press.

Steedman, C. (1986) *Landscape for a Good Woman*. London: Virago.

Stephenson, R. and Debrix, J. R. (1965) *Film as Art*. London: Penguin.

Stonier, G. (Autumn 1961) 'Review of *A Taste of Honey*', *Sight and Sound*, 30 (4), p. 196.

Storey, D. (1963) 'Journey Through a Tunnel', *The Listener*, 1 August 1963, pp. 159–61.

Strachey, R. (1978, first pub. 1928) *The Cause: A Short History of the Women's Movement in Great Britain*. London: Virago.

Taylor, J. R. (1974) *Masterworks of the British Cinema*. London: Lorimer.

Taylor, J. R. (1972) *The Pleasure Dome. The Collected Film Criticism of Graham Greene*. London: Secker and Warburg.

Taylor, N. (1973) 'The Awful Sublimity of the Victorian City', in H. J. Dyos and M. Wolff (eds) (1973) *The Victorian City, Images and Realities*, Vol. 2. London: Routledge and Kegan Paul, pp. 431–48.

Thompson, E. (1980, first pub. 1963) *The Making of the English Working Class*. London: Gollancz.

Thompson, K. and Bordwell, D. (1994) *Film History: An Introduction*. New York and London: McGraw-Hill.

Truffaut, F. (1968) *Hitchcock*. London: Secker and Warburg.

Turner, V. (1969) *The Ritual Process: Structure and Anti-Structure*. Chicago: Aldine.

Turner, V. (1977) 'Variations on the theme of Liminality', in S. Moore and B. Nyherhoft (eds) (1977) *Secular Ritual*. Assen: Van Gorcum, pp. 36–52.

van Gennep (1960, first pub. 1907) *The Rites of Passage*. Chicago: Chicago University Press.

Wandor, M. (1987) *Look Back in Gender*. London: Methuen.

Watney, S. (Spring 1983) 'Gardens of Speculation: Landscape in *The Draughtsman's Contract*', *Undercut*, 7–8, pp. 4–9.

Weeks, J. (1979) *Coming Out*. London: Quartet.

Westergaard, J. (1965) 'The Withering Away of Class: A Contemporary Myth', in P. Anderson and R. Blackburn (eds) (1965) *Towards Socialism*. London: Fontana, pp. 77–113.

Westwood, G. (1960) *A Minority*. London: Longman.

White, B. (1974) 'Interview with Walter Lassally', *The Journal of the University Film Association (USA)*, 26 (4), pp. 61–2, 79.

Whitebait, W. (1958) *International Film Annual*, 2, London.

Wildeblood, P. (1957, first pub. 1955) *Against the Law*. Harmondsworth: Penguin.

Williams, R. (1961, first pub. 1958) *Culture and Society: 1980–1950*. Harmondsworth: Penguin.

Williams, R. (1973) *The Country and the City*. London: Chatto and Windus.

Williams, R. (1980) 'The Bloomsbury Faction', in *Problems of Materialism and Culture*, pp. 148–69. London: Verso.

Williams, R. (1983) 'British Film History: New Perspectives', in J. Curran and V. Porter (eds) (1983) *British Cinema History*. London: Weidenfeld & Nicolson, pp. 9–23.

Williams, R. (1989) 'The Future of Cultural Studies', in T. Pinkey (ed.) (1989) *The Politics of Modernism*. London: Verso, pp. 151–62.

Wilson, E. (1985) *Adorned in Dreams: Fashion and Modernity*. London: Virago.

Winchester, C. (1933) *World Film Encyclopedia*. London: Amalgamated Press.

Winterson, J. (1985) *Oranges Are Not The Only Fruit*. London: Pandora.

Wohl, R. (1980) *The Generation of 1914*. London: Weidenfield and Nicolson.

Wolfenden (1957) *Report of the Committee on Homosexual Offences and Prostitution*. London: HMSO.

Wollen, P. (December 1975) 'The Two Avant-Gardes', *Studio International*, 190 (978), pp. 171–5.

Wollen, P. (1980) 'Introduction: Place in the Cinema', *Framework*, 13 , p. 25.

Wollen, P. (1993) 'The Last New Wave: Modernism in the British Films of the Thatcher Era', in L. Friedman (1993) *British Cinema and Thatcherism*. London: UCL Press, pp. 35–51.

Wood, R. (1965) *Hitchcock's Films*. London: Tantivy.

Wood, R. (1989) *Hitchcock's Films Revisited*. New York: Columbia University Press; British edition (1991) London: Faber and Faber.

Wright, P. (1985) *On Living in an Old Country: The National Past in Contemporary Britain*. London: Verso.

Yeo, S. (1986) 'Socialism, the State and Some Oppositional Englishness', in P. Dodd and R. Colls (eds) (1986) *Englishness: Politics and Culture, 1880–1920*. Beckenham: Croom Helm, pp. 308–69.

Young, M. and Willmott, P. (1957) *Family and Kinship in East London*. London: Routledge and Kegan Paul.

Index